D1112366

Find a Way

Find a Way
Valpo's "Sweet" Dream

by Shawn Malayter with Homer Drew and Rob Rains

Foreword by Scott and Bryce Drew

Diamond Communications, Inc.
South Bend, Indiana

Find a Way: Valpo's "Sweet" Dream

Manufactured in the United States of America

Diamond Communications, Inc.
Post Office Box 88
South Bend, Indiana 46624-0088
Editorial: (219) 299-9278
Fax: (219) 299-9296
Orders Only: 1-800-480-3717
Website: http://www.diamondbooks.com

Library of Congress Cataloging-in-Publication Data

Malayter, Shawn, 1972-
    Find a way : Valpo's "Sweet" Dream / by Shawn Malayter,
Homer Drew, and Rob Rains : foreword by Scott and Bryce Drew.
        p.   cm.
    ISBN 1-888698-23-3 (hardcover)
    1. Valparaiso University--Basketball--History. 2. Drew, Homer,
1944-   . I. Drew, Homer, 1944-   . II. Rains, Rob. III. Title.
GV885.43.V35M35   1998
796.323'63'0977298--dc21   98-43645
                                                                  CIP

Contents

For Eileen

Acknowledgments

The authors wish to thank the many people who have made this project possible. First and foremost, we want to thank Jill Langford and Shari Hill at Diamond Communications for their tireless efforts and their belief in this book.

Thanks to the supportive staff at Valparaiso University who provided an unbelieveable amount of help. President Dr. Alan Harre, Athletic Director Dr. William Steinbrecher, Assistant Athletic Director Carl Hensley, Sports Information Director Bill Rogers, Trainer Rod Moore, Assistant Sports Information Director T.R. Harlan, Robb Vessley, Jerry George, Denise Criswell, Paul Twenge, Nona Richardson, and Dick Harlan.

We would also like to thank the 1997-98 Crusaders: Bryce Drew, Cory Gibson, Monte Gordon, Aric Graham, Bill Jenkins, Bob Jenkins, Jason Jenkins, Jared Nuness, Jay Phifer, Marko Punda, Chris Sparks, Jamie Sykes, Aaron Thomason, Antanas Vilcinskas, and Zoran Viskovic. Your honesty, thoughtfulness, and candor were crucial to writing this book.

In addition, we would like to thank the assistant coaches, Scott Drew, Steve Flint, Jim Harrick, Jr., and student assistant Mark Morefield. Thanks are also in order to the team managers: Jason Baldwin, Matthew Couser, and Paul Ziemba, as well as to team secretary Sherry Williams.

Gratitude is also extended to members of the local media: Sean P. Hayden, Mike Hutton, Todd Ickow, Paul Jankowski, Mike McCardle, John Mutka, Sam Riche, and Dan Weber. Your professionalism and courtesy throughout the season were a credit to your publications. We also wish to thank everyone at the Mid-Continent Conference and at the NCAA for their accommodations during their respective tournaments.

Thanks to all who were interviewed during the course of writing this book, but we want to especially thank Gene Bartow, Dale Brown, Ken Rochlitz, and Tom Smith.

Last, but certainly not least, the authors wish to thank the other members of the Drew family: Janet, Dana, and Casey. Thank you for opening your home and heart and allowing the authors to tell your fascinating story to the world.

Shawn Malayter wishes to send special thanks to both Homer Drew and Rob Rains. He will be forever grateful for Homer's enthusiasm and contributions on this project. Without Rob's direction and guidance, Malayter is certain that this book would never have seen the light of day.

He wants to thank his wife, Eileen, for her love, support, and, most importantly, her patience over the past 18 months while this project was being completed. He wants the world to know that it was her foresight and loving confidence that allowed him the courage to even embark on this project.

Malayter also sends thanks to his family for their love and support: his mother, Delayne Malayter; his father and stepmother, James and Ali Malayter; his mother and father-in-law, Janet and Raymond Ryan; his brother, Ryan Malayter; his sisters, Amanda and Rachelle Malayter, and Aislinn Fen Malayter. Also, he would like to thank brothers-in-law Ken Jahnke and Robert Lee, sisters-in-law Sandra Jahnke and Debbie Lee, and nephews, Matthew Jahnke, Michael Jahnke, and Andrew Lee. Thanks to all his relatives, as well.

Malayter also wishes to thank friends and colleagues who have supported and helped him, with this project and over the years. This group is too numerous to mention everyone, but it includes: Ray Begovich, Dan Clark, Dan Davis, Noah Hahn, John Hanson, Howard Hewitt, Leo Joint, Carl Kozlowski, David Knott, Chad Lindley, Mark Lucas, Fred Newton, Marc Ransford, Web Riter, Greg Smith, Jama Vincent, Kelly Young, Gloria Zimmerman, and Brian Zink.

Foreword

Growing up as the son of a college basketball coach was enjoyable for me. As far back as I can remember, Dad's teams were successful and provided our family with a great deal of enjoyment.

When Dad told us he had made a decision to become the coach of Valparaiso University in 1988, I knew it was going to be a challenge. He was facing a tremendous rebuilding since Valparaiso University had never had a winning season since joining NCAA Division I.

Watching Dad's teams struggle his first few years was hard for everyone in the family. We knew he was working as hard as he could to make the Valpo program successful, and it's always frustrating when you think you are doing everything you can possibly do and still are not generating the results you want. Everybody in our family tried to think of what else we could do to help Dad in whatever way we could, and it was when I was a senior in college that I knew what my contribution could be.

I was a political science major at Butler University and was preparing to go to law school. I still was involved with basketball, working as the student manager of the Butler team and following Dad's team as closely as possible. Being around basketball, as I had all my life, was what I enjoyed more than anything. It struck me one day that I was close to having to leave it behind after graduation, and I didn't want that to happen. Law school could wait; I wanted to go into coaching.

Valparaiso Univerity was able to hire me as a graduate assistant and that's when I dedicated myself to doing whatever I could do to help make Dad's team successful. I broke down film for the players and coaches. I helped players during individual workouts. I worked with videotaping, scheduling travel, working to exchange film with other coaches, and, yes, I even did my share of dirty, sweaty laundry. There may have been some parts of my job that were more enjoyable than others, but the biggest reward came with the wins started to come.

Most people, given a similar choice, would do the same thing I did. They would want to do whatever they could to help their dad or any other family member. I was fortunate that I had the chance to do that, and I'm very grateful for it.

Those early, struggling days at Valpo now seem a long, long time ago. We have built a winning tradition, and come into each season with the expectation that we are going to be better than the previous year.

Of course, we have never had a bigger challenge to make that come true than we face this season. The magical ride which was Valpo's 1997-1998 season was one that everybody will remember and cherish for the rest of our lives. The happiest part for me was that I got to enjoy it first-hand with my dad and brother. I wouldn't have missed it for the world.

Scott Drew
October 1998

My first impression of Valparaiso University was from the backseat of the family car on a sunny spring day. It was a Sunday morning in 1988, and we had driven over to check out the school where my dad was so eager to coach. It was a big decision for our family, as Scott and Dana were in high school. Moving the family and starting everyone over in a new school with new friends was a big step, and my dad wanted to make sure it was the right step.

As we walked around campus, Dad stopped a student who was walking by and asked him what he thought of the school.

"Oh, it's great!" the student replied.

You should have seen my dad's face light up. He gave us this huge grin, as if his desire to coach at Valpo had just been given an additional stamp of approval.

After he got the job at Valpo, several people warned him that "you can't win in Division I at Valpo." Dad never scoffed at those remarks, but instead took them as the supreme challenge. We all believed he could do it. After all, this was his dream!

During my dad's first season as coach, it appeared everything was on track. Valpo upset a ranked Notre Dame team, and they set a single-game Division I record for three-pointers. However, the next season brought some struggles, and it was tough for all of us. I remember sitting in the stands at the games and looking up at the top section of the Athletic Recreation Center. I remember wondering what it would be like to fill those seats every night and have a winning team at Valpo.

Meanwhile, Valparaiso became my home. I was blessed with good friends, outstanding coaches at Valparaiso High School, and with the warmth and kindness of the city's people. No matter where I go in my life, I will feel like Valparaiso, Indiana, is always my home.

My senior year at Valparaiso High School, my brother made the decision to pursue the court of basketball instead of a court of law. He bought into the dream of what we could achieve at Valpo, and he recruited me. Coming to Valpo to play for my dad was the best decision I've ever made.

When I arrived at VU, the team set goals and we steadily improved. My freshman year, we won a triple overtime game to win the conference title. We didn't receive an NCAA bid that year, but we established a tradition of winning.

My sophomore year, we finally made it to the NCAA tournament. Unfortunately, the team was in awe when we got there, and we struggled against Arizona. The next year, we fought hard to get back to the tournament, but we lost again, this time to Boston College. This loss was much harder to take, because everyone on the team felt it was a game we should have won.

Finally, this past season, we made our dreams come true with our trip to the Sweet 16. I'll always remember this season, and what it meant to the Valpo community and basketball fans. I'll always be thankful I had the opportunity to play for my father and brother. I'll always be thankful for the Valpo fans, alumni, teachers, and friends who have been so supportive of my family and our team over the years. Most importantly, I'll always be thankful to God for blessing me with such a wonderful family. Mom, Dad, Dana, and Scott: I love you all very much.

The time has flown since the end of the season. Getting drafted by the Houston Rockets happened so fast, it still hasn't quite sunk in yet.

I know I'm entering a new journey in my life, and I know this journey will take me all over the country, and possibly the world. Yet, it's reassuring to know that as long as I keep everyone in Valpo close to my heart, I'll never be too far away from home.

Bryce Drew
October 1998

CHAPTER ONE

A Chance to Dance

"I will get ready and then, perhaps, my chance will come."
–John Wooden

The team bus wound through the streets of Oklahoma City. Inside, a group of young men silently focused on the task that lay ahead. Some stared out the windows at the overcast sky. Others stared at the seatback in front of them. Still others closed their eyes and visualized the goal, a goal six of them had pursued relentlessly for four years.

For these young men, the Valparaiso University Crusaders basketball team, the goal that day was a victory. That an athletic team would have such a simple, solitary goal was not surprising. What would separate this victory from all others was the meaning and significance it carried.

The game these Crusaders would play was a first-round matchup in the 1998 NCAA basketball tournament, and victory on this day would mean many things: respect for a program and conference; validation for a group of seniors who had been told such a feat was impossible; and achievement of a dream that had been set by players and coaches, yet had eluded their grasp. However, the most significant reason the Crusaders wanted to win on this day is that, for them, a win in the NCAA Tournament would be the fulfillment of a lifelong dream.

Yet, victory on this day would be a tall order. The Crusaders' opponent was the University of Mississippi, a team seeded fourth compared

1

to Valpo's 13th. Many pundits were touting the Rebels as a Final Four team. They were the champions of the Southeastern Conference's Western Division. They had been eliminated in the first round the year before. They were hungry.

Still, the Crusaders were not newcomers to playing at this level. They had qualified for the NCAA Tournament the previous two seasons, but had lost in their first-round games both years. In 1996, Arizona defeated the Crusaders in Tempe. In 1997, the Crusaders suffered a tough seven-point defeat at the hands of Boston College in Salt Lake City. On the strengths of their fourth straight Mid-Continent Conference title, the Crusaders had earned another opportunity to take the national stage in the "Big Dance."

As the bus glided into the loading dock of the Myriad Convention Center, the players and coaches gathered their duffels and rose to exit. Head Coach Homer Drew looked around at his team. There was no hint of fear or nervousness in their eyes. Good, he thought to himself. Drew did not know what awaited the team that day, but he was reassured to see that they were ready.

The team changed into their bright gold uniforms and took the floor for warmups. There was very little conversation, especially among the seniors. They knew this was their final opportunity to achieve their goal. Someone had printed up T-shirts to underscore the point. The shirts read: "We May Never Get Another Chance to Dance!"

This was a special group of seniors. They had achieved every goal except one. They liked going "dancing," and they wanted to make certain this wouldn't be the last song.

Bryce Drew, the All-American candidate who was the head coach's son, had provided the foundation for this team with his sharp shooting and his steady, oncourt leadership. Bill and Bob Jenkins, the outgoing twins who rotated at forward for the Crusaders, had dominated many teams with their rebounding skills, and provided the team with emotional fire in tight situations. Jamie Sykes, the ultra-quick guard, had dazzled many opponents with his defensive intensity and his dribbling prowess. Antanas Vilcinskas, the 7-foot center, provided a bedrock in the middle for Valpo with his strong post-up game. Finally, Jay Phifer, who missed the entire season with a shoulder injury, infected his teammates with his positive and upbeat attitude. All six were unique and special in what they had accomplished, but they all knew that this was their final opportunity to win a game in the NCAA tournament. The game was important to all of the other players, too, but for the seniors, the added significance was there. It could be their last game in a Valpo uniform.

The game started, and the Crusaders demonstrated that they weren't going to let go of their dream without a fight. They battled the heavily favored Rebels rebound for rebound, three-pointer for three-pointer, and dunk for dunk. Neither team was able to pull away from the other. With just under two minutes to go and trailing by just one point, the Crusaders missed a golden opportunity to score when a Valpo shot was blocked and then corralled by a Mississippi player. Timeout was called. Valpo fans agonized in the stands.

Inside the huddle, there was no panicking and no self-pity. The players looked at one another and then at their coach. Looking into their eyes, Homer Drew saw the fire and confidence still burning. The players knew what they had to do to win, it was a matter of executing during the game's final minutes.

Each player and coach reached into the huddle and clasped hands. The players broke from the huddle and headed back out on to the floor. They had just over 90 seconds to make their dreams come true.

But now, there was no more time for dreaming—it was time to make their own reality.

CHAPTER TWO

Basketball Roots:
The Team, The Town, and The Dream

This is the beginning of a new day
God has given me this day to use as I will.
I can waste it–or use it for good,
But what I do today is important because
I am exchanging a day of my life for it.
When tomorrow comes, this day will be gone forever
Leaving in its place something I have traded for it.
I want it to be gain and not loss;
Good not evil; success and not failure;
In order that I shall not regret the price
I have paid for it.

–Author Unknown

The small child is out in the family driveway, bouncing a basketball. It's a cold November afternoon, but the boy doesn't notice the weather. His sneakers are worn; his gloves are threadbare from the constant pulse of dribbling the ball. As he passes the ball to himself off the garage door, the boy's winter coat slides off his shoulder.

The only sound is the frigid wind outside, but in his head, the boy hears the clock ticking and the crowd cheering. As he fakes an imaginary defender, the child dribbles two more times and pushes a shot with all his might toward the rusty hoop. In his head, the buzzer sounds as the ball rattles through the tattered net. He leaps for joy, the champion of his own imagination.

As the boy grows older, many people will tell him that he's not big enough, not fast enough and not good enough to make the team, but this child knows better. He lives in Valparaiso. He has witnessed with his own eyes that dreams can come true.

Valparaiso, Indiana, is a small city located in northwest Indiana, 55 miles southeast of Chicago. The county seat of Porter County, it sits 15 miles south of Lake Michigan, and 30 miles east of Gary.

By all measures, it is a great place to raise a family. The crime rate is low, the public school system is among the best in the Midwest, and there are plenty of well-manicured subdivisions filled with grand houses, stately trees, and parks.

Despite being a quiet, suburban college town, Valparaiso experienced enormous growth beginning in the mid-1980s. Like several other cities in the area, including Munster, Merrillville, and Crown Point, Valparaiso saw a steady influx of Illinois natives moving across the border. There were many reasons behind this, namely the fact that the hour-long commute from Valpo to Chicago was the same as many Chicago suburbs, and the property taxes in Indiana were much lower. Add the outstanding local school systems to the mix, and it comes as no surprise that the region has become such a popular destination for former Chicagoans.

However, long before the migration of Illinois expatriates, indeed, long before there was much of a town present, Valparaiso University established itself as the local higher education leader. Founded in 1859 and nestled on 310 acres on the city's southeast corner, Valparaiso University began offering degrees in several fields. Based on the principles of the Lutheran Church, the outstanding academics helped earn the school its nickname, "Little Harvard of the Midwest."

In 1917, the school fielded its first intercollegiate basketball team. Under head coach Sidney Winters and led by captain Allan Dalrymple, the team won seven of the nine games it played. The team played only three games the next season before finally lining up for a full slate of 20 games in the 1919-20 season under new coach George Keogan.

The team had several stellar seasons during its first few decades. In 1923-24, Coach W.P. Shadoan's squad went 24-4. The 1930-31 team, coached by J.M. Christiansen, compiled a 42-16 record between 1930 and 1933. Captain Bob Dille's team in 1944-45 amassed a 21-3 record under the direction of Coach Loren Ellis. Ellis had one squad that was spotlighted in *Life* magazine as the "World's Tallest Team," because several players were over 6-7 in height.

The team was known by two monikers at that time, the "Fighting Crusaders" and the "Uhlans." A uhlan is a medieval German soldier armed with a lance. The symbol represented the university's heritage as a German Lutheran school. During World War II, however, university officials replaced the uhlan with the Fighting Crusader symbol. At that time, there was strong anti-Nazi sentiment in the United States which discouraged Germanic associations.

Two decades later, Gene Bartow took over the Valpo program as head coach prior to the 1964-65 season, replacing Paul Meadows, who had gone 64-79 in six seasons and was coming off a 9-15 season. According to Bartow, the process of filling a head coaching vacancy at that time was a bit simpler than it is today.

"I was coaching in Missouri at a small college there," Bartow said. "I met Athletic Director Dick Koenig, and shortly after that the job opened up at Valparaiso. Dick offered me the job and I took it."

Bartow quickly turned the program around. His first season the Crusaders posted a 13-12 record, and, in 1965-66, his second year on the bench, Valpo went 19-9. Led by co-captains Richard Enyon and future Valpo head coach Tom Smith, the Crusaders advanced to the second round of the NCAA Division II tournament, where their season ended with a loss to North Dakota. However, the highlight of that season for Valpo was a 114-96 victory over Purdue at venerable Hilltop Gym.

"When I came to Valparaiso in 1964, they had two or three losing seasons in a row and the program was perceived as being not that good," Bartow said. "But we found some good players and had a few good recruiting years and over the six years that I was there, we went to the NCAA (Division II) tournament three times...one year we made it all the way to the final eight in Evansville, so I enjoyed being at Valparaiso."

That "one" year was 1966-67, Bartow's third season as head coach. Valpo went 21-8 and defeated Southern Colorado and Indiana State in the NCAA small college tournament (now known as Division II) before finally losing to Southwest Missouri State, 86-72, in the national quarterfinals.

"That was a great team," Bartow said. "Vern Curtis was the leading scorer and Ken Rakow was another big part of that team. I still keep in touch with those guys.

"Of course, we also had several other very good players. That was a fine group, they did a lot of good things for the university."

Bartow notched 93 wins in six seasons at the helm of the Crusaders. He stepped down as Valpo's head coach in 1970 and went on to coach Memphis State to an NCAA Final Four appearance in 1973.

Bartow's successor, Bill Purden, coached the Crusaders through the early 1970s, and they didn't seem to miss a beat. Every Purden-coached team at Valpo finished the season at or above the .500 mark, with the exception of his last season as coach, the 1975-76 team that ended up 12-14. When Purden stepped aside, his young protégé and assistant, Ken Rochlitz, stepped in as head coach. He went 13-12 in his first season, but more importantly, university officials had given the go-ahead for Valparaiso to make the big move to Division I.

Rochlitz had no illusions: he knew that making the step up was going to be a difficult journey. There were two main obstacles hindering success at the start: a facility that was ill-suited to attracting top-flight recruits, and a murderous schedule due to a lack of conference affiliation.

First, old Hilltop Gymnasium, built in 1927, was a bandbox by just about any definition. With a capacity listed at 3,500—just over 4,000 with fans shoved into every nook and cranny and fire marshal in absentia—Hilltop clearly fell into the category of "cozy." Indeed, fans were seated so close to the floor that one time a man sitting in the second row simply leaned forward, without leaving his seat, and tapped on a referee's shoulder to give him an earful for a bad call a few minutes earlier. In addition, there were several exit doors a few feet behind one baseline. When players would chase a ball out of bounds on that end of the floor, they often had to run straight out the door to avoid a collision with a wall. "Out the door" didn't mean out into a hallway or lobby—it meant out into the parking lot and the cold, wintertime air.

These quirks may have been considered a home-court advantage by some, but the gym was definitely viewed as a liability by potential recruits. Rochlitz made no bones about Hilltop's impact on recruiting.

"It was a big negative," he said. "It was just a horrible facility for Division I basketball."

There also was the issue of scheduling. Valpo started in Division I as an independent, which allowed for flexible scheduling and powerhouse opponents—with a major catch.

"Since we were an independent, everybody in the world wanted to play us...on their floor," Rochlitz said. "No one would play us at Valpo, except for Ray Meyer at DePaul, who agreed to play in Valpo once if we played there twice. It made for some very difficult schedules."

Also not helping Rochlitz' cause was the fact that several of Valpo's traditional, longtime opponents were becoming national powerhouses at the time.

"It seemed like a lot of the teams we played were in their heydeys at that time," he said. "Notre Dame was in the Top 10 every year and they had Kelly Tripucka. DePaul had Mark Agguire and was ranked #1 off and on during that time. Indiana State had Larry Bird and they were making their great runs back then nationally. It made it very tough on us."

Valpo's records during Rochlitz' tenure reflected the growing pains of the schools transition to major college basketball. Its first season in Division I, Valpo dropped to 6-19. While the Crusaders defeated Navy and Xavier (to add to their victory over Tulane the year before), the change was reflected in losses to Northern Colorado, Tennessee Tech, and Wisconsin-Milwaukee.

The next year, the Crusaders struggled through a 4-21 season. The four victories that season were (in order): Gustavus Adolphus, Baltimore, Arkansas-Little Rock, and St. Joseph's (Indiana). Among the teams that bounced the Crusaders were Carthage, Northern Colorado, St. Joseph's (Indiana) (Valpo won the rematch at Rensselaer), and DePauw. The 1979-80 season, Rochlitz' final season as head coach, the team improved to 8-18, but losing had taken its toll on the coach, even though he harbored realistic expectations about a fledgling Division I program.

"I knew it was a situation where we would have to crawl before we could walk, but boy, did we do a lot of crawling," he said.

Rochlitz moved on to the wide open spaces of Powell, Wyoming, to take the head coaching job at Northwest Junior College. He has been there ever since, and he has had a tremendous amount of success. In 1997-98, his squad was nationally ranked and finished with a 24-6 record. He has taken his team deep into the NJCAA playoffs on several occasions. Now, he reflects back on his days in Valparaiso with some fondness, despite the struggles his teams had.

"Looking back, there were a lot of fun things that happened back at the time," he said. "And I like to think, in some small way, our staff played a hand in the success they would have down the road."

Valpo turned to one of its own for its next head coach. Tom Smith, an All-American on Bartow's 1966-67 team, had been the head coach at Central Missouri State prior to arriving at Valpo. He had built Central Missouri State into a national Division II powerhouse, and his team earned a 26-2 record—and the number one ranking in Division II for two months—the season before taking the head coaching reins for the Crusaders. He posted 12-15 and 9-18 seasons, respectively, in his first two years on the bench. At the start of the 1982-83 season, Valpo made its first big step since joining Division I—hooking up with a conference.

Along with Eastern Illinois, Western Illinois, Northern Iowa, Illinois-Chicago, Wisconsin-Green Bay, Cleveland State and Southwest Missouri State, Valpo was a charter member of the Association of Mid-Continent Universities (AMCU-8). According to Smith, the formation of the new league signaled a new era in Valpo basketball.

"We really needed a league," he said. "The schedule as an independent was very difficult. We were getting paid to go places and play, like Montana and Florida. Whenever that happens, you're not going to be successful. The conference added stability."

In its first season of conference play, Valpo posted a 13-15 mark. The following year, the Crusaders were 9-19 in their final season at Hilltop Gym. To start the 1984-85 season, Valpo would move next door into the sparkling, $7.25 million Athletics-Recreation Center (ARC). The seating capacity was enlarged and the amenities were first-rate. However, Smith said the new arena wasn't quite home at first.

"The university was pretty adamant that it didn't want it to be 'too basketball,' because it was to be used as recreation facilities by the students," he said. "As a result, it was pretty sterile at first. It took a year or two for the place to begin to feel like a home court."

In their first two seasons playing in the ARC, the Crusaders went 8-20 and 9-19, respectively. Smith said recruiting was hampered by a lack of resources.

"We had not yet made the financial commitment to compete at the Division I level," he said. "There was not nearly as much advertising around the arena as you see now. There was no active fundraising that went directly back to basketball."

Smith also said that there were little things that signaled Valpo was still experiencing growing pains from the move up to Division I. One particular memory sticks out in his mind.

It was December 1984, and Valpo was playing in the Dedication Game of the ARC against Notre Dame. A sellout crowd was on hand and a regional cable network was broadcasting the game live. Like many schools do, Valpo removed the "Home" and "Guest" from the scoreboards to replace them with the team names. However, for reasons unknown, work crews only replaced one of the names. During the game, the scoreboards read "Home" on one side and "Notre Dame" on the other.

While that might seem to be a trivial detail, it made a big difference, according to Smith. A prized recruit was visiting campus that afternoon, and when he passed on Valpo a few weeks later, he told Smith one of the main reasons why.

"You couldn't even put 'Valpo' on the scoreboards in your own gym?" the recruit asked incredulously.

Another problem facing Smith: he could never recruit any big men. Size was always a problem with Valpo teams then, who went into many games undersized, and, frankly, outmanned.

"I just wanted to get on equal footing with other teams in our conference," Smith said. "I never felt like my gun was loaded."

After two more losing seasons, Smith resigned following the 1987-88 season. He said he never felt in danger of losing his job, which was a big problem in his eyes.

"The thing that bothered me was that no one cared enough to put that pressure on me," he said. "No one cared that we were losing, the local media didn't seem to care that we were struggling, nothing."

Smith moved back to Missouri and took the head coaching job at Missouri Western, where he has built that program into a Division II powerhouse. Although he is disappointed that he was never able to win at his alma mater, he said he never got down on himself.

"We had kids that played hard, but we just didn't have the athletic ability, so I never had a problem holding my head up," Smith said.

"I have an opportunity to perhaps be remembered around here at Missouri Western, and I'd rather have that than to go off chasing a rainbow which may not be there and start all over again," he said. "But would I do it all over again? Yeah, I would. At that time in my life, I wanted that shot."

Smith compiled an 84-138 record over eight seasons as head coach. With his departure, there was a vacancy to be filled at Valpo. Enter Homer Drew.

Homer W. Drew was born September 29, 1944 in St. Louis. His parents, Alice and Homer Drew, were most supportive of his love of sports. Drew recognizes that he was blessed to have had wonderful parents. His father was a hard working provider for the family, and his mother was very strong in values and principles and yet possessed a tender, loving heart in raising Homer and his sister Diane.

Growing up in suburban Webster Groves, Drew learned an appreciation for the game of basketball from his next-door neighbor, John Russell. Russell, who would go on to receive a full-ride scholarship to play at Vanderbilt, was four years older than Drew, yet Russell allowed the little kid from next door to play in pick-up games with the older boys from the neighborhood.

"I was always the last guy picked when they were choosing teams," Drew recalled. "But I loved playing those games against older kids in the backyard; I enjoyed basketball thoroughly."

Like most boys his age, Drew played all sports growing up. In the spring and summer, he played baseball. In the fall, it was football time. During the winter months, everyone played basketball. Drew played and enjoyed basketball more, however, and he was talented at the game. He played in high school and earned a grant-in-aid to William Jewell College in Liberty, Missouri.

Drew played on two conference championship teams ('64 and '65) and two second-place teams ('63 and '66). Adjectives that come to mind when describing Drew, the player, include: smooth, smart, instinctive, creative. A master of the bank shot, the 6-foot-tall Drew would be called a "combo" guard by today's standards because he could play both the point and two-guard positions. He did, in fact, lead the Cardinals not only in scoring and assists but also in rebounding during his senior year.

Drew, a co-captain, was the complete guard at both ends of the floor. He finished his career with 1,261 points (No. 5 on the career-scoring list at the time—he currently ranks No. 19). His 43-point performance at Central Methodist in 1965 stood as the single-game scoring record for 10 years (It was broken in 1976 by Charlie Funk who scored 49 points vs. Graceland, which remains the record).

In addition, Drew was a first team MCAU All-Conference selection three times. He was Jewell's first basketball player to be an NAIA Honorable Mention All-American selection three times.

While at William Jewell, Drew's teammate, Bob Ulrich, was dating Jo Ann Demark. Ulrich set up Drew on a date with Jo Ann's sister, Janet. They went on one date to the Basketball Banquet during Drew's freshman year. The following year, Janet Demark transferred to the University of Missouri to finish up her degree and graduate magna cum laude. Drew received his bachelor's degree in physical education and social studies from William Jewell in 1966. The next year, Drew began pursuing his master's degree from Washington University in St. Louis. In 1967, he re-met Janet Demark who was teaching elementary school in St. Louis. The two began dating again, and the rest, as they say, is history. Drew and Demark were married, and Drew set off to find a career.

Drew enjoyed being around the game of basketball, and he enjoyed teaching, so he figured coaching might be something he would be interested in. He began coaching high school basketball in Missouri, where his passion for the game and for teaching young people made him decide to pursue coaching jobs. In 1970, Janet Drew gave birth to the couple's first child, Scott.

Shortly after Scott's birth, Drew took an assistant coaching position at Washington State University in Pullman, Washington. In Pullman, Drew met fellow assistant Dale Brown, who would become a mentor and close friend.

"He was like the older brother I never had," Drew said. "He was an excellent people person and he treated everybody with a genuine interest."

The feeling was mutual, according to Brown.

"Right from the moment you meet Homer, you know there's something special about him," Brown said. "He just loves people."

In 1972, Brown accepted the head coaching job at Louisiana State University. The first person Brown hired to be a part of his staff was Drew.

"He's the kind of person you want to have coach your own sons and grandsons," Brown said. "He had this great sense for the game... he's not a cynic, and there's not a selfish bone in his body."

"He's a very spiritual man, and he's so genuine," Brown added. "What you see is what you get."

The pair were inseparable during a four-year stretch in the bayou. Louisiana is football country, so selling basketball to the local fans was not an easy task. As part of a campaign to tell the state's residents about LSU basketball, the two traversed the state, passing out purple-and-gold basketball nets and schedule cards, complete with a whimsical poem that Janet Drew had written and was published in *Sports Illustrated*. The initiative was called, "The Tiger Safari," and the goal was to increase awareness and support of the team.

JOIN THE TIGER BASKETBALL SAFARI

Basketball is the name of the game
To those who practice, it can bring much fame.
But more than that, it's a GREAT sport to play
Its rewards can come in every way.

LSU Basketball wants YOU to know
It's thinking of YOU and a sport that will grow
So use wisely this net from the purple and gold
To play a great game that will never grow old

by Janet Drew

In 1976, Drew himself received the opportunity to be a head coach. He jumped at the possibility. Only this time, he had to pack up and move a family of five across the country. Daughter Dana was born in 1972 and son Bryce was born in 1974, both in Baton Rouge, Louisiana. Now they would all be heading north so Drew could become head coach at Bethel College in Mishawaka, Indiana

While Drew's teams at the NAIA school experienced great success, it was the progress in his spiritual life that he valued most about his tenure at the Christian institution. Drew had been raised with solid Christian beliefs by his parents, but he felt he grew even more spiritually in the religious environment of Bethel. Those values were passed on to his children, who carry their faith to this day.

The faith carries over into the locker room. After each game, Drew's teams, led by the captains, recite the Lord's Prayer. The idea, Drew said, is to keep basketball in its proper place and to make sure that God is present. Drew invites guests in to share a thought and prayer prior to each game, as well. Local businessmen such as Paul Van Tobel, Harley Snyder, Bruce Leetz, Dr. Greg Gates, Dr. Jim Malayter, Dave Hollenbeck, Dr. Rob Behrend, Denny Hyten, and Ron Landgrebe; Valpo family such as Pres. Alan Harre, Paul Schrage, Jerry Petzer, Jerry George, Ed Lloyd, Dr. Bill Steinbrecher, Rod Moore, and Charles Gillespie; celebrities Dale Brown, Tommy Lasorda, and Rich Telander, all have helped share "thoughts and prayers" with the basketball team.

"It's my belief that you should pray to play to the best of your ability and to be injury free," Drew told the coaching journal *Championship Performance*. "I'm not sure God takes sides out there. He has a plan for each one of us and that is what is taking place."

"For I know the plans I have for you," declared the Lord, "plans to prosper you and not to harm you, plans to give you hope and a future."
—Jeremiah 29:11

Enjoying his family, Drew could spend more time at home. Rather than meeting the grueling travel demands of a Division I job, he and Janet could watch their children grow up. Drew and Janet made it clear that each child could find activities that suited them best while they were growing up.

"I enjoyed reading several of Dr. James Dobson's books, and one of the important messages I remembered is that every child should find a niche," Drew said. "So when the kids were young, we made sure they could try all sorts of different things: piano lessons, the guitar, basketball, football, baseball, fishing, math...the list goes on and on. Psychologists tell us that for a child's self-esteem to be high, children need to know they can do something well or at least be part of something good."

Not surprisingly, two of the children picked up basketball. Dana was the first child to show an interest in the game.

"Dana really started playing the game in earnest during her eighth and ninth grade," Drew said. "She was such an intense competitor, she just had this feistiness about her when she played. She was very goal-oriented and determined to do well."

A few years later, Bryce fell in love with basketball, as well.

"He was good in baseball and excelled in tennis," Drew recalled. "But basketball is the game that really got into his blood."

The love spilled over onto the family basketball courts, where many a competitive one-on-one game emerged.

"They used to head out there on snowy nights, shovel off the court and cut the fingertips off their gloves," Drew said. "Then they'd play for hours."

At Bethel College, Drew received District and National Coach of the Year honors. His 252-110 record over 11 years averages out to almost 23 wins a season, which along with making it to the NCCAA and NAIA play-offs every year, allowed Bethel College to become known as a "small college giant."

After leaving Bethel College, Drew coached one year at Indiana University-South Bend, leading the Titans to the first-ever winning season.

After Smith's resignation, from his home in Mishawaka, Drew quickly found out about the opening, but not through a phone call, an agent, or any of the typical job-search techniques of a Division I coach.

"I read about it in the newspaper," Drew said. "I wrote a letter to Bill Steinbrecher, the athletic director, and then he called and we had a meeting with Dick Koenig, who was then vice president. I met with those two, and went through an interview off-campus at the Holiday Inn in LaPorte (Indiana)."

Drew said the reason for the off-campus rendezvous wasn't anything covert—it was merely a method for getting to know one another.

"It was just so there wouldn't be the distractions and the rumors around campus of who was being interviewed," he said. "Plus, LaPorte was a good halfway point between Valpo and Mishawaka."

Drew liked what he heard. He enjoyed the sincerity of Athletic Director Bill Steinbrecher and the vision of Dick Koenig. He also liked what he saw and the people he met when he visited campus shortly thereafter. Following his formal interview, Drew walked into Valpo's campus landmark, The Chapel of the Resurrection, and kneeled down for a moment of prayer.

"I was just praying and I said, 'Lord, if this is where you want me, let the doors open,'" he recalled. "Driving home, we had a 'Family Forum' where the entire family—Homer, Janet, Scott, Dana, Bryce—talked about the pros and cons of the job. We even got Janet's mom and dad, Lee and Tom Demark, involved by seeking their opinion. After much talking, it was a consensus: If they offered the position, I would accept. I got a phone call within the week offering the position, and I accepted."

The task in front of Drew was daunting, though. His job: rebuilding a program that had never really been built in the first place. The Crusaders had never had a winning season in Division I basketball, and had 11 straight losing seasons with only three 20-win seasons in the history of Valparaiso University.

Of course, the Crusaders were guaranteed of doing better in attendance for at least one game in the 1988-89 season, since they had a home game scheduled with Notre Dame. The larger issue of cultivating a local fan base still remained.

When the season finally started, Drew had a team with a size problem. The tallest player stood only 6-7, and most of the players were under 6-4. He had two veteran leaders, seniors Scott Anselm and Jim Ford. However, the team lacked athleticism, especially against some of Valpo's early opponents.

The Homer Drew Era got off to an auspicious start in a 30-point loss to Butler at historic Hinkle Fieldhouse in Indianapolis. The Crusaders followed up that game with a 19-point home loss to Evansville. After the

Evansville loss, players were amazed by the positivity of Homer Drew. There was no yelling in the locker room after the game. There was no blaming or finger-pointing. There were no angry glares. Instead, the sum of Drew's post-game message was this: "I'm proud of you guys as long as you play hard and don't quit. We need to try to improve in a few areas, but I'm proud of your effort. Keep playing hard and the wins will come."

After starting with a 2-5 record, the Crusaders improved. Playing at home against Ball State, the Crusaders battled the Cardinals to the wire before falling 63-56. Ball State, coached by Rick Majerus, would go on to have a 29-3 season and advance to the second round of the NCAA Tournament. After the game, Drew consoled his players by applauding their effort and desire against a much bigger and more athletic foe.

Unfortunately, there was no reason to believe that win number three would arrive with their next game. The Crusaders would be facing 19th-ranked Notre Dame at the ARC.

In the years leading up to 1988, Valpo's play against Notre Dame had been an exercise in futility. The last time Valpo had beaten the Irish, Warren G. Harding was in the White House—the 1920-21 season. Notre Dame won the next 30 meetings over 67 years. In addition, the Crusaders hadn't even been within single digits of the Irish in decades.

To make matters worse, Notre Dame headed into the 1988 game undefeated, with wins over Indiana and Kentucky in the early season. Led by highly heralded freshman LaPhonso Ellis, many observers felt this was the season that Notre Dame would return head coach Digger Phelps to the Final Four for the first time in 11 years.

A crowd of 4,913—a school record at that time—filed into the ARC on a snowy Saturday evening. Several of the Valpo players had final exams earlier in the afternoon, so preparation for the game had been lacking—not a good sign against such a powerful opponent. Still, the crowd was excited by the prospect of playing a ranked team at home and by the cable television broadcast—still a rarity for Valpo at that time.

As the pre-game clock hit the 10-minute mark, the Crusaders gathered and headed into the locker room for final instructions. When the team entered the dressing room, many of the players shot puzzled glances at one another.

Drew stood smiling before the chalkboard, clad in a Los Angeles Dodgers jacket. The jacket, as it turned out, was a gift from Dodger manager Tommy Lasorda to former Valpo athletic director Koenig. Koenig let Drew borrow the jacket as a good luck charm for the game—but Drew's pre-game talk would have nothing to do with luck.

"You all remember the World Series this year—no one gave the Dodgers a chance to win against the Oakland Athletics...but they did," he said. "No one thought Orel Hershiser would be able to pitch like he did. But his teammates called him 'Bulldog' for this reason: he never gives up, he never stops fighting, he plays with the intensity of a bulldog.

"Tonight, you need to be bulldogs. You need to fight on the boards and chase after every loose ball. Dive on the floor," he said, eyes glowing with excitement. "They may be the bigger dogs, but you be the bulldogs tonight. This is a great opportunity for us, men. Let's play hard and have fun. Be Bulldogs!"

After a quick prayer, an inspired group of Crusaders headed out onto the ARC floor—and demonstrated some inspired play. Outhustling, outshooting, and outplaying the Irish, Valpo took a three-point lead at halftime. After Notre Dame had its traditional strong second-half start, Valpo proceeded to do something they hadn't done in years: they proved the traditions wrong. Notre Dame fought back, and a dunk by Ellis put the Irish up by five points with less than 30 seconds left. Desperate, the Crusaders needed a quick three-pointer. Sophomore Curtiss Stevens, a Michigan City, Indiana, native, heaved up a trey from the right side that looked like it might come down in Lake Michigan. The shot was way long.

However, the ball slammed off the backboard and ricocheted through the net. The Crusaders were within two at 64-62 with 15 seconds left. Valpo signaled for a timeout. In the timeout, Digger Phelps tried to soothe his rattled team. The ARC crowd was now going crazy. Valpo was within a possession of the mighty Irish with less than a minute left. This wasn't supposed to be happening. Phelps had to verbally reassure his team.

"Don't worry, we're going to win," he said in the huddle.

In the Valpo huddle, Drew was cool and collected.

"The rebound is the game," he said in the huddle, smiling the whole time. "Rebound, then get the ball to Scott or Mike, then push it up quickly and get the best shot you can. Jim spot up, and, Curtiss, go straight for the bound so if we miss, you tip it in. We can do this!" As the team broked the huddle, Drew had a final reminder: "Get this rebound!"

Once again, a Notre Dame player stepped to the line with a chance to seal the game, but the free throw bounced away, no good. Valpo freshman Scott Blum tracked down the loose ball and flipped it to Mike Jones. Suddenly, Valpo had a two-on-one fast break.

Jones dribbled upcourt. When he reached the free-throw line, he dished off to his former Valparaiso High School teammate Anselm. Anselm tipped the ball back to Jones, who was wide open for a layup at the buzzer. Tie score. Overtime. Bedlam.

In the overtime, with just under a minute left, senior Jim Ford put the Crusaders ahead to stay on a rebound dunk. As the final Irish shot bounced off the rim as the buzzer sounded, pandemonium ensued. Valpo students mobbed the floor. Drew shook hands with the Notre Dame coaches, then turned to the celebration. He raised his arms. For the first time in 67 years, Valpo had a victory over Notre Dame. In the locker room, the seniors were in tears, not believing what they had accomplished.

"You guys just had a special night that you and this school can treasure forever," Drew told them after the game. "You really earned it. Congratulations."

The next day, local papers dubbed the game the "Miracle on Union Street." It was the first taste of national attention for a Valpo program that had worked long and hard for it. It was only December 17, but Christmas had arrived on campus.

More importantly, the gutsy win endeared the Crusader program to the community of Valparaiso. For a long time, the campus and community had existed as separate entities when it came to basketball. Packed houses were the norm across town at Viking Gym for Valparaiso High School games. The ARC was deserted on many game nights. Finally, a win over a nationally ranked opponent paved the way for Valpo to bridge that gap.

"That win really got our foot in the door with the community," Drew said. "It took us a while to build a program...but that was the first step where the community stayed with us and they supported us from then on in the good times and the bad times. That's what's so special about our community—its loyalty to Valparaiso University."

While the win was something that the community would treasure for a long time, there was still a season ahead. While the team finished the season with a 10-19 record and a 4-24 record the next season, Drew wouldn't give up. However, after posting 5-22 seasons in both 1990-91 and 1991-92, Drew returned to the Chapel of the Resurrection where he originally prayed for guidance prior to taking the Valpo job.

"Lord, are you *sure* this is where you want me to be?" he asked.

The answers came later that season. Casey Schmidt and David Redmon, two former Valpo High standouts, were unhappy in their current situations at Arizona and Arkansas-Little Rock, respectively. Both decided to come home and transfer to Valpo. The reality of a winning team set the wheels in motion, and Drew credits Athletic Director William Steinbrecher and University President Alan Harre with making the financial commitment to Division I basketball at Valpo, allowing for the basketball staff to fundraise and to enable a bigger recruiting budget. After a 12-18 season in 1992-93, Drew welcomed a familiar face to his staff: his son Scott.

Scott had graduated from Butler University, where he had played and been a manager for the basketball team. During his senior year over the Christmas holiday, he broached the subject with his father, which was a change in Scott's career plans.

"Dad, I think I want to try coaching," Scott Drew said.

"Great! After you finish law school I think that would be wonderful," Dad replied.

"No, Dad, you don't understand. I want to start coaching now," Scott Drew said.

Drew made his son a deal. He would hire Scott Drew as a graduate assistant, but only if he promised to pursue his master's degree from Valpo at the same time. Scott Drew agreed.

The next season was a breakthrough in more ways than one. The Crusaders compiled a 20-8 record, their best ever in Division I. They came within five points of a shot at the NCAA Tournament. Finally, the coaching staff was compiling talent for the following year's team. Scott Drew was completing his master's and showing that he was going to make an excellent addition with his recruiting abilities and knowledge of the game.

"I always like to say recruiting is like shaving," Drew said. "You miss a day, and you look like a bum."

Being the first to contact a player is crucial to gaining an inside track for landing a top prospect, according to Drew.

"If you're one of the first to do that, you have a good shot to be one of the last," he said.

Despite the fact that the recruiting process seems interminable to most coaches and fans, Drew said really there are three steps to recruiting.

"July is a time to evaluate players. After evaluation, you line up home visits to meet them and their families. The next step is to invite them to campus and meet Valparaiso University."

While there are a number of variables coaches will look at when evaluating high school players, Drew offered a quick checklist of qualities that are consistently applied to each Valpo recruit.

"First, we look at if he has the ability to play at the Division I level," he said. "Next, we see if he has the grades to make it at Valparaiso University. If his grades are not good enough to get into our university, we stop right there and move on to the next player.

"If his grades are good enough, then we send him information about Valpo. We go to his home in September, to his hometown, to get to know him and his family better. If that goes well, we invite him to come visit our campus. If everything goes right, when the early signing period rolls around, he'll be signing with Valparaiso University."

Starting off the recruiting season was a pair of athletic, muscular twins at Nicolet High School in Glendale, Wisconsin. Bill and Bob Jenkins were three-sport stars: basketball, volleyball, and baseball. They were being recruited for both volleyball and basketball. Some Big Ten and Pac-10 schools recruited them for both sports, however, no school was offering a scholarship to both Bill and Bob. Valpo came in and offered a scholarship to both young men. They accepted, although they confessed to being a little nervous. They also didn't know what to make of Drew.

"Your first reaction when you meet him is 'is this guy for real?'" Bill Jenkins said. "But he isn't phony or insincere...he's an all-around nice person."

Next up, Scott Drew said, was a super-quick guard from Kankakee, Illinois, named Jamie Sykes. Sykes was a phenomenal athlete and a terrific defender.

"We were hoping he could come in and play the same type of role as [Valpo all-time scoring leader] Tracy Gipson," Scott Drew said.

Then came the final piece of the recruiting puzzle: Bryce Drew. Bryce had developed into one of the nation's hottest prospects during his high school career.

Bryce had overcome some long odds to become a top player. During his junior year, Bryce battled a heart condition, A-V node re-entry tachycardia, which caused his heart to race at 260 beats per minute. His parents were informed about his condition by Dr. Eric Prystowsky, a specialist in the electrical system of the heart, when Bryce was a high school freshman. The condition never hampered his playing basketball very much until that year. While medication was effective in controlling the tachycardia for two years, it often left him too lethargic and unable to play basketball to his potential.

"It was necessary for him to take the medication," Drew said. "But after he took it, he would just come home and lie around which was totally opposite of Bryce's personality."

To correct the problem, the summer before his senior year, Bryce underwent three heart ablations, procedures in which a catheter inserted through his groin was used to locate and "zap" the faulty circuitry of his heart. The third surgery on the first day of his senior year proved a success. Bryce was finally ready to resume his playing career.

It was a ray of sunshine into what had been a tough year for the Drews. While Bryce was struggling with his heart condition, his junior year in high school, Dana had blown the anterior cruciate ligament in her right knee at the start of her junior year and was out for the season, interrupting her All-American career at the University of Toledo. The family came together as a team, determined to get through the tough times.

"Through it all, we just supported each other and drew our support from God," Dana Drew told the *Indianapolis Star*. "Our family is special and I think for all of us it's made all the difference in the world."

Bryce, with a clean bill of health, rebounded his senior year to lead his team to a 28-1 record, ending with a heartbreaking overtime loss in the state championship game to South Bend Clay. He was named Indiana's Mr. Basketball; however, he was undecided as to where he would play ball in college. Stanford, Syracuse, Notre Dame, LaSalle, Wisconsin, and, of course, Valpo were all schools in the chase. Slowly, but surely, Bryce pared down the list. All of the schools had many different things to offer in terms of education and basketball tradition, but none of them could offer his family. Case closed.

Prior to the announcement of his college choice at a high school lecture hall, Bryce let his brother in on the wonderful secret.

"We're going to the NCAA Tournament," Bryce said.

It certainly looked that way, but another roadblock was thrown in Valpo's way. Just before the start of the 1994-95 season, several members of the renamed AMCU-8, the Mid-Continent Conference: Cleveland State, Illinois-Chicago, Northern Illinois, Wisconsin-Green Bay, Wisconsin-Milwaukee, and Wright State, all defected to the Midwestern Collegiate Conference. Even though the Mid-Continent scrambled to find teams to join the league, the league's automatic NCAA Tournament bid was revoked for one year due to the changes.

Valparaiso went on to post another 20-8 record that year, winning its first conference regular season and tournament titles. The Crusaders were snubbed by both the NCAA and the NIT tournaments.

The next season, the bid was reinstated, and the Crusaders again had something to shoot for. Valpo's inside game was also bolstered by the presence of newcomer Antanas Vilcinskas, a 7-0 Lithuanian native who Scott Drew picked up on during a visit. Later that year, Valpo signed 6-11 center and Croatian native Zoran Viskovic to help provide for the future with inside play.

Despite the obvious hardwood talents of the foreign players on the team, Drew insisted there was a more important benefit to having players from different cultures coming together on a team.

"Basketball is truly a global sport," he said. "Our foreign players are good students and intelligent people, and that's important.

"The next generation has to understand the diversity of our world. You have to be able to understand the conflicts in the Middle East, China, Japan, and other areas of the world. Sports and young people competing together with people from different backgrounds helps us to understand other cultures."

Drew then rattled off a statistic to illustrate his point.

"I read where 50 percent of the world's population in the year 2000 will be under the age of 18, so our youth is the key in learning how to get along with other cultures," he said. "I believe basketball can be a catalyst to that end, and hopefully help kids to understand this world a little better."

During the 1995-96 season, Valpo fought to a 21-11 record. More importantly, they fought their way to the NCAA Tournament with a win over Western Illinois. Valpo was defeated by Arizona in Tempe, Arizona, 90-51. While the lopsided margin of victory disappointed many fans, the Crusaders accomplished a major goal: making it to "The Big Dance."

The following season, the Crusaders repeated the feat, going back to the NCAA Tournament before losing to Boston College, 73-66, but not before Bryce put on a shooting display. He ended up with 27 points, impressing Bob Ryan of the *Boston Globe*, who called him "dazzling" and said his shots were so perfectly arched, it "looked as if they would touch the comet Hale-Bopp" on the way down. The Crusaders led most of the game before the bigger, physical BC team came back for the win.

With everyone coming back for 1997-98 from that team, the future looked bright. However, one of Drew's athletes was so talented that the pros couldn't wait to get him.

In early June of 1997, the Crusaders were dealt a big blow when Jamie Sykes was selected in the 11th round of the Major League Baseball draft by the expansion Arizona Diamondbacks. Since he was drafted so high, the Diamondbacks weren't about to let him play basketball in the off-season. Despite having a year of eligibility left, Sykes—along with his senior leadership, defensive quickness and 42-inch vertical leap— seemingly had played his last basketball game in the brown and gold.

Even though it was disappointing to have the team's starting guard leave early, Drew couldn't help but be proud of Sykes.

"We're very happy for him," Drew said. "Make no mistake, we would have loved to have kept Jamie for another year...he's a great defender and a great player on the perimeter, but he's got a future to play baseball in the major leagues! With a brand new club, no less. What a great draft choice for Jamie!"

Meanwhile, Bryce was receiving a national honor, as well. He was selected to play for Team USA in the World University Games in Sicily over the summer. Along with some of the top college players from around the country, Bryce helped lead the team to victory.

Team USA won the gold medal at the World Games, and Bryce scored 10 points in the championship game, but he seemed more satisfied with getting to play against top-notch national and international competition.

"It was a tremendous experience," he said. "I'll probably never get another chance to represent my country and win a gold medal, so it's a great honor and something I'll cherish forever."

Something that Bryce felt would help in the upcoming season was the fact that he had to adjust his game for international rules.

"It's a totally different style, so you have to adjust your game, which is good to learn how to do," he said. "But it was a completely different game over there.

"The biggest thing we [Team USA] had trouble with were traveling calls. It seemed like every time we went right and didn't put the ball on the floor right away, we got called for traveling. I like to shot fake and go right, so I got called for traveling a lot at first.

"It was a tremendous experience. I'll probably never get another chance to represent my country and win a gold medal, so it's a great honor and something I'll cherish forever."–Bryce Drew

"Another thing is that in America, we play defense with our hands. Over there, they spread the floor more. You can't even touch them or it's a foul, so I had to step off of my man a lot more."

Bryce said that, defensively at least, the international rules grew frustrating.

"I'm used to making contact," he said. "The game in America is definitely more physical than in Europe."

While Bryce loved visiting a new country and enjoying the delicious local cuisine, he did slightly injure his knee during the championship game. It wasn't a big deal, he insisted.

"It's a little sore," he said two months before the start of pre-season practice. "I'll get some therapy on it, and I'll be fine."

As pre-season practice started, something bothered Sykes, however. He hung around the Crusaders' first few practices of the season—and it killed him inside. He desperately wanted to play for his senior season.

A few days later, Sykes couldn't stand the sidelines anymore. He called up the Valpo coaches and told them he was going to ask the Diamondbacks to give him a release. They did. Sykes headed straight down to Drew's office.

"He walked in smiling and said 'I got permission,'" Drew said. "And I just told him, 'Welcome back.'"

While Drew said Sykes took the initiative to get everything worked out on his own, he said the process was made easier by the Diamondbacks' organization, including Director of Player Development Mel Didier.

"Everyone, especially Mel, was excellent to work with, and we want to have them as our guest at a home game this year, so they can all see Jamie play," he said.

Sykes told the local newspaper, the *Vidette-Times,* that his love of hoops was the reason for the change of heart—although he did say that the school would likely pay for his full tuition by suiting up.

"I just don't want to be 10 years down the road and have any regrets, saying, 'man, I should have played,'" he told the newspaper. "Hanging around the guys and watching practice was killing me now [in October], so you can imagine what it would be like in January or February."

Later, Sykes explained the frustration of having to sit out until he got his release. Without obtaining his release from the Diamondbacks, he could not play on scholarship at Valpo.

"Everyone's really gone out of their way to help me here. I just wanted to figure out a way that I could play this year and have my education covered, that's all."

As pre-season practice started, Drew knew he had a team with the experience and talent to potentially be the school's best ever.

"If we stay healthy," Drew said before the season. "This could be a very special year."

Like the little boy shooting baskets in the driveway, the Valparaiso Crusaders had some "dreams" of their own.

CHAPTER THREE

Life without Bryce

"How we prepare for today will determine our tomorrow."
–Author Unknown

As the start of pre-season practice slowly approached, and the glow of winning the gold medal at the World University Games was wearing off, Bryce Drew noticed something alarming: his knee, which he had sprained in the semifinal game, still hurt. It really hurt.

He had been undergoing treatment for the soft tissue sprain—ice, rest, therapy, etc.—to little avail. His knee felt a little better, but it was affecting his mobility in a major way, and until an MRI turned up negative, Bryce had been told by the medical staff to prepare himself for the possibility of surgery.

Slowly, but surely, Bryce's knee started to heal, despite the rigors of two-a-day workouts. While he was far from peak level, his mobility was getting better as practices wore on. Still, Homer Drew felt concerned enough to air his worry on the topic two weeks before the first exhibition game.

"His knee is very sore...we've been giving him a little more rest than everyone else," he said. "He's not even close to being 100 percent yet - he's limping down to the ice machines after practice. He has such a high pain tolerance that it's hard to keep him of the floor."

Over the next few days, however, Bryce's knee showed gradual improvement. While it didn't look like he would be at full strength by the start of the regular season, he felt he could play with the injury.

Enter another roadblock. During practice, Bryce suffered an injury to his right leg, likely by a kick to the shin. Valpo's sports medicine people, as well as Bryce, thought it was a bruise, until it still bothered him a week later. As it turned out, Bryce had a strained anterior tibial tendon. Dr. James Malayter, team physician, described the pain involved with the condition as "more advanced shin splints." Rod Moore, team trainer, is one of the best and continues to work with Bryce.

At the start of pre-season practice, Drew said one of the keys to the upcoming season was to keep the team healthy. To see his star player and son go down before his team had even taken the court for an exhibition game was nerve-wracking.

With the injury on everyone's mind, the Crusaders set off on their first exhibition journey without their floor leader. Kouvot-Finland visited the ARC on November 6 to kick off the pre-season. As the two teams took the floor, Bryce, dressed in street clothes, hobbled to the end of the bench and sat down. Fans behind the bench applauded his entrance.

Before the game, Drew looked around the room at his shorthanded team and offered a pragmatic assessment.

"We believe in you, but we will make mistakes tonight," he said. "Just keep hustling through it and try to make something good happen. This game will help prepare for the stronger schedule that awaits us."

As the game started, two things were immediately apparent. First, the six new players on the Valpo roster had some jitters to work out. Secondly, Jamie Sykes was glad to be back. He didn't stop smiling until a good two minutes into the game.

As could be expected, the first 10 minutes of the game were sloppy. Turnovers, fouls and missed shots were the order of the early going. The Crusader offense lacked any kind of rhythm, but Finland's shaky ball-handling kept the game close. Finally, late in the first half, the Finnish long-range shooters started heating up, draining four three-pointers in the half's closing minutes. Meanwhile, at the other end, Valpo suffered through 35 percent shooting and was getting killed on the boards by a smaller Kouvot team. Buoyed by a 30-12 rebounding advantage, the Finnish team opened up a 40-25 lead at halftime.

To top it off, Bob Jenkins headed to the locker room a couple minutes before intermission with a severe gash on his hand. He sliced it open on the rim, producing a wound that required 10 stitches. Later in the game, Aaron Thomason cut his hand slightly on the same rim, prompting Drew to demand an inspection and repair of the offending rim. Bob Jenkins seemed upbeat after the game as he related his injury, despite its gruesome details.

"I cut it open on the rim...cut it right to the bone," he said as he ducked into the training room. Several bystanders in the hallway winced as he clutched the wound.

Valpo came out in the second half with more defensive intensity, playing a tighter man-to-man defensive scheme. But the Crusaders' shooting woes continued, especially from long range. Valpo missed its first eight three-point tries, while Finland's big men rotating to the perimeter presented problems for Zoran Viskovic and Tony Vilscinkas. Finland's hot outside shooting continued, and Valpo could never get closer than eight points the entire second half. Kourot walked away with a 77-61 win. While no Valpo fans were pushing a panic button, they were audibly restless as the game clock ticked down.

During the game's waning moments, Bryce Drew sat expressionless with his head in his hands. After the game, his father wore the same expression as he addressed reporters in the hallway outside the locker room. One got the feeling that he wasn't as upset about the loss as he was about a possible glimpse into this team's near future with his star player, and now possibly Bob Jenkins, sidelined with injuries.

"Well, we've only had two weeks of practice, so we knew that we would be ragged," he said. "We will get better, but we need to learn that you can't live in your past. We have to execute and play harder."

Through four straight 20-win seasons and back-to-back NCAA tournament bids, there were two constants in Valparaiso University basketball, both of which Drew felt his team was lacking at the moment. The first, and most obvious factor was that the team was not healthy. The second factor was the team's intensity. While there wasn't much he could do about the injury bug, Drew labored for a solution to the intensity quandary.

"Obviously, the first step is to get people healthy," he said. "But we have to return to our days of playing with intensity instead of living on our past accomplishments."

While many people think of intensity in terms of the physical, Drew said that mental intensity was just as important.

"Intensity comes from not wanting to let yourself or your teammates down," he said. "That requires communication, and one of the problems we need to overcome is team communication. Communication is a powerful weapon that will help lead to teamwork and unity. The difference between an average team and a good team is the chemistry factor and we need to start with a foundation of good communication."

One of the ways Drew likes to get his team to communicate is through community service projects. At the start of the season, the players and coaches were involved with the Heart Walk to help raise funds for the local American Heart Association. In the past, Drew's teams had bagged groceries to benefit cancer research, helped out at the local Boys and Girls Club, as well as speaking to inmates at a local juvenile detention center.

In addition to providing a platform for the players to get to know one another off the floor, volunteering in the community serves a more important purpose, Drew said. "All of these experiences allowed our athletes to understand how fortunate God has been to them to give them the ability to play the game of basketball," he said.

Outside of the volunteering, Drew also scheduled other outings to help the team grow together and bond away from the game. From canoe trips to NBA games to softball games against members of the media, players were offered the opportunity to build unity, and, in turn, build teamwork.

Teamwork is a key to success in basketball, a main reason why Drew loves the game so much. The ability of a team to come together and work together largely determines its success, which is not unlike many other things in life, Drew said.

"Life is teamwork," he said. "For any position, or any job, we must learn to work with others. This holds true in most situations, from work to family to basketball. I always ask myself the question, 'how can we make this team function better?' The answer is to start with communications and grow from there."

In another effort to improve team communications, the coaching staff decided to start showing up at practice early, and begin meeting with each player individually.

"I knew I needed to set up team meetings with our captains to help them focus on communicating with our young players," Drew said. "I could also see that it was going to be a year where I was going to have to visit with some parents and convince them to encourage their sons to sacrifice and do what is best for the basketball team.

"There's an old proverb that says, 'a tree that bends with the wind will grow strong.' I knew we were going to have some strong winds hit our team and bend it, but I still had a great feeling that this team could become the greatest in the history of Valparaiso University if they allowed themselves to grow strong together."

Drew has always been described as an optimist, always seeing a glass half full when some see it half empty. He says, "I look at the sunny side of life and that comes from my faith in God."

Drew was a believer in positive reinforcement. Some coaches rant and rave on the sidelines and in practice. Others single out players for criticism, but not Drew. His philosophy is to strengthen existing positive behaviors with praise. He took his cue from an ancient parable.

"I remember Aesop's fable in which the wind and the sun argued over which one was stronger. The wind claimed to the sun that he could make an old man walking on earth take off his coat quicker than the sun could," he recalled. "The sun agreed to go behind a cloud while the wind blew up a storm. However, the harder the wind blew, the firmer the old man wrapped his coat around him. Eventually, the wind gave up; and the sun came out from behind the clouds and smiled kindly upon the old man. Before long, the old man mopped his brow, pulled off his coat and strolled on his way. The sun knew the secret: warmth, friend-liness and a gentle touch are stronger—and more effective—than force and fury."

In developing better habits for the team, Drew employed several techniques. First, he utilized some quotes, as well as bringing guests in to speak at practice. In addition, Drew showed the team several videos to encourage the players to develop a better work ethic to accomplish their goals. Finally, Drew used a technique he referred to as "cueing."

"Cueing is one of my favorite techniques and it involves starting on a positive note," he said. "For example, if we are working on free throws, I remind the player to follow through before the shot instead of correct-ing after the shot was taken. I need to employ a lot of cueing to develop new, positive behaviors for this basketball team."

"I remember Aesop's fable in which the wind and the sun argued over which one was stronger. The wind claimed to the sun that he could make an old man walking on earth take off his coat quicker than the sun could. The sun agreed to go behind a cloud while the wind blew up a storm. However, the harder the wind blew, the firmer the old man wrapped his coat around him. Eventually, the wind gave up; and the sun came out from behind the clouds and smiled kindly upon the old man. Before long, the old man mopped his brow, pulled off his coat and strolled on his way. The sun knew the secret: warmth, friendliness and a gentle touch are stronger—and more effective—than force and fury."–Homer Drew

---

While Drew said he was happy with increased defensive pressure in the second half of the game against Finland, Valpo's offense needed a lot of work.

Drew especially felt the rhythm of the offense was off-kilter. He knew that Valpo had to have everyone back from injury in order to develop a true rhythm and flow to the offense, but he thought the team needed to do a better job of recognizing each other's strengths, and then set each player up for his favorite shots. However, just as it would take time to get the team communicating, it would take time and willingness on each player's part to sacrifice a little for the benefit of the team.

"We have to get better shots, no question," he said. "Also, no one's exploding to the ball to get rebounds right now. I don't know how good we are, but at least this shows what we need to work on."

A few minutes after his father's post-game comments, Bryce Drew sat in the training room with his leg in a bucket of crushed ice.

He shrugged his shoulders and shook his head when asked about his injury.

"It's terrible," he said feebly. "It's going very slowly. Especially with this being my senior year, it's frustrating. And tonight was frustrating to watch."

As he squirmed a little from the chill of the ice—and anyone who has ever sprained an ankle can attest to that uniquely hellish sensation of a bare foot sitting in a bucket of ice, slowly losing feeling while the nerve endings scream the whole way to numb—Bryce admitted his leg was improving slowly.

"The pain has gone down, but I have no idea when I can play," he said. "When it feels a lot better, I can play, but I don't see it being better for a while. All I can really do is pray and hope it gets better."

Due to his two injuries, Drew had only gotten to play basketball full-speed for 12 days since the end of August. After he was asked if Purdue was one of those "big games" where one plays with an injury, no matter what, he shook his head vehemently.

"I would need assurances (by the medical staff) that it wouldn't do any permanent damage," he said. "I can play with pain, but this injury could cause permanent damage, so to play in a situation where you could do some permanent damage would be total stupidity."

Bryce said he hoped his teammates could use his absence as a rallying point in the early stages of the season.

"I just want the team to get better, especially the freshmen, because they can't rely on me [next year]," he said. "Hopefully, they can learn from the games that I'm not there."

Five nights later, the Crusaders returned to the ARC for their second exhibition game, against an Athletes In Action team that had already disposed of Michigan and Indiana during the pre-season. With Bryce already injured, Drew decided to take no chances. Every player who was banged up watched the game in street clothes. Joining Bryce on the bench were Bob Jenkins, Zoran Viskovic, and Jay Phifer.

Even the youngsters weren't immune from the injury plague. Jared Nuness, the freshman point guard out of Hopkins, Minnesota, sat out with a slight sprain in his ankle. As one might expect, Valpo suffered a long evening against the experienced AIA team that featured ex-Notre Dame standout Ryan Hoover, former Miami (Ohio) star Landon Hackim, and Southern Illinois graduate Aminu Timberlake. Prior to transferring to Southern Illinois from the University of Kentucky, Timberlake earned a spot in college basketball folklore as the player who was stepped on by Duke forward Christian Laettner during an infamous incident in the 1992 NCAA Regional Finals.

AIA shot 64 percent to Valpo's 33 percent in the first half to jump out to a 51-33 advantage. The Crusaders played AIA to an even second half, but Valpo could never get closer than 12 points. Athletes In Action coasted to an 88-73 win. Perhaps not wanting to tempt fate in the face of the injury explosion, Drew removed Bill Jenkins from the game when he tweaked his hamstring slightly. Both Bill Jenkins and Sykes watched the final eight minutes from the bench.

Afterwards, Drew said he was pleased with the increased defensive intensity in the second half, but he was handcuffed by the lack of personnel.

Drew acknowledged that his team was short-handed and promised they would be more competitive in the season opener against Bethel the following Saturday. But he also added a caveat, with a bit of foreboding in his voice.

"Finland and AIA got up and down the floor quickly, and Bethel will do the same thing," he said. "Their whole team shoots the three very well...it's not going to be an easy game for us."

While the team was upset with the loss, everyone seemed more concerned with Bryce Drew's status. He had visited Dr. John Hefernan, former Chicago Bulls team physician, earlier that afternoon. Hefernan was unusually cautious about his injury and set a recovery timetable of more than five weeks.

Bryce announced the update to the disappointed ARC crowd at halftime, and most of the questions in Drew's post-game press conference involved his son.

"I don't want to bring him back too soon, because it could get injured worse and then we lose Bryce for the season," Drew said. "I want to take a conservative approach to his rehab... we're not looking for him to be back until mid-December."

Going by that timetable, he would miss games against Purdue, Wisconsin-Green Bay, and Illinois-Chicago. Bryce would also miss the Big Island Invitational featuring potential games with Stanford, Oklahoma, and Wisconsin. While losing all of those non-conference games wouldn't affect its conference standing at all, it would seriously damage Valpo's hopes of getting a good seeding if they made the NCAA Tournament again. Moreover, it would virtually wipe out any shot of an at-large bid if the Crusaders were to lose in the Mid-Con tournament.

Bryce smiled and said he was slightly relieved as he left the training room after the game, immediately following a 20-minute meeting with trainer Rod Moore, dad Homer, brother Scott, and team physician Malayter to determine a plan for rehabilitating the injury.

"It's going to take six weeks to heal, but he [Hefernan] was real vague. I guess my injury is a freak thing...he said he had never seen anything like it in that part of the leg," he said. "But at least I've got a set rehab program, and I should be able to start practicing by December 1st at the latest."

Missing the big home game against Purdue wasn't going down with Bryce as easily, however.

"I feel like I'm letting the whole team down," he said. "We've all been looking forward to playing Purdue, but God has a plan for it."

His father concurred.

"I remember the Bible accenting in the books of Jeremiah and Romans that God has a purpose and a plan for our lives, and I have learned that God's timing is better than mine...but I sure wish Bryce would get back soon," he said.

Five days later, Valpo opened the regular season at home against Bethel College, an NAIA school from Mishawaka, Indiana. Of course, this wasn't an average NAIA team. For one thing, Bethel was the defending NAIA Division II national champions. For another, Bethel has strong ties to the Drew family, for it is where Homer Drew got his start as a head coach, leading the Pilots to a 252-110 record over 11 seasons. And Bethel's head coach, Mike Lightfoot, played for Drew during the 1976-77 season. "Mike was a tenacious competitor and it has carried over to his coaching as he is one of the best in his division," Drew said.

With all these family connections floating around, one would think the basketball game would be a giant love-in. Not quite. Bethel came out in a furious full-court press. With Bryce Drew on the bench in street clothes again, Valpo jumped out to an early lead, but the Bethel press took its toll. Jamie Sykes picked up two fouls within a matter of seconds, and then reached in to pick up his third personal foul—with 16:56 left in the first half. Jared Nuness hopped off the bench and entered the game. The freshman would get an early test.

The Crusaders exploited their size advantage in the game's early minutes, throwing the ball in to Tony Vilcinskas, whose easy shots in the lane helped Valpo grab a seven-point lead five minutes into the game.

Later in the half, Bethel, trailing by 10 points, regained its composure. A quick three-pointer by Ryan Bales pulled the Pilots within seven, and after a couple of turnovers and a missed layup by the Crusaders, Bethel had pulled to within one. An offensive foul and two turnovers later, and Bethel held a five-point advantage. With Bethel College being only 60 miles from Valpo, several hundred BC fans had made the trip. Fans dressed in Bethel blue were going crazy.

Behind the late momentum of a Bob Jenkins' dunk, Valpo pulled to within one at the half.

The two teams battled evenly in the second half. Valpo could not break the Bethel press with any consistency and was plagued by turnovers. Vilcinskas struggled in the post the entire half, missing five lay-ins in the half alone. Moreover, the Crusaders couldn't stop Rico Swanson, Bethel's NAIA All-American point guard. His slashing drives left Valpo's defenders dazed for most of the second half.

The two teams traded leads for most of the half. With just under four minutes left, VU held a 73-72 lead. Coming out of a timeout, both teams were clearly exhausted. Most players had their hands on their shorts gasping for air. However, it was only Valpo who looked tired during the final three and a half minutes of play.

While Swanson scored two straight baskets, Valpo couldn't convert on three straight possessions, and Bethel's angel-faced Ryan Bales stuck a dagger in the Crusaders by draining a three-pointer with just over 90 seconds left. Valpo missed another shot, and Bales buried another jumper with 43 seconds left to put the Pilots up by 10 and send Crusader fans scurrying for the exits. The Bethel fans screamed with delight.

As the final seconds of the game ticked away, Bryce leaned back in his chair and stared blankly at the scoreboard. Final score: Bethel 85, Valparaiso 75. The Bethel players mobbed each other at mid-court as their coaches hugged on the bench. The Crusaders walked quickly and silently to the dressing room after shaking hands, most of the players looking directly at the floor the entire way.

The back breaking statistic for Valpo wasn't hard to spot: Valpo committed 27 turnovers for the game against Bethel's staggeringly tenacious press.

Despite a huge win for his program, Bethel head coach Lightfoot was modest in the post-game press conference.

"This one's special because of what Coach Drew has done here at Valparaiso," he said. "He's really built this program."

Surprisingly, Drew lightened the mood as soon as he walked into the media room.

"Does anyone have any eligibility left?" he joked.

Despite the disheartening loss, Drew said, that it was no time for his players or Valpo fans to panic.

"We're excited to get our team back together and healthy, because we're struggling right now," he said. "But I have faith in this group. They will get better."

Not lost on Drew was the fact that Purdue, ranked in the Top 10 and playing a style of basketball similar to Bethel's pressing defense, would be invading the ARC in 48 hours.

"We didn't have the poise today," he said. "And what's really scary is that Purdue does the exact same thing as Bethel, except they're bigger, stronger and faster...hopefully, this will make us a better basketball team."

After the game, Bryce was once again sitting on a table in the training room, receiving an ultrasound treatment on his leg. He looked completely crestfallen.

"You can come in," he told a reporter. "But the quotes won't be very long."

He could barely muster enough words to describe having to watch the upset loss from the bench.

"Terrible...just terrible," he said as an assistant trainer glided the ultrasound wand over his gel-covered leg. He had begun a shooting regimen, so the natural question was if the long layoff was affecting his shot at all.

"No, my shot is fine," he said, somewhat tersely.

It was pretty apparent that Bryce didn't want to talk about the game, especially since he wasn't able to play. A few players had mentioned that they were pleased that freshmen Jared Nuness and Jason Jenkins got some experience under adverse conditions, and that it could turn out to be a positive for the team in the long run. Bryce nodded briefly at that notion, then shrugged.

"Well, I guess so...but I'd rather win and have them get that type of experience later," he said with a hint of a smile. "I'm not sure if any good can come out of this kind of a loss."

One thing was for certain on this chilly Saturday: if there were any other Valpo players as down in the dumps as Bryce, they had better shake it off quickly, because Gene Keady's Purdue Boilermakers were about to storm into town. No rest was in sight for the weary Crusaders.

CHAPTER FOUR

The "Learning Thing"

"If we can look in the mirror after the game, and we can say that we tried our very best, we are winners."

−Homer Drew

A group of Valpo students milled around the ARC on a frigid Monday afternoon. Walking up the snow-covered side streets near campus, one could sense something that was fairly new to the city of Valparaiso: big-time atmosphere. The ESPN trucks were parked next to the arena, and a few fans were hanging around the VU Bookstore next door waiting to purchase souvenirs, even though it was more than four hours to tipoff.

Many Valpo fans wondered what adjustments Coach Drew could possibly make in such a short time to allow the Crusaders to challenge the highly ranked Purdue Boilermakers. Indeed, the morning before the game, the *Vidette-Times* summed up the local sentiment with a banner headline. It read: "Bring On Purdue?"

About two hours before tipoff, Drew spoke about the game from home, and he sounded fairly pessimistic about his team's chances.

"Our problem is that we're learning as we go," he said. "We've had all these new freshmen come in, and from opening day on, we haven't had the chance to all play together. Thanks to injuries, we've never been able to have all of our top five players practice together." Plus Coach Gene Keady is one of the most successful coaches in Division I. His knowledge and "will power" permeates to his players.

While the challenge of facing the ninth-ranked Boilermakers excited Drew, he said his team wasn't even close to where he wanted it to be.

"We've got to regroup, and we're going to use this game as a learning thing," he said.

Was the head coach holding out any hope for another home-court miracle, like the one against Notre Dame in 1988? Drew laughed.

"Well, we need some magic," he said. "Anything can happen on any given night, so if we play our very best and Purdue doesn't play its best, maybe we'll have the second miracle in the ARC."

Putting his younger players in such an emotional game early in the season was another source of worry to Drew.

"The emotion factor is a huge disadvantage to us...it's like we're throwing them [the freshmen] into the fire because they just haven't had that type of experience yet," he said. "It'd be like if you or I started a new job, and then you're thrown into a really tense situation on the very first day. That's pretty much what our freshmen are doing tonight."

There were rumors—or at least wishes—around town the previous few days that Bryce Drew might make a dramatic entrance, injury be damned, and play against Purdue. His father shot that theory down instantly.

"No, he's not playing," Drew said. "It's really hard for him. He was in tears the other night, because he loves big games, from the high school Final Four, to the World Games, and the tourney game with Boston College last year. For him not to get a chance to play is just devastating to him."

Later, at the ARC, the certain record-breaking crowd filed in. Valpo officials had added more than 800 temporary seats for the game, virtually ensuring the largest crowd in school history. As could be expected, there was a sizable contingent of Purdue fans who had made the 90-minute drive north from West Lafayette. Even Purdue Pete, the school's hard hat-wearing mascot, made the trip.

As Valpo took the floor, a huge roar engulfed the ARC. University students held up banners to try to get on television. Purdue, obviously, was accustomed to nationally televised games. For the students and citizens of Valparaiso, however, this was special. They were determined to make the most of it, even if their team was going to have to fight just to keep the game close.

Drew knew that two freshmen, Jared Nuness and Jason Jenkins, would play key roles against the Boilermakers. He wanted to get the young players experience in a big game, and he needed them to play with more confidence than they had displayed so far. Drew knew that the freshmen needed to play heavy minutes against Purdue for both themselves and the team to improve. It definitely was an opportunity to learn.

"When an injury comes along, it allows other people the chance to play, and those people have to be ready," Drew said. "The important role of the bench is to have someone be able to step up and take advantage of that opportunity. Mentally, physically, and emotionally, a player must be ready to go in and do the job when injuries happen to a team."

Drew believed in the power of the bench. Two of his favorite examples of why the bench is so vital to a team are from the National Football League. One is Earl Morrall, the backup quarterback under Baltimore Colts legend Johnny Unitas. After an arm injury sidelined Unitas in 1968, Morrall was thrust into the position of filling Unitas' shoes. Fans wondered if Morrall could maintain the level of play that Unitas had established. Due to the fact that he worked hard in practice, the well-prepared Morrall not only sustained the level of brilliance at which his predecessor had performed, he was named the NFL's Most Valuable Player in 1968.

"I am living proof that being willing to pay the price everyday can payoff. And I suppose that's true of any kind of job you have to do, whether it's playing football, selling suits, or running a business."–Earl Morrall

Drew's other favorite story from the bench is the tale of Frank Reich, the backup under Buffalo Bills quarterback and certain future Hall-of-Famer Jim Kelly. During the 1993 AFC Wild Card Game, the Bills trailed the Houston Oilers, 35-3, in the third quarter before Reich replaced an injured Kelly and led the Bills to a 41-38 win—the greatest comeback in the history of professional football.

A modern success story off the bench was UCLA's Cameron Dollar. He replaced an injured Tyus Edney and promptly led UCLA under Coach Jim Harrick to the NCAA National Championship.

"The bench is vital and each person must be ready so that when his number is called, he is in the best possible shape physically and mentally to do what is best to help the team, and eventually help himself to receive more playing time," Drew said. With Bryce injured, there was an opportunity for the bench to step up big against Purdue.

Purdue spurted out to a 10-2 lead, but Valpo cut the lead to 10-7 and trailed only 12-8 when play was stopped for a television timeout. The fans rose to their feet as the teams headed for the benches.

Out of the timeout, Viskovic hit a short jumper in the paint to bring Valpo within two and the Crusaders stayed close for a few minutes, trailing only 18-16 when suddenly the team began to stumble.

Purdue's pressure defense started to take its toll as Valpo committed three quick turnovers and then compounded the problem by fouling Purdue's Brian Cardinal, an outstanding free-throw shooter. Cardinal drained six straight free-throws, and then added a three-pointer, pushing Purdue 11 points ahead.

To make matters worse, Valpo started missing shots—all of its shots. Long jumpers, short tip-ins, everything. Miller, who had been quiet since the game's opening minutes, hit a few tough baskets in the lane. When Viskovic finally converted a three-point play with 1:21 remaining in the first half, it broke a 16-point run by Purdue. The Crusaders trailed by 13 at a halftime, 34-21.

When the two teams returned for the second half, it was obvious Purdue wasn't changing its defense at all. The pressure forced a Valpo turnover on the inbounds pass to start the half. Bill Jenkins and Cardinal tussled briefly near midcourt. After Jaraan Cornell hit a three off a kick-out play to push the Boilers' lead to 16, Bob Jenkins hit a jumper and then Vilcinskas drew a charging foul. However, on the ensuing possession, Jared Nuness threw the ball away. Bob Jenkins quickly stole it back and Nuness made up for his mistake by draining a three.

After a Purdue miss, Vilcinskas was fouled by Cardinal and went to the line, to the delight of the partisan Valpo crowd. As Vilcinskas stood at the line, Valpo students teased Purdue's rough-and-tumble forward.

After a Purdue basket stretched the lead back to 17, Nuness hit another three from the left side of the key. You could see the freshman's confidence grow as he trotted downcourt waving for the fans to make noise. Valpo forced a turnover by Purdue and Jason Jenkins converted a transition layin to cut the Purdue lead to 12. The ARC crowd exploded. Keady instantly and frantically signaled for a timeout. With 11:23 left, Valpo—minus its All-American—was making a furious run at a Top 10 team, and on national television to boot.

After the timeout, Valpo kept the defensive pressure up. Purdue missed its only shot on the possession, and Valpo came down with the rebound. The crowd roared, sensing that the Crusader run would continue. On the offensive end, Valpo operated methodically, running the shot clock down. Viskovic broke free underneath on a back cut. Jason Jenkins sent a bounce pass to him, but the pass bounced off Viskovic's knee and out of bounds. The house groaned. Valpo had missed a golden opportunity, and the players knew it as they slunk off the court for a television timeout.

Out of the timeout, Valpo's defense came through again, as Nuness drew an offensive foul on Jaraan Cornell. Nuness knocked down both free throws to cut the Purdue lead to 10, 47-37, with just over 10 minutes left in the game. The crowd rose to their feet as Purdue brought the ball up the floor. A defensive stop here could change the momentum for the balance of the game, and the fans realized it. They responded by chanting, pounding on the wooden bleachers, and making lots of noise.

Valpo forced Purdue to work for the shot. The Boilermakers tossed the ball around the perimeter. The crowd grew louder as the shot clock ticked down. Finally, Chad Austin launched a bail-out three. It looked off—way off. As the Crusaders scrambled for position to grab a long rebound, the ball glanced off the glass and splashed through the net. Purdue went back up by 13, and the ARC seemed to deflate.

The teams exchanged baskets, and after a Viskovic free throw, Purdue's lead stood at 10, 52-42, with less than eight minutes to go.

Once again, the Boilermakers came up big when they needed it. Gary McQuay, who hadn't been much of a factor all night, slammed home two points and was fouled. The completed three-point play put Purdue back up by 13. Slowly, Valpo chipped away again. The teams traded free throws, and after two Cardinal free throws gave Purdue a nine-point lead, Bill Jenkins hit a reverse layup to pull Valpo within seven with just over four minutes to play. As Valpo came back on defense, Nuness slapped the floor to fire up the defense and the crowd. This was Valpo's chance to take the game to the wire.

Yet one more time, the Boilermakers hit the big shot. Chad Austin shook loose off of a screen and nailed a three-pointer, pushing the lead back to 10 and effectively finishing the Crusader rally for the evening. Valpo then turned the ball over three consecutive times. The comeback had been thwarted.

Purdue closed the game with a 12-2 run to make the final score 73-56, in favor of Purdue. Valpo headed off the court to a standing ovation from its fans. Following the post-game handshake, Bryce Drew quickly walked with his teammates off the court. Despite a gallant effort, Valpo was still 0-2 and would have to work its way out of an early-season hole.

Still, the display by the fans did not go unnoticed by Valpo coaches and players.

"What special fans we have," Drew said. "For them to stand and provide a standing ovation after a losing effort when we were short-handed really says what is special and unique about Valparaiso, Indiana. They appreciate good effort. They knew that we played the best we possibly could on that day."

The final stats would point out one glaring factor as to why Valpo lost the game: turnovers. The Crusaders finished the game with a whopping

30 turnovers. In the post-game press conference, however, Drew was still upbeat.

"I'm very proud of our basketball team," he said. "Since October 17, we have never had our top five players practicing all together. For one of our exhibition games last week, we had seven players sitting there on the bench in dress shirts."

"We've had no time together, and so you get 30 turnovers," he said.

He was also proud of the freshmen, Jason Jenkins and Jared Nuness, who he brought into the media room with him. The "learning thing" was that the freshmen realized they could contribute to the team with their shooting and defense, and that the rest of the team could play with confidence, even after losing its star player to an injury.

"They did a nice job handling the basketball and shooting some threes," Drew said. "Our guys didn't hang their heads. They tried and tried to get back into the ballgame, so I'm really proud of them."

"This game gave us great confidence because we showed a lot of heart and didn't give up," Nuness said. "We're tired of losing...but we're learning under fire. We became a better basketball team tonight."

After the game, Drew had shared his "two scoreboards" theory with the players. The first scoreboard, he said, was what the fans and media see as the final score. The second scoreboard is in the players' hearts.

"If we can look in the mirror after the game, and we can say that we tried our very best, we are winners," Drew said.

Even Gene Keady was impressed with the way Valpo performed without its leading scorer.

"We had to fight through as a team tonight...," he said. "We knew those guys [Valpo] would be warriors. They're well coached, so we knew they would play better."

Chad Austin, who hit several big shots to keep Valpo at bay, said that the ARC was a big-time basketball environment, and he was proud of his team for pulling through.

"We knew they'd have a good ball club and that they would be fundamentally sound," he said. "And here the crowd is right up on the court. To win in that type of atmosphere is good for our team."

Austin didn't care to speculate on the outcome if Bryce Drew had been playing.

"They could have gotten closer. They might have beat us," he said.

Bryce stood in the hallway outside the training room after the game. He was in good spirits, but he was obviously disappointed that he had been unable to play.

"There is a sense of loss," he said. "Because it was a great opportunity for us tonight...not being out there was tough."

"In a sense, I'm glad the game's over with because of all the talk," Bryce continued, referring to his injury. "But I'm still mad that we're 0-2 to start our season. A loss is still a loss."

A reporter asked Bryce if sitting out against Purdue was tougher than the 1994 loss in the Indiana High School State Championship game. Bryce smiled.

"Tonight was the worst night for me, because I tend to thrive off big crowds," he continued. "Not having the opportunity to play really hurt. I've been looking forward to this game for such a long time. I mean, I'd rather play and lose than not play at all."

Bryce echoed his father's sentiments about Jason Jenkins and Jared Nuness, however.

"If they aren't ready to play, we aren't going to be very good," he said. "So we've been trying to give them a lot of encouragement so they won't doubt themselves."

"We took Jared upstairs and worked on some shooting and ball handling drills," Drew said. "Jared's in a tough situation, but he's a good player, so this will only make him better."

Overall, each player felt the Purdue loss was a moral victory of sorts. While they had still lost by 17 points in a game that so many people had been targeting since the schedule was drawn up, they were proud that they were slowly improving. Also, they were proud that they learned how to compete and execute their gameplan with their best player and floor leader sidelined. They were proud that even while shorthanded, they were able to put a scare into a Top 10 team. Leave it to Tony Vilcinskas to bring back a little of the swagger of the previous two seasons' championship teams, and put the "learning things" in perspective: more confidence.

"It was all in our heads," he offered as a reason for the team's early struggles. "But we have more confidence in ourselves now. We had lost it, but tonight, we got our confidence back."

While Drew was proud of his players for the way they battled, he wasn't quite sure the confidence level was where it needed to be.

"Success breeds success."-Homer Drew

"Confidence is such a tricky word," he said. "Confidence comes from experience...it comes from success and in knowing that you can be successful. Yet, how do you become successful? Through experience and through winning. It can be a vicious circle, but it's one that is important in the life cycle of a team. The best way to gain confidence is to continue to try and be persistent and once success is found, then success breeds more success."

Regardless of what level of confidence the team was playing with, the process of blending six seniors with five freshmen was taking much longer than Drew had hoped.

"We have tried team meetings and one-on-one meetings, and we are making progress slowly, but not as quickly as our staff would like," he said. Drew sensed that the level of trust between the players was lower than it needed to be.

"One of the things we discussed with the team is that we want them to find the good in one another, in other words, to be tolerant of one another and find the power in themselves that will allow our team to be successful," he said. "But right now, the maturity and experience gap between the older and younger players is tremendously wide.

"We have to understand the true acronym of the word 'team,'" he said. "It means, 'Together Everyone Achieves More.'" Citing as an example were

TEAMWORK

An Editorial Without Words

the previous five NBA Champions. After winning the 1994 title, Houston Rockets center Hakeem Olajuwon said bluntly, "Teamwork won it." When the Rockets repeated as champs in 1995, guard Clyde Drexler told reporters that "we think as a team." Despite the presence of the game's greatest indivdual player, Michael Jordan, the Chicago Bulls, who won three straight titles in 1996, 1997, and 1998, epitomize team play through their "triangle" offense and full-court defense. Drew wanted his players to begin thinking as a team.

Still, there was a simple way for the Crusaders to get better: get healthy.

"Injuries can turn your season if they happen to key players," Drew said.

"Without Bryce, we could not handle the double team or quickness of Purdue."

Published reports had stated that Bryce would be unavailable to play until December at the earliest. However, several people around the team had mentioned that his injury was healing quicker than anticipated, and that the injury itself may have turned out to be less serious than originally feared.

The Crusaders' next game would be in Hilo, Hawaii, for the Big Island Invitational Tournament over Thanksgiving weekend. Valpo was slated to play Montana in its tourney opener, but national powers such as Stanford, Oklahoma, and Wisconsin were also in the field; so unless Valpo wanted to start the season 0-5, there needed to be a spark. A few hours before tipoff of the Montana game, Drew confirmed over the phone that the rumors were true, giving every Valpo player, coach, and fan something to be thankful for.

"Yes, Bryce will play tonight," he said.

Regaining Respect

"If you want a rainbow, you've got to put up with the rain."
—Author Unknown

While the entire Crusader team was excited by the prospects of Bryce's return, they were less than thrilled by what greeted them when they arrived on the lush, tropical Hawaiian islands: an illness.

A virus of unknown origin befell approximately a dozen people in the Crusaders' travel party, including Homer Drew. The viral infection also kept Tony Vilcinskas, Bill Jenkins, and Marko Punda on the sidelines during the Crusaders' first few days in paradise. Those hampered with the illness were too nauseous to keep down any of the local Polynesian cuisine, or anything else for that matter. Indeed, Drew's voice was weakened and hoarse when he relayed the news of Bryce's availability.

"We're going to see how he feels," Drew said. "If he plays and it feels okay, we'll leave him in. If not, we'll go back to our original timetable."

While the constant rain and illnesses shortened planned sightseeing trips during the team's first few days on the islands, Drew still made sure the team got a chance to enjoy the beautiful culture of Hawaii. The team went snorkeling in the crystal blue waters and coral reefs and then also traveled up the mountain to see the volcanoes. Tony Vilcinskas especially enjoyed the water activities with his high dives and slides off the boat. Scott Drew and Steve Flint did their sport fishing off the back of

53

the boat while Coach Harrick enjoyed watching the dolphins. Perhaps the favorite, however was the Polynesian BBQ. "Enjoying the beauty of nature and learning about different regions and cultures I think is important," Drew said.

"Whenever we're on a basketball trip, we like to take in the educational and geographic environment," he said. "To me, that is important because it will help them develop into well-rounded individuals, which will help them be successful when their playing days are over."

When Valpo took the court against Montana at Hilo's Afhen-Chinook Civic Center, Drew feared that his son might try to do too much and re-injure himself. He was also worried that Bryce's return could throw off the rhythm of the entire offense if they didn't ease him into the offensive framework.

"We have to be careful," Drew cautioned. "We must take time to blend him into the offense or else it may cause problems with our motion and rotations."

Bryce started slowly, as did the rest of the team. The team shot poorly, and, at halftime, the Crusaders trailed Montana, 34-28. Less than one minute into the third quarter (all pre-season basketball tournaments were experimenting with four 10-minute quarters instead of two 20-minute halves), Montana's leading scorer, center Ryan Dick, picked up his fourth foul. The Crusaders capitalized on the big man's absence, going on a 19-6 run to push their lead to seven.

The big plays during the spurt were courtesy of Bryce, who hit a three and was fouled to achieve the rare four-point play, and Jamie Sykes, who followed Bryce's play with a trey of his own.

"That 3-pointer gave us the momentum to finish strong and win the game," Drew said.

Valpo cruised the rest of the way and won, 70-58, its first victory of the season. Bryce finished with 23 points and six assists in 35 minutes of playing time. Drew fretted that he had left his hobbled superstar on the court for too long.

"I really played him too long," he said after the game. "Fortunately, his leg isn't swelling and isn't too sore."

Bob Jenkins, however, felt Bryce's value to the team merited the health risk.

"We were a lot more comfortable because you know he's out there on the floor...," he told the *Vidette-Times*. "It takes a lot of stress and pressure off us and gives us a mental edge."

While the Crusaders were ecstatic to have finally cracked the win column, there was little time to celebrate. Valpo had another game the following evening, this time against yet another Top 20 team: Stanford University.

The Cardinal had lost its lightning quick point guard, Brevin Knight, to the NBA. Still, what Stanford lost in speed, they made up for in size. Mark Madsen and David Young, two players who hovered near 7-foot, anchored their muscular front line. They were undefeated and ranked 15th in the country entering the game.

While the opponent was formidable, Crusader players refused to be intimidated. In fact, they relished the challenge. Practically the only goal that the Valpo seniors had set for themselves that hadn't been achieved was upsetting a team from a major conference. They had fallen just short on several occasions. The game was also a chance for Valpo players to reclaim some of the respect that fans felt they had relinquished with the loss to Bethel.

"We keep getting the chance to play bigger schools," Bob Jenkins told the *Vidette-Times*. "We want to go out there and compete, but we want a shot at winning."

The Crusaders hit the court with an intensity that had been lacking in the season's first two games. After the first quarter, Valpo and Stanford were tied at 15. In the second quarter, the Cardinal's defense clamped down, limiting Valpo to eight points as Stanford opened a 33-23 lead.

In the third quarter, Valpo was able to cut into the lead, but not without getting the entire frontline in foul trouble. Stanford drew a foul nearly every time it went inside and it frustrated the Crusaders. The Cardinal, an outstanding free-throw shooting team, drained the charity shots and kept the Valpo rally at bay throughout the third and the majority of the fourth quarter.

One by one, gold jerseys headed to the bench after fouling out. Zoran Viskovic, Bill Jenkins, Tony Vilcinskas, Aaron Thomason, and, finally, Bob Jenkins were all disqualified before the game ended.

With Valpo trailing by eight with three minutes left, Bryce led one final push.

Bob Jenkins stole the ball near mid-court and dished to Bryce, who pulled up from 25 feet and knocked down a three to cut Stanford's lead to 56-51. On Stanford's ensuing possession, Bryce stole the ball again and drained another NBA-style three. The score was now 56-54 Stanford with 2:20 remaining.

Stanford set up on offense and threw the ball into the post. Once again, Jared Nuness fouled Young, and a Stanford player returned to the free-throw line. Hitting both shots, Young pushed the lead to 58-54. With 1:30 remaining, Bryce countered, leaning between two defenders to hit another three-pointer. The Stanford lead was trimmed to one point. Even Valpo radio announcer Todd Ickow, who had witnessed many of Bryce's greatest moments, was awestruck.

"What Bryce is doing tonight is just mind-boggling," Ickow said. "This is why he's being promoted as an All-American candidate, folks."

After a Stanford timeout, the Cardinal returned to their inside game. Young spun for a short jumper and was fouled by Bob Jenkins. The shot fell, and Young converted the three-point play to put Stanford up by four. The Crusaders missed their next shot, and Young was fouled yet again when he posted up Aaron Thomason. Two free throws later, the Crusader deficit was six with 59 seconds left.

Jason Jenkins stepped up to hit a three and pull the Crusaders back within three with 47 seconds left. In the backcourt, Bob Jenkins fouled Kris Weems. More Cardinal free throws. Drew shook his head in frustration with the call of the touch foul.

Bryce dribbled the ball upcourt with just over 30 seconds remaining for Valpo's last stand. However, as he drove the left side near the baseline, Bryce slipped and fell. The referee whistled a traveling call. Valpo's threat was over.

The final score, 70-65, was remarkable considering that Stanford shot 48 free throws compared to 19 for Valpo.

"If I were an official," said Valpo sports information director Bill Rogers, who was doing the radio commentary for the game, "I would be ashamed of myself to have been a part of a game where you had five players foul out from one team and none on the other, in addition to that foul shot discrepancy."

Even after a good night's sleep—or perhaps a sleepless night—Drew couldn't shake off that statistic, especially after his players had come up just short against a major opponent again.

"Our players deserved to win that game," Drew said the next day. "I don't understand why the game was called the way it was. I'm really disappointed, because it was not called fairly at both ends of the floor. It completely wiped out all of our outstanding offensive plays."

Drew wasn't the only one who held that opinion, either. One NBA scout attending the tournament approached him outside the locker room after the game.

"He told me that it was the worst-officiated, most one-sided game he's ever seen at this level," Drew said. "And this guy's seen a lot of basketball, so that's a strong statement."

Despite the loss, Drew still saw many positives in his team's play.

"This game really helped our confidence, because it showed our team that we are capable of beating a Top 20 team," he said. "Only time will tell if it will have a lasting effect, but if we get stronger and healthier and continue to hustle, then we'll continue to improve."

In addition, the Valpo squad had made a name for itself among the local fans in Hawaii. During the final minutes of the Stanford game, the crowd began chanting, "Val-po! Val-po!" Even after the game, the crowd rose to give the team a standing ovation as the players left the floor.

The Crusaders had one more game in Hawaii, and it was less than 24 hours after the end of the Stanford game. The Crusaders would take on the University of Pacific in the tourney's third-place game.

Pacific had defeated Wisconsin in the tournament's first round and was led by 7-1 center Michael Olowokandi, who would go on to become the top pick in the 1998 NBA Draft. The short turnaround after an emotional loss concerned Drew, especially facing a Pacific team that had gone to the NCAA Tournament the year before.

"We are simply exhausted as a team," he said. "It was an heroic effort by our basketball team last night, but Pacific's a quality basketball team. This is going to be a real challenge for us."

The Crusaders showed few ill effects, however, in the game's early stages. They battled Pacific basket for basket, and at halftime trailed by only one point, 37-36.

In the second half, however, Pacific began feeding the ball inside to Olowokandi, who dominated the paint. He finished with 24 points and helped Pacific build a 10-point lead with 2:15 remaining. With 1:37 left, Drew called a timeout. Valpo still trailed by eight, 70-62. Jason Jenkins hit a three to pull the Crusaders within five. Valpo fouled Pacific's Earl Clark, a 30-percent foul shooter. He hit one of two free throws to make it 71-65. Jamie Sykes buried a three to cut the lead in half. Once again, Valpo fouled Earl Clark, who hit one of two free throws to make the Pacific lead 72-68. Sykes scored another three-pointer. Valpo trailed by only one point with 46 seconds left.

"If you continue to hustle, good things will happen."–Homer Drew

Jared Nuness stole the ball from Clark and was fouled. His two free throws gave Valpo the lead. After another Earl Clark free throw to tie the score, Valpo readied itself for the final possession. Pacific set up in a zone defense and was clearly most concerned with Bryce. Two defenders shadowed him the entire play. With the clock running out, Nuness drove the lane and kicked the ball to Sykes, who was standing on the left wing. Sykes took two dribbles and then launched a fadeaway jumper that rippled through the net as time expired. Valpo had won, 75-73. Sykes was buried under an avalanche of happy teammates.

Drew felt the dramatic ending offered compelling evidence why basketball has become the world's number one game. To quote Yogi Berra, "it ain't over 'til it's over."

"What a wonderful example of persistency and a team never giving up," Drew said. "Even though we were down by eight points, our team never lost heart and never lost the will to compete."

Pacific coach Bob Thomason expressed no regrets for the zone defense after the game.

"We didn't want to go with a man defense because they'd just get it to [Bryce] and let him take it..." Thomason told the *Stockton (California) Record*. "He barely got the shot off. We made them go to the guy that we wanted them to go to."

That proved to be Pacific's demise that evening. Pacific forward Barry Marvel told the *Record* that he was impressed with the teamwork that Valpo displayed down the stretch.

"You know they have an All-American three-point shooter, but it was everyone else that beat us at the end," he said.

Sykes, who had been in a shooting slump in the first few games, picked an opportune time to snap out of it. He didn't have a field goal in the game until the final 1:37. Sykes thought that Pacific may have let up a bit too early.

"Pacific knew they had the game won," Jamie told the *Vidette-Times*. "They were in celebration mode."

Drew was thrilled with the last-minute comeback.. More importantly, he felt it taught his team an important lesson. He likened it to the pre-championship era Chicago Bulls, who did not win many titles despite Michael Jordan often scoring 50 points a game. It was only after they surrounded Jordan with better players, who were willing to sacrifice for championships, that the Bulls achieved greatness. Team play is what Drew witnessed against Pacific, and that was what allowed the Crusaders to make such a comeback.

"A team is *always* in a game, as it truly takes a team to win," Drew said.

"This showed them that we are never out of a game, no matter how far behind we may be, if we continue to hustle," he added.

Drew also was excited at some of the gelling he witnessed in the Aloha state.

"This was a great step in blending our basketball team as our younger players made great contributions," he said. "We are getting better, but we need to continue to improve and work on our team chemistry."

Drew was reminded of this passage from Kipling's Second *Jungle Book* when reflecting on the Hawaiian tournament:

> *Now this is the law of the jungle, as old and as true;*
> *As old and as true as the sky;*
> *And the wolf that shall keep it may prosper,*
> *But the wolf that shall break it must die.*
> *As the creeper that girdles the tree trunk,*
> *The law runneth forward and back.*
> *For the strength of the pack is the wolf,*
> *And the strength of the wolf is the pack.*

Drew knew his team had plenty of experience and that they had good people at each position. However, he also knew team chemistry is an extremely fragile commodity. Talent alone would not allow this team to become the best it could be. Only through outstanding chemistry could the Crusaders become a team of destiny.

Drew derived his theory of team chemistry from two of the greatest coaches in basketball history: Red Auerbach, who won eight NBA titles as coach of the Boston Celtics in the 1950s and 1960s; and John Wooden, who won 10 NCAA championships during the 1960s and 1970s at UCLA.

"Red Auerbach had a great quote, 'some say you have to use your five best players, but I found out that you win with the five who fit best together as a team,'" Drew said. "John Wooden, perhaps the greatest coach in the history of the NCAA, states it this way: 'our titles would not have been possible without the unselfishness displayed by all of our team. The team wins, not the individuals.' In Hawaii, we took a giant step forward, but now we must continue."

Drew thought the emotional lift of the Pacific win provided an opportune time to offer advice to the players.

"Now is a perfect opportunity to reinforce the good behavior that we saw out on the floor, and also to correct things that we need to work on in the future," he said. "After a win is a wonderful time to make people improve themselves because people are very receptive and in a good frame of mind then."

Off the floor, however, Drew felt the players still were not communicating as a team. At the airport on the way home, he noticed that several players were sulking, unable to enjoy the success of their teammates, even though the team was doing well. Drew thought that it was important for the players to put aside any personal displeasure at this critical juncture in the team's development. It was his belief that positive thoughts and actions lead to positive results.

"Although it may sound odd, I truly believe that you can at least fake some enthusiasm, even though it may hurt inside, for the betterment of the team," Drew said. "There are only 14 players on this team, so each person must find a way to support the team."

Although Valpo was returning home with a losing record, and some players were still upset with the close loss to Stanford, the Crusaders had gone a long way in re-establishing themselves as a team with the potential to live up to the greatness expected by their fans.

On the plane ride home, Drew shared a quotation with the team which he felt summed up the trip to the Hawaiian islands:

> *I am not what I ought to be,*
> *Not what I want to be,*
> *Not what I am going to be,*
> *But thankful that I am not what I used to be.*

Upon their return to Valparaiso, the team found that among the fans and the local media, the progress they had achieved outweighed the struggles of the first two games.

"The Crusaders may have lost some respect after being upset by Bethel in the season opener. But they certainly gained some of it back in Hawaii," wrote Paul Jankowski in the *Vidette-Times.*

Five days after their return from Hawaii, the Crusaders were set for their first home game of the season with Bryce Drew in the lineup. In addition, the game would be against Division III opponent Elmhurst College, which was coached by former Valpo assistant Mark Scherer. Drew set up the game as a favor to Scherer and Elmhurst in return for all of the "big" schools who were willing to schedule Drew's teams during his years as the coach at Bethel. While some Valpo fans criticized having a Division III team on the schedule, Drew defended the game.

"I feel it's the absolute least we can do," Drew said. "When I was at Bethel, there were Division I teams, including Valpo, that were willing to schedule us and I'm eternally grateful for that, because it made us a better team and a better program. Even now, we're grateful that Gene Keady was willing to bring Purdue here for a game. Not too many Top 10 teams are willing to come to the ARC for a game. So, if this game helps Mark and Elmhurst College, it's worth it because it means we're doing a good turn for another school, and many schools have done that for us."

The crowd at the ARC welcomed back the Crusaders for the Saturday afternoon game. Bill Jenkins started the game with a fiery passion, scoring Valpo's first six points, two on an authoritative slam dunk from Bryce.

Valpo led from the early minutes, and owned an 18-point lead over Elmhurst at halftime. In the second half, the Valpo lead never was less than 10 points. With less than four minutes remaining, Bryce's two three-pointers propelled a 12-2 Valpo run that pushed the lead back to 20 points. Valpo walked off with its first home victory of the season, 85-70. Although the win appeared easy, Bill Jenkins owned up to some nervous thoughts when Elmhurst chipped away at the lead late in the game.

Rather than having separate press conferences, Drew and Scherer sat side-by-side in the media room. Drew put his arm around Scherer as they began their comments.

"It's great to be back here," Scherer began. "I don't get a chance to see [Valpo] play very often anymore. This is emotional for me, because I still care about them very much."

Despite the loss, Scherer was taking the positive view of the matchup with the Crusaders.

"We'll use this game the rest of the year…we'll look at how hard Valpo played and try to do the same," he said. "In the second half, we just wanted to hang in and keep the score even, which we did. I learned from Homer not to put unrealistic goals on players. As a result, we'll take some positives away from this game."

Scherer marveled at the growth and development of the players he helped to coach during his tenure as a Valpo assistant from 1992-1996. He singled out the Jenkins twins for special praise, but said the team had the total package.

"Being around a team is like raising a child—you don't always recognize the day-to-day progress," he said. "But now that I've been away… you see that there is so much maturity and senior leadership on this team. This is Valparaiso's year if they stay healthy."

The Elmhurst coach also credited Drew with helping him land his first college head coaching position, as Drew offered a personal recommendation for Scherer when he applied at Elmhurst.

"Coach Drew played a big part in helping me get that job," he said. "In this business, you have to have people who are willing to put their reputations on the line for you."

Drew said that while Scherer's comments were gracious, they were not necessary. In his role as a head coach, Drew believed in the saying, "Each One Teaches One," which means that coaches have an obligation to serve as mentors for their younger counterparts.

"Give a man a fish and he will eat for a day…Teach a man how to fish and he will eat for a lifetime."

"One of the most important things that I do as a coach, which I enjoy, is helping one another," he said. "It has been a true joy to see Mark and others that I have had the privilege of coaching and working with go on and be very successful."

Heading into two tough road games—at Wisconsin-Green Bay and Illinois-Chicago—Valpo had evened its record at 3-3. Two of the losses were to teams ranked in the AP Top 15. More importantly, Bryce Drew was back on the floor contributing. While he wasn't 100 percent, his mere presence on the court made Valpo better.

In Drew's view, the team's togetherness was growing, but he was aware that it took three steps to accomplish true togetherness.

1) *Coming together is a beginning.*
2) *Working together is progress.*
3) *Staying together is success.*

"We are working together and showing progress," Drew said. "Now the key is staying together and persisting in our improvement so that we can truly enjoy the success that this team is craving to have."

Valparaiso may have been slowly regaining respect lost in the early season defeats, but the team's success and confidence in Hawaii appeared to be letting Valpo grow at a much faster rate.

CHAPTER SIX

Overcoming the Seeds of Dissension

"We make the choice everyday to get "bitter or better."

–Author Unknown

With their renewed optimism, the Crusaders headed north to Green Bay, Wisconsin, to take on UWGB. Drew knew this game would be a challenge for his team, for several reasons. First, Bryce Drew was still nursing a sore knee that he banged up during the Stanford game, in addition to his original leg injury, which still was not 100 percent healed. In addition, Brown County Arena, where the UWGB Phoenix played their home games, was regarded as one of the tougher home courts in the country. Lastly, Valpo would have a revenge factor to deal with: the Crusaders scored a six-point victory when Green Bay visited the ARC during the 1996-97 season.

Nevertheless, Drew felt his team was gaining momentum since the Hawaii trip. Since Green Bay used to be a member of the Mid-Continent Conference, there was no mystique or unfamiliarity for the team to face in a hostile road arena. Moreover, Drew had developed a close friendship with former Green Bay coach Dick Bennett. Bennett took over at the University of Wisconsin in 1996, but his assistant, Mike Heideman, was promoted to head coach at UWGB and continued the winning tradition.

However, when the game started, the Crusaders were revisited by a nemesis that had plagued them all season: foul trouble. Valpo was whistled for the first eight fouls of the game. After the Stanford debacle, Drew said such a statistic could understandably make even a veteran player frustrated.

"When you look up at the scoreboard, and it's 8-0 in fouls, it makes it very difficult as a player to tune out the officiating," he said. "It's total inequality, and it's irritating."

Even so, the Crusaders were able to rebound in the first half, aided by the tempo that Green Bay set. Methodically low-scoring games were a trademark of Green Bay's teams, and as a result, Valpo trailed by just two points, 24-22, at the half.

In the second half, Valpo was able to keep up with the Phoenix. With just over ten minutes to play, Valpo grabbed a one-point lead. However, the Crusader frustration was about to boil over.

Tony Vilcinskas got tangled up with Green Bay's Kevin Olm and was called for his fifth foul with just under 10 minutes remaining in the game. Before departing the game, Vilcinskas huddled with his teammates in the lane. Olm, in either a display of one-upsmanship or a moment of absent-mindedness, strolled through the Crusader huddle. Vilcinskas took exception and gave Olm a shove.

The referee's whistle blew again. Technical foul on Vilcinskas. Vilcinskas had allowed his temper to get the best of him.

The Valpo coaches had worked with Vilcinskas to improve his agility, post-up moves, and defense, all with degrees of success. However, the one facet of Vilcinskas' game that Drew and other coaches felt he needed to learn how to deal with was frustration during the heat of battle. "Tony is such a competitor which we love in him," Drew said, "and he is getting better at handling those frustrations." Against Green Bay, the lack of composure cost Valpo free throws and the lead. Olm hit all four of his foul shots, and UWGB never looked back.

After that point, Valpo was forced to play catch-up. Although they pulled within two points late in the game, Green Bay sent its fans home cheering a 60-52 win.

While Drew was pleased that his team had played hard, he wasn't happy with what he viewed as a lack of composure down the stretch. In order for the team to reach its goals, the coaching staff knew that the team needed to work on concentration and composure in close games. Drew summed up what he wanted the Crusaders to learn from the Green Bay game with four simple points.

"I wanted our team to admit it, learn from it, don't repeat it, and then, move on," he said.

"We need to eliminate careless fouls," he said. "And even though we've had some calls that haven't gone our way, we've got to just play through it and not let the officiating bother us...we're getting into too much foul trouble right now. Learn it and then move on...that's an important life fact."

"Admit it, learn from it...move on. That's an important fact of life."
                                                              –Homer Drew

To make matters worse, the team wasn't getting any healthier. Bryce sprained his ankle slightly and Vilcinskas injured his calf in the three days leading up to the game at Illinois-Chicago. UIC would be Valpo's toughest opponent since Hawaii. The Flames, another former Mid-Continent Conference team, came into the game with a record of 7-1, including a 12-point victory over eventual Big Ten Champion Michigan State. Their only loss was a one-point decision to Illinois in Champaign. UIC actually had a final shot to beat the Illini, but couldn't get it to go down.

Second-year head coach Jimmy Collins had facilitated a complete turnaround of his club from the year before, when the Flames started the season 1-8. Playmaking guard Mark Miller and sharp-shooting guard Anthony Coomes led UIC. Bryant Lowe anchored a bulky, athletic front line. The senior-laden squad also had a score to settle with the Crusaders, as Valpo had dominated them during a visit to the ARC the year before. Valpo led by as many as 24 points in that contest before finally registering a 77-68 win. Many UIC players, especially Miller, said that they felt they had something to prove against Valpo.

UIC liked to score a lot of transition baskets, and that was a point of emphasis for Drew coming into the game.

"We have to keep them from getting easy shots, especially off of their fast break," Drew stressed. "That won't be easy. This is the best team they've ever had here. They're ranked in the 40s in the power rankings."

Not to mention that UIC was playing in the friendly, not to mention cold, surroundings of their home arena, the UIC Pavilion. The Pavilion is a 10,000-seat arena tucked into the surroundings on Chicago's near West Side. The arena was the gem of the Mid-Continent Conference when it was built in the early 1980s, completely modern and comfortable compared to the high-school style barns that were the norm in the league at that time. The building's opening also ended the one-sided dominance that Valpo had enjoyed during the first several meetings between the schools, when UIC was known as "University of Illinois-Chicago Circle."

Essentially, Valpo started losing to UIC when the Pavilion opened, and the Crusaders never had much success there. In fact, in 13 games at the arena, Valpo had won only once. Even though the Crusaders had notched several victories over UIC on their home court during that span, the Pavilion still remained a psychological obstacle for Valpo. Despite the fact that hundreds of concerts and wrestling matches had left the arena as a worn-out shell of the jewel that opened just 15 years earlier, there was still a perception among Valpo fans that the team simply can't win there.

Drew didn't buy that there was a psychological factor in playing there, however.

"It's got nothing to do with the building," he insisted. "UIC's had some good teams over the years, that's all. And it's very difficult to win on the road in college basketball."

If the Crusaders were to win on this afternoon, they'd have to do so in addition to fighting off frostbite. It was freezing inside the Pavilion prior to tipoff. Noticing that the ice rink below the floor had been removed (UIC had dropped hockey as a sport a few years earlier), several reporters on press row looked around to find the source of the cold.

"I think someone left a door open," said a member of the Pavilion staff. "Are you guys cold?"

The reporters, some of whom were still wearing winter coats despite the fact that tipoff was minutes away, nodded vigorously.

A door being left open on a day with sub-zero wind chills. Exactly what Valpo's banged-up players needed: a tougher time getting stretched out and warmed up.

However, after Ray Clay, the UIC public address announcer who is best known for his "Annnd Nowwww....." introductions of the Chicago Bulls at their home games, announced the lineups, Valpo started the game with confidence, playing UIC evenly for the first half. Both teams played airtight defense, forcing altered and off-balance shots by their opponent. The result was a surprisingly low-scoring half.

Bryce found himself double-teamed frequently, and, as a result, had trouble getting into the offensive rhythm. In front of Chicago Bulls' general manager Jerry Krause, as well as scouts from the Toronto Raptors, Orlando Magic, New York Knicks, and Phoenix Suns, Bryce and the team were struggling to score.

UIC led by four late in the half. Just before intermission, Bryce hit a running one-handed jumper in the lane and Vilcinskas drained two free throws. Officials waved off a Bryce layup at the halftime buzzer, over the guard's pleadings. Nevertheless, the Crusaders held a one-point lead, 26-25. Even though the first half was far from a work of art, Drew was happy with his team's defensive effort.

"Our defense is simply playing awesome," he said, walking toward the dressing room. While a score in the 20s was in Green Bay's favor a few nights earlier, a similar score was going the Crusaders' way this afternoon. This was the tempo Valpo wanted for this game.

In the second half, the teams exchanged baskets at the start of the 20 minutes. Then, with UIC leading 32-30, Viskovic lost the handle on the ball and turned it over. UIC responded with a Bryant Lowe dunk that pushed the lead to four and swung the momentum clearly to the Flames.

UIC applied full-court defensive pressure, and Valpo seemed to wilt. Valpo turned the ball over on several occasions, missed key free throws, and watched UIC convert each mistake. After Jaime Sykes missed a wide-open eight-foot jumper, Coomes buried the second of back-to-back threes. With just over 10 minutes to go, UIC had the biggest lead of the game at 51-37.

Rather than responding with a run of their own, as they did against Pacific and Stanford, Valpo seemed to collapse. The turnovers against the press continued. The Flames continued to get wide-open three-point shots. The frustration-induced "silly" fouls continued. The UIC lead grew.

Meanwhile, the Crusaders resembled a team that was on its way to obscurity and many losses. The team sulked its way through the game's final minutes, and when the final horn mercifully sounded, the Flames had earned a 72-51 win. The Crusaders, who had started the season with such high hopes, stood at 3-5 and on the precipice of digging themselves a huge hole if play didn't improve in the next week's Mid-Continent opener at Missouri-Kansas City.

After the game, Drew was clearly agitated by his team's play. Prior to meeting with the press, Drew gave a stern address to the players in the dressing room. He was most perturbed by the lack of effort and emotion in the second half.

"In the second half, we gave up too many rebounds, we committed multiple turnovers...we just never were able to mount a spurt," he said. "UIC deserved to win, their defense was superb and their athleticism really hurt us...but the tempo of the game just got away from us."

Drew had a laundry list of areas that he wanted his team to improve upon.

"We have to start shooting the ball well...we can't count on Bryce to do all the scoring," he said. "Yes, we've had a difficult schedule early, but the test is going to be whether it helps us down the road." Drew knew that losing was contagious, and he also knew that no one wanted such an affliction to spread.

"We've tried so many different things," he said. "I think we've got to just get good shots and hit those. Also, we weren't really quick to the ball tonight—they got 19 offensive rebounds. It's frustrating."

Drew thought the biggest frustration was that he had no doubt his team was better than its recent performance.

Bryce was similarly frustrated, but placed most of the blame on himself. He said there was no one area the team could point at in order to correct its woes.

"There are a lot of things that need to be done to take care of the problem," he said. "I'm capable of playing so much better. I wasn't at my best today. The way I'm playing now, I'm just like dead weight."

As he spoke, Bryce chewed nervously on his lower lip. The frustration in his eyes and in his tone of voice was obvious. He answered reporters' questions abruptly and he shook his head frequently as he tried to come up with the answers to why the Crusaders fell flat in the second half. Adding to his frustration was the fact that Valpo had played better against two Top 15 opponents than they had against their current competition.

"We're struggling now," he said before adding almost sarcastically: "I almost think we're better off playing against the big guys...we seem to show up for those games."

Jamie Sykes also conveyed his frustration with the team's play. He had a rough night, scoring just three points on one-for-six shooting. While he was disappointed in his own performance, he also made it clear that Bryce shouldn't have to take the Valpo team upon his shoulders every game.

"Everybody's gotta check themselves right now," Sykes said. "All of us seniors have to lead the team better...we're not just a one-man team."

As the Crusaders packed up their belongings and headed toward the bus loading dock, Bryce sat by himself on the blue carpet underneath the arena, leaning against a metal barricade. With an ice bag resting upon his sore knee, he buried his head in his hands. He looked like the loneliest guy in the place.

When the team returned home, the frustration finally boiled over the next day. Drew called a team meeting, and it was time to lay a few things on the line.

"The UIC game was a bitter pill for us," Drew said. "We lost to a good team, but we did not play well. We had a team meeting to just bring out some cold, hard facts in order to play better." Drew needed to find a way to bring the team back together again and turn the loss into a positive.

Drew brought up three main points in the locker room at the Pavilion the day before.

"I started with the team meeting after the game. Players had to hear the truth," he said. "First, we did not play together. Second, we did not play with intensity. Finally, we did not play with a passion or love for the game."

Before delving into the issues any further, however, Drew gave his players a night off to cool down.

"In a fragile situation like this, I knew to take a little while longer before we met," Drew said. "It's better to wait than to act too quickly without getting everyone involved in the solution. I wanted to find a process where the team could share their input and try to bring everyone together in a win/win situation."

The next day, Drew visited with the coaching staff. He felt it was imperative that all of the coaches were on the same page before holding a team meeting with the players.

"If a team has assistant coaches who are negative, complaining, and downbeat, it can destroy a team from reaching its goal. I have always attempted to communicate with my staff and not dictate," he said. "I expect and encourage them to share their opinions and I want them to share in the ownership of the decisions."

Assistants Scott Drew, Jim Harrick, and Steve Flint were all surprisingly upbeat and anxious to find solutions. The fact that the staff was not angry or hanging their heads was cause for Drew to be thankful.

_____

Assistant coaches need to:
1) Be loyal
2) Possess a high level of energy
3) Evaluate and project talent
4) Have knowledge of the game
5) Be communicators

"I knew I was blessed to have men around me who were competent, loyal, and wanted the best for these young men—'the best' meaning they were ready to help the players achieve their goals and dreams," Drew said. "I knew that a united staff could help to lead us out of the adversity we were in, and help us evolve into something very special as a team. And that's due to Scott Drew, Jim Harrick, and Steve Flint and also to Steve Johnson and Mark Scherer for helping us get to this point. These coaches have been loyal with a high level of energy and been the backbone to our success."

Finally, Drew met with his team to ask for its input on issues surrounding togetherness, intensity, and passion. Drew opened the floor up to his players, and the emotions flew. Players aired their feelings about what would correct the team's course.

Drew sat back and took it all in. What he saw was too many personal agendas getting in the way of the team's goals. He saw possibly the school's most talented team ever on the verge of disintegrating into dissension. He saw veteran leaders too concerned with statistics instead of the team's success. Drew knew that many great teams had been torn apart by internal chaos once the seeds of dissension had been sown. Something had to be done to put the team in the right focus, and quickly. Once everyone had an opportunity to speak their mind, Drew wanted the team to talk things over without the coaching staff in the room—a move many coaches would consider risky. However, Drew decided to trust the qualities that had drawn the players to his program.

"I knew the team was made up of good people, and I knew they wanted to be successful just like the coaches did," he said. "By letting them talk this over by themselves, I was trusting that their heart for the team would prevail. I was trusting that they would treat their teammates as they would like to be treated. Robert Schuller had a great quote: 'What happens to good people when bad things happen to them? They become better people!'"

"I needed people who were willing to sacrifice for this team. Players needed to quit worrying about their playing time and quit worrying about their personal interests. They needed to start worrying about what's best for this basketball team."

Drew also wanted the seniors on the team to set an example for the younger players. Complaining about playing time and the number of shots each player was taking was not the way to do that. Nor would it help get the team back on track. The bottom line was simple: personal glory must be put aside for the common good.

Fortunately, the seniors on the team took the message to heart. Bill Jenkins called the meeting "a big wake-up call." After the veterans met briefly later that day, they came to a few conclusions based on their coach's advice.

"We all agreed that we know what it feels like to win and we know the expectations and what it takes to get there," Bill Jenkins said. "And we all agreed that we weren't doing squat. And we agreed that it was time to stop being a bunch of babies and to start playing ball like we knew how."

Bill Jenkins felt the team meeting achieved the desired effect: bringing the team together. He credited Drew's decision to have an open forum discussion when the team was in such an emotional state.

"The meeting was good because we got everything on the table, and as a result, we were able to get a lot of the individual differences put aside," he said. "We were ready to move ahead as a basketball team."

Moving ahead meant gearing up for the conference portion of the team's schedule, which would make or break the team's season. After winning three consecutive championships, the Crusaders were "the hunted," as Drew liked to put it.

"It's as if we have a giant bull's-eye on our chests and each team gets to line up and take their best shot at us," he said. "But I'm confident that this team will respond."

Drew knew that the Mid-Continent opener would be critical, and that falling behind in the conference race early in the season could be fatal to the Crusaders' post-season hopes. So after making the trip to Kansas City—a trip that took twice as long as normal, due to bad Chicago traffic which led to a missed plane flight and as Coach Flint has said, "Nothin comes easy for this team"—Drew decided a theme for the game would be important. A theme would be something for the players to rally around after the potentially divisive team meeting.

On the way to Kansas City, Valpo players enjoyed the movie, *Wyatt Earp*, starring action hero Kurt Russell. At one particularly dramatic point during the film, Russell's character says, "the thunder's coming." Drew knew he had found his theme.

Before the game, Drew told the team to "bring the thunder to the game." In other words, bring the intensity, the desire, the heart, the effort, and the work ethic. Bring the execution on offense and the hustle on defense. Bring all the things together in order to leave the chapter of dissension behind.

The Crusaders were slow to respond to this advice at first. In the first half, UMKC jumped out to an early advantage, and held a five-point lead at the half. Inside the locker room at halftime, it was Scott Drew's turn to give the team an earful. He let the team know, in no uncertain terms, that if they lost this game on the road it would be difficult to win another conference title. This was a road game the team absolutely had to have, and Scott Drew wasn't going to let the team hit the court for the second half until they knew it. Even his father was taken slightly aback by Scott Drew's vocal dressing room outburst.

"Coach Scott got pretty emotional in there," Homer Drew said with a grin, "and he truly got the team to focus second half which was important to us because UMKC with Coach Bob Sunvold is a well-coached team."

The verbal motivation worked, though. After giving up the first basket of the second half, Valpo went on a 14-0 run. Clamping down on the defense, crashing the boards, and buoyed by a career-high 20-point, 12-rebound effort from Bill Jenkins, Valpo never looked back. The closest the Kangaroos got the rest of the way was six points. The final score was 80-68.

"We know we are going to get everybody's best performance," Drew told reporters after the game. "We have to be ready to meet that challenge."

The Crusaders met that challenge in the second half, mainly due to an "outstanding team defensive effort," as Drew called it. However, what also had to please him was the team offense. For the first time all season, four Crusaders finished with double-digit scoring. Even more important than that was the fact that Valpo had started the conference season off on a winning note—as a team.

Scott Drew's halftime speech was given high marks by the head coach.

"His talk played a vital role in winning our first conference game," Drew said. "We had taken a giant step forward, but we're still not the team that we can become."

Part of Drew's leadership style includes allowing his staff to share in the motivation of the team, like Scott Drew had. Both Flint and Harrick had played that role in similar situations, both successfully.

However, Valpo didn't have much time to savor their return to the victory column. Two nights later, Valpo would travel to Nashville, Tennessee, to take on Belmont University in the first game of a home-and-home non-conference series. Most Valpo fans scratched their heads quizzically when they received their season schedules in the mail and saw an unfamiliar school such as Belmont, especially when it was listed twice. However, there was a reason that Valpo slated the two games against the Bruins' program.

Belmont, a team moving to Division I in basketball, would be looking for a conference. The small, religiously affiliated school was viewed as fitting in well with the Mid-Continent Conference, and it would give the Mid-Con a presence in another major television market. The two games were booked in hopes of getting Belmont familiarized with the conference should it be interested in joining.

In any case, Valpo wanted to finish off before the holidays on a winning note. The game was being played on December 22, so Drew feared the players might have their thoughts on sugarplum fairies and hanging their stockings by the chimney with care instead of the task at hand. Before the game, Drew stressed the need to stay focused.

"I told the guys why I thought the game was important, and we came to the consensus: this could be a turning point for us," he said. "We decided as a team to try and keep the momentum we had going in."

That turned out to be easier than expected, thanks to an unexpected source: the hot hand of Jared Nuness. Nuness hit his first two three-point attempts of the game, and his shooting streak continued for the rest of the night. The Crusaders opened up an 11-point halftime lead. Belmont cut into the lead early in the second half, but another Nuness trey helped put the game squarely under Valpo's command. Valpo went on to win easily, 78-62. Nuness finished with 18 points, while Vilcinskas added 14 and Bryce scored 10.

Drew should have known such a scoring display was at hand. During the morning shootaround at Belmont's Striplin Gym, Nuness barely missed a shot.

"Coach, I feel good in this gym," Nuness told Drew. "I like the shooting background."

Drew theorized Nuness' comfort was due to the fact that the gym reminded him of cozy high school fieldhouses back home in Minnesota. Whatever the reason, the Crusaders got to head home for the holidays happy and on a winning streak.

"This was a wonderful Christmas gift for the players and coaches," Drew said. "I'm giving the players four days off now to go home and be with their families over the holiday. The win makes everything more pleasant."

Valpo wouldn't play another game for nine days, a New Year's Eve tilt on the road at Western Illinois. Although the Crusaders had assembled back-to-back road wins, Drew cautioned that the team chemistry and execution was not yet of championship caliber.

"We're nowhere near where we need to be right now," he said. "We still need to improve in a lot of areas, especially continuing to improve on defense. But it's nice to win as a team and it's wonderful to be going home for the holidays."

Drew thought this was an opportune time for the team to build on its strengths. The Crusaders had shown resiliency in defeat, something that characterized a champion, according to NBA coaching legend Pat Riley.

"You have no choice about how you lose," Riley once wrote. "But you do have a choice about how you come back and prepare to win."

Regardless of the areas where the Crusaders were still lacking, the fact that the frustration-riddled aftermath of the UIC loss was clearly in the past was a relief to Drew. The Crusaders were at least playing as a team once again and attacking the court with a winner's intensity. Through open, honest communication and togetherness, the seeds of dissension—which threatened to divide the team just 10 days earlier— never had the opportunity to take root.

CHAPTER SEVEN

Setting the Table for Success

"There are no secrets to success. It is the result of preparation, hard work, learning from failure."

–Gen. Colin Powell

During a time of year known for resolutions, the Crusaders arrived at Western Illinois University displaying their resolve. It was New Year's Eve, and Valpo had a late-afternoon conference game against the rival Leathernecks.

The team had shown poise in rebounding from the Illinois-Chicago loss with two straight road wins. This game would be a much tougher test, however. The Leathernecks had been ousted by the Crusaders for three straight seasons from the Mid-Continent Conference tournament, each time in the finals. Western players felt, rightfully so, that the only hurdle standing between them and the NCAA Tournament was Valpo. They relished the chance to play Valpo on their home floor.

Valpo jumped out to an early five-point lead, but Western responded with a rally and built its own 10-point lead. Tony Vilcinskas and Zoran Viskovic both got into foul trouble in the first half again, which slowed the Crusader frontcourt scoring. Thanks to seven points from Jamie Sykes, however, Valpo pulled within one point at the half. Drew stressed one aspect in his halftime comments to a television reporter: converting on easy chances.

"We have got to convert some of the easy shots that we missed in the first half," he said. "That will give us some inside action to go with the outside shots."

Early in the second half, Western went on a 14-4 run and led by as many as 11 points before a Bryce Drew three-pointer brought Valpo back within eight. Slowly, Valpo climbed back within a point. After several missed Valpo free throws, Western extended its lead back to five points. The lead hovered in that area until Bryce hit two foul shots with 51 seconds remaining in the game. Western led by one, 59-58. Valpo knocked a loose ball out of bounds off of a Western player to gain possession. With 20 seconds left, Bryce drained a baseline jump shot to give Valpo its first lead of the half. But with 14.1 seconds left, Bill Jenkins fouled Alexander, who hit both of his free throws to hand the lead back to Western. The Crusaders set up on offense.

With three seconds to go, Bryce took a pass and pulled up from the top of the key and buried the shot. Bryce's foot was correctly ruled to be on the line, so two points were awarded instead of three. Western quickly threw an inbounds pass downcourt, caught by Mark Buckingham, who threw up an off-balance shot. The rebound caromed off early and long, and Buckingham grabbed the rebound and was fouled as he tried a tip in. Only 1.3 seconds remained.

Buckingham calmly sank both free throws to give Western a one-point lead. A long pass downcourt was tipped away. The buzzer sounded, and Western players mobbed each other along the bench. Final score: Western Illinois 63, Valparaiso 62. It was a gut-wrenching loss for Valpo, but Drew felt there was no point in agonizing over the game's final play.

"It angled right back to [Buckingham]. It was a bang-bang play," he told the *Vidette-Times*.

Although Drew told reporters he was disappointed with the team's play in the first half, he was proud of the fact the team didn't quit. The determination and perseverance of the team would pay dividends down the road, he thought. The defeat could be a valuable educational tool for the players as Valpo faced close games later in the season.

"The comeback showed their true character," Drew said. "I knew that character would prevail, even though we were going through a challenging time. If this team continues to persist and press on, I knew better days were ahead."

Press on.
Nothing in the world
Can take the place of persistence
Talent will not;
Nothing is more common
Than unsuccessful men
With talent.
Genius will not;
Unrewarded genius
Is almost a proverb.
Education will not;
The world is full of
Educated derelicts.
Persistence and determination
Alone are important.
                    –Author Unknown

The bad news was that the Crusaders were shooting only 44 percent from the field—lower than Drew wanted, especially with two big inside players. The good news was that Valpo was finally coming home after being on the road for nearly an entire month.

"The road wears you out," Drew told the *Vidette-Times*. "We haven't seen our own gym in 28 days. It will be wonderful to play at home."

More importantly, the Crusaders would get to play in front of their home fans. Every one of the coaches and players recognized the vital role that the home crowd had played in Valpo's success.

"Our fans are special," Drew said. "They have been there to support us through the wins and the losses. They love the effort of our team.

They help bring out our best, and they are very knowledgeable about the game."

Another reason for the Crusaders to look forward to a brief homestand was that they would be facing Chicago State, a struggling Mid-Continent Conference foe. Although the Crusaders were wary that a wounded animal is quite dangerous, they were also confident that playing Chicago State three days after the heartbreaking loss at Western Illinois could help them rebound quickly.

On a cold Saturday afternoon, the crowd at the ARC witnessed a hungry Chicago State team. Head coach Phil Gary had his Cougars come out in a box-and-one defense—a rarely used set designed to limit shot opportunities and touches for one particular player. Quite obviously, the target of the defense was Bryce.

Alternating between the box-and-one and a triangle-and-two defense (where floating defenders hounded both Bryce and Sykes), the Crusaders were caught off guard. Drew confessed after the game that both sets were unfamiliar.

"It made it very difficult for us to move the basketball and get our offense into a good flow," he said.

As a result, the Crusaders were not able to build more than a five-point lead throughout the entire first half. In fact, with just over three minutes remaining in the half, a Rashaan Mitchell three-pointer gave the Cougars a brief lead, illustrating Drew's point that Chicago State could be dangerous. Valpo rallied quickly however, and a Bill Jenkins' layup gave the Crusaders back their five-point advantage at the intermission.

In the second half, the Crusaders continued to struggle against the trick defenses. Valpo went up by nine points, only to miss seven straight shots and see the lead whittled to five again. Chicago State wasn't giving in.

With just under 10 minutes to play, Valpo solved the box-and-one riddle by making an adjustment in strategy, in large part by working the ball inside to Vilcinskas. He scored seven points in a five-minute span as Valpo built its lead from five to 19 points. The Crusaders' defense also clamped down on Chicago State's outside shooters, aiding the run.

Valpo never looked back from that point, going on to an 82-62 victory to even its record at 6-6.

Drew was pleased with the way his team didn't panic in the second half as the Cougars continued to hang around. He was also pleased that they were able to make adjustments against the surprising defensive strategy.

"I was very pleased with the poise we displayed in the second half," he said, noting that Chicago State's record was a bit deceiving. "They're a scary team to play because they are quick and athletic. If all of a sudden they put it together for 40 minutes and get emotionally involved, you never know what can happen. You don't want to be the first one to get beat by them."

Bill Jenkins agreed, saying that it was merely important to get a victory, no matter how difficult it might have been.

"This game was big, simply because we lost our last game. It would have been easy to start complaining about the Western game and not pick any way to go out and improve," he said.

"I have a feeling that's not the last time we're going to see that this year," Bryce said, noting the defense's effectiveness. If that occurred, though, Bob Jenkins said that it would be the rest of the team's responsibility to help Bryce get open shots.

"Bryce is our primary scorer," he said. "If we can't get the ball in his hands at first, we have to find a way to get it in his hands somehow."

The Crusaders' respect for Chicago State's defense was a compliment to coach Phil Gary, who faced one of the most daunting tasks in college basketball: building a winning program with no resources and a small facility. The athletic department was financially strapped, hampering Gary's ability to recruit top-notch Division I players.

Chicago State was an NAIA powerhouse in the 1980s, posting winning records year after year. In 1984, the school decided to make the leap to Division I. The move made sense at the time—Loyola and DePaul's programs on the city's North Side were beginning to fade from national prominence, and UIC on the city's West Side was just starting to ascend. There was reason to believe that a Division I program on the city's South Side, rich in basketball tradition, could succeed and capture the city's attention. There was reason to believe excitement could be brought to the corner of 95th Street and King Drive. In a January 1998 profile of the school's basketball program in the *Chicago Reader*, writer Sridhar Pappu explained that hope is always a major ingredient at the university. He wrote that there was "a belief among the students that hard work and dedication can pay off—that from here there's nowhere to go but up. That same sense of possibility has long surrounded the basketball team..."

However, ever since making the step up, the Cougars have struggled mightily, aside from two winning seasons at the start of their Division I tenure.

One of the admirable things about Gary was his ability to keep a sense of humor through it all. He had a difficult task to start with—replacing former Chicago Bulls star Craig Hodges the season before when Hodges left the head coaching position in mid-season. Despite the rough start, Gary continued to stay upbeat. When a close call went Chicago State's way early in the game, Gary clapped and joked that the call was "a New Year's gift." Later in the game, he and Bryce shared a joke and a laugh during a break in the action. However, he turned serious when the subject of the school's financial constraints came up after the game.

Drew sympathized with Gary's plight. Drew understood being in a situation with limited resources. When he first arrived at Valpo, he was faced with similar problems. Fortunately for Drew, the leadership of university president Dr. Alan Harre and athletic director Dr. Bill Steinbrecher came to the fore. They got permission from the board of trustees for the athletic department to raise funds. This allowed Valpo the opportunity to be competitive in Division I basketball, as Valpo could now regularly recruit outside of the Midwest.

"Phil's in a very difficult situation there," he said. "A lot of pressure is being put on him to win there, but he doesn't have the resources necessary. It's not fair, but unfortunately, that's the nature of our business."

In his book, *The Coaches*, Bill Libby wrote of the naturally precarious position of most coaches, and the emotional wringer that many are put through.

"Having seen them exultant in victory and depressed in defeat, I have sympathized with them," he wrote. "Having seem some broken by the job and others die from it, one is moved to admire them and to hope that someday the world will learn to understand them."

After the win over Chicago State, Valpo had to turn around two days later and take on Northeastern Illinois, another Chicago school, at the ARC. Valpo-Northeastern had developed into a heated rivalry in the previous two seasons, with Valpo winning three emotional, hard-fought contests the year before.

Two of the Crusaders' victories the year before came in overtime. At Northeastern, Bob Jenkins caught a three-quarter-court, left-handed pass from Bryce and won the game on a last-second slam dunk. In the semifinals of the Mid-Continent tournament, Valpo scored an 88-84 overtime win in one of the most physical battles in the conference's history. Early in the game, Northeastern forward Daveeno Hines flattened Bryce with a forearm to the head as Bryce drove to the basket. Bryce crumpled to the floor as a flagrant foul was whistled.

The sight of his son lying on the floor with a concussion, coupled with the fact that Hines was not ejected from the game for the cheap shot, prompted the most emotional sideline response that Valpo fans had ever seen from the normally unflappable Drew.

"Is he being thrown out?" Drew asked the official. The referee shook his head.

"WHY?" Drew demanded to know. "WHY?" Drew recalled later that barely keeping his cool in that situation was tough, and that was one of the few pitfalls of coaching his son.

"As a father, when I saw him lying there, I wanted to run out on the floor and defend my son," Drew said. "But I knew if I did that, I would be hurting the entire team. That was very difficult for me."

Bryce ended up playing the rest of the game in a dazed state, and he played with a pounding headache in the finals the next night. Still, memories from the event lingered.

Northeastern Illinois was wounded, but in a unique manner. Their university had decided a month earlier to drop athletics altogether at the end of the season. In their lame-duck state, Northeastern had gotten off to a slow start. However, Bryce knew that you threw out the records in a rivalry game. He summed up the game in three words.

"Huge. Huge. Huge," he said.

Northeastern-Valpo games had developed a reputation for intensity, and this game was no exception. Behind the hot shooting of Brad Bestor, the Golden Eagles built a 37-28 halftime lead. Bryce came up big in the second half, hitting a key three-pointer down the stretch. He finished with 22 points and five assists.

It was the Jenkins twins who turned out to be the heroes of the evening. The pair combined for 20 points and eight rebounds. Bob Jenkins also had four steals and a blocked shot. It was also Bob who scored the biggest basket of the game. With less than 20 seconds remaining and the score tied, Bob drove the lane and drew a foul as he shot. He hit the free throw to complete the three-point play. The score provided the winning margin, as Valpo squeaked out a 72-69 win. Drew knew the win was crucial.

"This was a big win for us because it allows us to continue our improvement and build up to a championship level of performance," he said. Finally, Drew saw the Crusaders beginning to harness their best performances each game and resist the pitfalls that the team had already been through. The coaching staff was excited and looking forward to the upcoming road trip. Drew wanted to win both games at Southern Utah and Oral Roberts, but he felt that given the quality of opponents and the extensive travel, if Valpo could salvage a split of the two games, he would be satisfied.

Southern Utah and Oral Roberts were new members of the Mid-Continent Conference. At least against Southern Utah, Drew knew one of the keys was going to be player substitution. Drew knew that his

Crusaders would get tired quicker in the thin, mountain air of Cedar City, Utah. So, he substituted frequently to keep his players fresh.

The strategy worked perfectly. After leading by just one point at halftime, and after trailing by two points with just under five minutes left, the Crusaders went on a 19-5 run and ended up winning, 79-70.

Bryce scored 23 points, and he finished the game as part of a Crusader three-guard offense with Sykes and Jared Nuness. Drew was forced to use such a lineup after both Jenkins twins fouled out with three minutes left.

Since the Illinois-Chicago game, Valpo had won five of the next six games to improve its record to 8-6. Another big hurdle loomed: Oral Roberts.

Oral Roberts University, named for the famous evangelist, has a strong tradition in basketball dating back to the early 1970s. Their home court, the Mabee Center in Tulsa, Oklahoma, has been the site of many victories over major opponents. The most recent was Arkansas, who lost there in the 1996-97 season. The Crusaders fell there that season as well, so Drew knew his team had its work cut out.

Drew holds ORU president Richard Roberts and Athletic Director Mike Carter in the highest esteem. Consequently, he was also familiar with their success in basketball and aware of the challenges presented by playing a game in ORU's home arena.

"They have a beautiful arena to play in and a very enthusiastic fan following," Drew said.

Valpo fell behind early, thanks to an 11-0 run by Oral Roberts. Valpo rallied back to pull within three points, but ORU finished the half strong, taking a 40-32 lead into the locker room.

In the second half, the Crusaders suffered from streaky shooting, heating up one moment and going cold the next. The ORU lead grew to 10 points. With just under eight minutes left, a Sykes' basket capped a run that brought the Crusaders within two, 52-50. Once again, the Crusader offense went cold, and ORU was able to build up another eight-point lead with two minutes remaining. Valpo had no late comeback on this night, and Oral Roberts won, 68-60. Three steps forward, one step back.

Bryce finished with 18 points, but got very little scoring help in the paint. The only bright spot of the evening came from the fact that Bryce closed within six points of becoming Valpo's all-time leading scorer, surpassing Tracy Gipson. He would have a chance to break the record against Buffalo—at home.

The Crusaders stood at 8-7 and 4-2 in conference play, not as good as the players and coaches were hoping for at the start of the season. Nevertheless, Drew was seeing more and more signs of team play, of selflessness, of all the intangibles that held promise of what this team could become. He wanted to see it more consistently, though.

"Having seen them exultant in victory and depressed in defeat, I have sympathized with them. Having seem some broken by the job and others die from it, one is moved to admire them and to hope that someday the world will learn to understand them."–Bill Libby

The Crusaders were about to enter a daunting stretch against two of the teams favored to contend for the Crusaders' Mid-Continent crown, with two tough non-conference games thrown into the mix. The season may not have hinged on the next four games, but they would go a long way in determining whether the Crusaders would be able to defend their conference title and make it back to the NCAA tournament.

Drew and his players had brought themselves back from the brink of early-season destruction. Through hard work and mental toughness, they had set the table for success. Whether or not they would get to dine on such a feast would be determined within the next few weeks.

CHAPTER EIGHT

Turning the Corner:
Valpo's Time Begins

"You can tell the character of a person by the choices made under pressure."
–Winston Churchill

Over the previous few seasons, the State University of New York at Buffalo had provided some of the most intense competition in the Mid-Continent Conference for Valpo. Head coach Tim Cohane's crew always played close against the Crusaders and always gave an all-out effort. Like several other teams in the conference, Buffalo viewed Valpo as the obstacle stopping them from great things. To get over the hump, the Bulls felt they had to go through the ARC.

The Crusaders were able to rest for a full week following the Oral Roberts game, which gave the community of Valparaiso plenty of time to get excited about Bryce Drew's near-certainty of breaking the university's all-time scoring mark. While Bryce was excited about the possibility, he didn't want his pursuit of Tracy Gipson's scoring record to become a distraction to his teammates. The game against Buffalo would be tough enough as it was—he didn't want his teammates to have to worry about the scoring record all afternoon.

As a result, Bryce came out firing. Twenty-seven seconds into the game, he pulled up from 25 feet away and launched an airball. Bryce jogged downcourt smiling and shaking his head. He knew he had forced that one. Homer Drew urged Bryce to be patient.

Three minutes later, Bryce broke into the scoring column with a layup to put Valpo ahead, 8-6. The Crusader offense kept humming. Bill Jenkins slammed home a lob pass from Bryce, and then Bryce took over on the next possession. He ran off a screen and drained a three-pointer to put Valpo ahead by seven. More important to the fans in the house was the fact that Bryce had tied the record. A little more than a minute later, he got his opportunity to break it—albeit in an unusual fashion.

As Buffalo guard Rasaun Young was whistled for a charging foul, Tony Vilcinskas inadvertently caught Bulls forward Zaid Alkhas in the mouth with an elbow. No foul was called. On the Buffalo bench, Cohane was outraged. As the two teams walked to the other end of the court, Cohane angrily scolded the referee and threatened to pull his team off the court for the non-call. As the referee walked away, Cohane took his argument a step further—and a step too far. Taking two steps on the floor, Cohane threatened Vilcinskas.

As a chorus of boos began to rain down on Cohane, the official blew his whistle and motioned to the scorer's table: technical foul on the Buffalo coach.

Bryce stepped to the line to shoot the technical free throws. The first shot bounced off the front rim and out. The second shot was true, and Bryce had the record. The ARC crowd rose for a standing ovation as Bryce acknowledged the fans' response.

As play resumed, the tone of the game was set. Players set punishing screens. Post players battled for position with arms, legs, and knees inside. Three or four players fought for nearly every rebound. A physical afternoon was in store for both teams.

Buffalo battled back from its early deficit, and trailed by only two points at the half. In the second half, three-pointers by Bryce and Jamie Sykes pushed Valpo to a six-point lead, only to see Buffalo keep the game close behind the lights-out shooting display of Young. No team was able to get more than a three-point advantage during the final 11 minutes of play.

After driving through traffic in the lane, Young lofted a soft, one-hand layup into the basket to give Buffalo an 80-78 lead with 54 seconds left. Just 17 seconds later, however, Bill Jenkins broke free underneath the basket and slammed home the tying basket off an assist from Vilcinskas. With 28 seconds left and the ball, Buffalo called timeout.

Not surprisingly, the Bulls ran an isolation play for Young, who had already blistered the nets for 32 points. What was surprising was that Young found himself with an open eight-foot jumper with seven seconds left—and he missed it. Bryce cleared the rebound and headed straight toward the basket at the opposite end. As the clock ticked down, he dribbled around one defender. With one second left, he leaned under another and let fly with an off-balanced, 12-foot runner. The ball splashed cleanly through the net as time expired. The crowd erupted. Valpo had won, 82-80.

After the Crusaders quickly celebrated the dramatic win, one could have easily thought the game had offered all of the drama it could muster. Not quite. As the two teams were shaking hands, Alkhas went after Vilcinskas. Alkhas lunged at the big center twice as he was restrained by teammates. A witness to the incident claimed that Alkhas was upset because Vilcinskas blew him a kiss as the teams were walking off the floor. In the *Post-Tribune*, however, Vilcinskas vehemently denied that accusation.

"I just said, 'see you later,' and I had my arms up," Vilcinskas told the newspaper. "I wouldn't do that. I know we have to play them in Buffalo."

Sykes said that occasional confrontations during the heat of a long season were inevitable.

"I didn't want it to be that physical, but everyone we play, especially Buffalo, is always gunning to beat us. You are going to have tempers flare from time to time," he said, before mentioning that Valpo would have to play at Buffalo in front of a fired-up home crowd in a few weeks. "Tony's probably going to have to wear body armor when we go to play at Buffalo."

In addition to the improved composure, another heartening statistic for Drew was that all five Crusader starters scored in double figures.

Bryce was the hero, with the game-winning basket, 23 points and eight assists. However, Bill Jenkins added 15 points and 10 rebounds, and Vilcinskas scored 11 points, grabbed nine boards, and blocked three shots. It was clearly a team win.

While Bryce said he was much happier with the victory than the scoring record, he did reflect on the accomplishment after the game. The record-breaking point was a nervous moment, he said.

"I stepped up to the line and I suddenly remembered that my sister broke the record on a free throw," he said, mentioning the all-time women's scoring record Dana Drew achieved at the University of Toledo. "Then I missed the first one, and I'm thinking, 'geez.' I'm happy the second one went in. It will make a nice memory."

However, even though he hit the winning shot, Bryce sympathized with Young, who had missed the crucial shot with seven seconds left. Bryce was asked if he would have taken a similar shot, even if it meant shooting earlier than planned and giving the opponent a chance to win the game.

"Wow, man...I don't know," he said. "If you see a shot like that open, it's really tough to pass on. It all happened so quick. I don't know."

Fortunately for Bryce, he didn't have to worry about such a scenario on that day. However, he did allow himself to look ahead to the next game: a non-conference game against Northern Illinois. The game would be special for Bryce because he would get to play against an old friend, NIU forward T.J. Lux, a graduate of nearby Merrillville High School. Bryce and Lux had become friends through basketball, playing together during the summer, and keeping up with each other's teams during the season. Bryce looked forward to seeing his friend come into the ARC for the game. He said he felt a kinship with Lux, because they were both high school standouts from the same area. Many in northwest Indiana believe the region gets short-changed by the rest of the state when it comes to exposure in basketball.

"When you're from northwest Indiana, it's harder for players to get recognized," Bryce said. "No one downstate sees you. They might hear about you, but they hardly ever see you."

Northern Illinois came into the game after earning a berth to the NCAA Tournament as the champion of the Midwestern Collegiate Conference. NIU was struggling against a higher level of competition in the Mid-American Conference, which they re-joined at the start of the year. Still, with Lux and play-making guard Donte Parker, the Huskies were a formidable foe. In addition, more than 400 friends and relatives of Lux were in attendance, insuring that NIU would have some fan representation at the game. A big crowd was on hand, and the game had high regional interest due to the Bryce-Lux connection.

However, as Valpo was taking warmups, Drew noticed that something was wrong with his team. They seemed distant, uninspired, and sluggish. When they returned to the dressing room, Drew delivered some fiery motivation. He told the players that they might as well just start preparing for conference foe Youngstown State, the team's next game, because they hadn't come prepared to play against NIU. Drew told the team that he didn't see the zest and excitement of a team that "wanted to be a champion."

Whatever funk the players were in, the pep talk snapped them out of it. Valpo stormed out of the gate to start the game. Within five minutes, they held a 10-point lead. NIU came back to within two points, and stayed within two possessions for the majority of the half. However, Valpo went on a 13-0 run to close the half, sparked by three blocked shots and two inside baskets from Zoran Viskovic. As the buzzer sounded, Valpo held a 46-27 advantage.

In the second half, Valpo didn't let up. Behind more blocked shots by Viskovic and Bill Jenkins, and stellar outside shooting by the Crusaders, the Valpo lead stretched to as many as 25 points. NIU didn't give up, but they were in too deep of a hole to come back. They pulled to within 12 with about two minutes left in the game, but that was it. Valpo won 87-73. Behind 27 points and seven blocked shots by Viskovic, the Crusaders were able to give their head coach a gift—his 400th career win, making Drew one of only 34 active coaches to accomplish this feat.

Drew, fresh from being presented the game ball, acknowledged all of the coaches and players who helped him along the way.

"There were a lot of great players who made this possible," he said.

More impressive to Drew than the personal achievement, however, was the way that the players were finally thinking as a team, due in no small part to some additional time put in by the players to improve.

"We want to get better as a team," Drew said. "So, the players have been working extra hard lately to accomplish this. This has been a major step for us. The coaching staff has been working extra hard on shooting and coach Scott Drew and coach Steve Flint have been creative in making up new finishing drills using foothold blocking pads and karate blocking pads. One of the drills, called 'the car wash,' has been fun and productive in helping us finish shots around the basket."

Perhaps no one personified this recent rebirth better than the all-star play of Zoran Viskovic. In the Buffalo game, he was seven-for-eight from the field. Against NIU, Viskovic shot 12-of-13 from the floor. He was literally dominating the paint on offense, nearly automatic once he caught the ball in the post.

"It's getting to the point that when Zoran misses a shot, we all wonder what happened," Drew said. "That's really a credit to him."

"' The Car Wash'–a finishing drill using foothold pads and karate blocking pads has helped the team complete baskets. It was created by Coach Scott Drew."–Homer Drew

---

Viskovic, however, wouldn't make a big deal out of his recent success.

"I've gotten a bunch of great assists, which make it very easy for me," he said. "I'm thankful to my teammates for that... it makes it fun to play."

He also felt the need to thank an assistant coach for his improved stamina in recent contests. Well, sort of.

"Coach Scott Drew is killing me with the jump ropes," Viskovic said with a weary grin.

In the locker room, all of the talk was about Viskovic's recent hot streak, specifically a dunk with seven minutes remaining that stopped the final NIU rally of the night. Although he stood 6-11, Viskovic rarely dunked in games, opting for soft layups and short jumpers instead. His teammates were encouraging him to take the ball stronger to the basket.

"Man, that dunk was nasty!" Bob Jenkins said gleefully, clearly meaning the term in a good sense. "He's been trying that in practice, so when he did it tonight in the game, you heard the reaction from the crowd. I was trying not to run on to the floor because I was so excited."

"I've been telling Zoran that he should dunk more inside," Bill Jenkins agreed. "I always tell him when he gets the ball alone underneath to make a 'game shot.' The dunk is a 'game shot.'"

"Oh, yeah, 'game shots,'" Viskovic said when told about his teammates' advice. "That's what we call it. Yeah, you could say it [the dunk] was a 'game shot.'"

The Crusaders would be in need of more game shots from all parties concerned a few nights later, however. A late January showdown with conference rival Youngstown State at the ARC loomed.

While YSU came into the game with a slightly better 12-5 mark than Valpo's 10-8 record, both teams had identical 5-2 conference records. A share of first place in the conference was on the line.

The quick start that Valpo launched out to against NIU did not repeat itself against Youngstown. In fact, the Penguins shot out to an early nine-point lead, before Valpo countered with a 10-0 run to take back the lead. After Valpo held the lead for approximately two minutes, a Desmond Harrison jumper gave Youngstown an advantage that they would hold until the final two seconds of the half, when Bill Jenkins would stuff home two points off a pass from Bryce. Valpo led 35-34 at the break.

The second half was a horse race. Neither team led by more than four points. However, Valpo's shooting went cold—down to 36 percent from the field. Still, the Crusaders trailed by only one point with less than a minute to play when Jared Nuness knocked down a three-pointer from the right corner. Youngstown's David Brown was fouled by Sykes, and hit both free throws to put Youngstown up by three with 27 seconds remaining. As Valpo took a timeout with 15 ticks remaining, the ARC buzzed. Everyone in Porter County knew that Bryce would be getting the ball to attempt a game-tying three. Could Bryce offer up game-saving heroics twice in seven days? Judging by the anticipation in the crowd, Valpo fans thought so.

However, there turned out to be one flaw with the grand plan: Youngstown played textbook, airtight defense on Valpo's play. Bryce came around a screen and launched a three-pointer, which was blocked. Youngstown's Harrison grabbed the loose ball and was fouled with nine seconds left.

Harrison missed both free throws, so Valpo would get a final shot. However, after getting the ball up the floor against the quick Youngstown defenders, the best shot that Valpo could muster was a running 33-foot heave by Bryce. The fell harmlessly away from the basket, and the Youngstown bench celebrated. Meanwhile, the capacity crowd in the ARC sat stunned. Final score: Youngstown State 69, Valpo 66.

A visibly dejected Drew and Bryce entered the media room after the game. Although they were disappointed in the loss, they gave all of the credit to Youngstown.

"They have the best eight-man rotation in our conference right now," Drew said. "Down the stretch, they made all the big shots. They earned the basketball game."

Earning big wins was something that the Penguins had done quite frequently in recent years. Head Coach Dan Peters had succeeded in transforming a struggling program into a conference title contender.

"Coach Peters has done a remarkable job of turning that program into a very competitive one," Drew said. "He deserves a lot of recognition for his team's performance."

However, coach, son and teammates all expressed frustration at the fact that Bryce wasn't getting to the foul line. Despite the fact that he was double-teamed, bumped, pushed and muscled around in most games, Bryce had attempted a total of three free throws in the past three games. He didn't set foot at the line once against Youngstown.

"I don't know what I have to do to get there...," Bryce said. "But if I can get a fair shake with the refs, we'll be okay."

Some of his teammates, however, were not shrugging off the statistic even that much.

"Bryce takes a lot of abuse out there," Bob Jenkins said. "I know that it's something we have to play through, but still, it does get frustrating to watch him get beat up, especially when there's nothing you can do about it. It's like watching your little brother get beat up."

The Crusaders worked hard to get Bryce open. Teams keyed on Bryce defensively and, as a result, Drew was forced to employ some creative screening schemes to get Bryce shots. Some of the plays came from Drew's brief visit with a famous coach the season before.

Following the Crusaders' loss to Indiana at the Hoosier Classic, Drew met up with Bob Knight outside the locker room. Drew asked Knight for advice on Valpo's offense. Knight gladly offered Drew a half-hour tutorial on screens and motion offenses on a locker room chalkboard.

"Bob Knight was the ultimate teacher," Drew said. "And I'm grateful that I had the opportunity to be his student."

One other aspect of the free-throw statistic irked Jenkins, as well.

"We're the number one team, so, of course, the refs aren't going to give us anything," he said. "That's okay, we expect that. But at home? That's what I find disturbing."

However, despite the irritation with the officiating, Drew felt good about his team's demeanor after the game. Despite losing a pivotal conference home game, no Crusader was moping in or around the locker room.

"This is not as big of a setback as people think," Bob Jenkins said. "Youngstown's a good team, and they're hot right now."

Sykes also refused to allow the game's ramifications to seep over onto future contests.

"I don't think this will be a big problem," he said. "Morale's a little low right now, but by Thursday, we should be back in the swing of things."

Of course, before they could get to Thursday and another conference matchup, the Crusaders would have to make a side trip to St. Louis. Another non-conference game awaited, this time against the Billikens of Saint Louis University.

Before a crowd of nearly 16,000 at the Kiel Center, Valpo knew it was going to be relying on a three-guard lineup for a majority of the evening. To top it off, Sykes and Viskovic were still banged up from the Youngstown game two nights earlier.

Nonetheless, Valpo came out with high emotion and played the host Billikens even for the first half. Valpo led most of the way, but a late three-pointer gave Saint Louis a 34-31 halftime lead.

The Billikens outscored Valpo 24-16 over the first 11 minutes of the half to take an 11-point lead. Valpo battled back to within three points with 2:50 left, but couldn't convert on two straight possessions that would have cut into the lead. Saint Louis regained its composure and put Valpo away with two late three-pointers. Behind 17 second-half points from 1998 NBA Draft lottery pick Larry Hughes, Saint Louis went on to a 77-66 win. Valpo's record dropped to 10-9, far below the team's own expectations. Bryce had 27 points in a lights-out shooting display that wowed the St. Louis crowd, but he was the only Crusader in double figures.

Yet, something happened on that Monday night in the shadows of the Gateway Arch. Drew felt his team come together like never before. He saw his team rally and nearly win a game that some people gave them no chance to win. He finally believed he had found a clear rotation to use for the rest of the season. The freshmen were finally blending with the upperclassmen. The pieces were falling into place. We finally have a team here, Drew thought.

On the way to St. Louis, Drew decided that the players would change roommates for the trip. This was an effort to allow players to get to know one another better and furnish a "comfort zone" for the team where the players could relate to each other and bond away from the coaching staff.

The bonding had paid off already. Drew felt the game could be a precursor of championships ahead.

"Tonight, with the rotation and the camaraderie of the team, I really believe this could be our turning point," Drew said.

Two nights later, on the northwest side of Chicago, it was time to find out if the team had indeed turned the corner.

Northeastern Illinois University's tiny gymnasium was about half full on a cold, blustery night. A good portion of Valpo fans had made the short drive into the city to follow their team. This would be the final meeting between the two rivals—Northeastern Illinois was ineligible to participate in the conference tourney. Northeastern was fading fast with a record of 4-14. Still, in a rivalry game, the records are thrown out. Hence, Drew wanted the Crusaders to make it a memorable evening with a victory.

In the locker room before the game, Drew told his players that they were running low on opportunities to get back into the conference race. Valpo's turn to make a run had to start right away. The players were eager to prove the Saint Louis game was the turning point in propelling the team forward.

"This is our time," Drew told the players. "This is our time!"

Wanting to get the losing streak behind them, Valpo shot out of the blocks quickly. After scoring the first nine points of the game, Valpo went on to take a 21-6 lead on a layup by Bryce. Northeastern was shooting poorly in the first half, and Valpo took advantage of it, leading by as many as 22 points in the first half. Valpo owned a 41-24 lead at halftime, but the play of the game came six minutes prior. In transition, Bill Jenkins caught the ball on the right baseline and went straight up in traffic. He buried a highlight-reel slam dunk and was fouled. The dunk was so authoritative that a group of Northeastern students sitting under the basket began throwing confetti and celebrating.

In the second half, however, the Golden Eagles mounted a furious rally behind the hot hand of Zachary Norvell. As Valpo began turning the ball over against the press, the Eagles slowly climbed back into the game. By the final minute of the game, they were within five points. Thanks to 13-of-13 free-throw shooting from Sykes, Valpo was able to keep Northeastern at arm's length and walk off with an 88-82 win.

Bryce finished with 28 points and Bill Jenkins added 14 points and nine rebounds. Only one stat mattered after this game, however: the one in the win column.

"This was huge," Sykes said. "We're not out of the race yet."

Sykes also had his dander up from an incident near the end of the game. A Northeastern assistant coach had been jawing at Sykes for most of the game and finally went a little too far for Sykes' liking. Sykes brushed him off with a couple of words and an annoyed glance.

"That guy's talked junk to me every game, every time we've played them," Sykes said. "I don't know what his deal is."

Two nights later, the Crusaders were in Chicago again, on the opposite side of town to take on Chicago State again. Much like their other game in the city, Valpo started quickly.

Exploiting their size advantage inside, Valpo sprinted out to a 15-4 lead. Chicago State called a timeout. In the huddle, Drew told his team not to let up.

"Don't be satisfied with the lead," he said. "Let's build on this."

Build they did. Thanks to more stellar post play and three-pointers from Sykes, Nuness, and Bryce, Valpo assembled a 49-32 halftime lead. In the second half, Valpo contrasted their performance from the game two nights earlier. Valpo blew the game wide open, and cruised on to an easy 102-74 victory. The story of the evening was Viskovic, who went a perfect 11-for-11 from the field.

There was a little bit of comic relief, too. With time dwindling and the game squarely tucked away in Valpo's favor, reserve forward Aaron Thomason was wide open for a dunk. As he rose up to slam the ball, the ball was pinned against the front of the rim. Thomason nearly fell flat on his back. His teammates on the bench doubled over with laughter.

According to Jason Jenkins, Thomason was forever boasting to his teammates about his outstanding leaping ability. Knowing that Thomason, the team prankster, would have to take a little ribbing struck the freshman as amusing.

"Oh, the teasing's already started," he said in the locker room. "It's going to go on the whole way home, too. This is too funny."

Thomason himself saw fit to laugh at the miss. When a Chicago State student teased him about the failed slam, he had a good laugh at his own expense, breaking out into an impromptu song.

"I got...no hops! I got...no hops!" he sang as he strolled out to the team bus. "Aaron is our 'inspirational leader,' Coach Drew would say later, "and, by the way, he is our best singer on the team as he performed the National Anthem before our game in the past."

On this night, Valpo could afford to laugh, and why not? They were on a winning streak, the team was playing its best basketball of the year, and it was finally heading home after a three-game road trip.

A few days later, news was handed down from the conference office: Chicago State, thanks to a scheduling error that had them playing too many games, was ruled ineligible for the post-season conference tournament. That meant there were only seven teams remaining that could play and also meant the team that received a top seed would receive a first-round bye. The Crusaders saw this as a golden opportunity that would help them get back to the NCAA Tournament.

Trailing by one game in the conference standings, Valpo geared up for a crucial battle at home with Oral Roberts, one of the conference co-leaders. The day of the game, the *Vidette-Times* summed it up with a banner headline that read, "The Race is On."

The Crusaders were ready for the homestretch of the season. The corner had not only been turned, it was fading fast in the rear-view mirror.

CHAPTER NINE

Return to the Top:
A Race to First Place

"Excellence can be obtained if you constantly strive for perfection and you care enough to do your best in everything."

–Author Unknown

Bryce Drew sat removing tape from his ankles in the cramped shower room following the decisive win over Chicago State.

"This was a long awaited night," he said. "We've been waiting for this team to get healthy and play like this all season long."

Like his son, Homer Drew believed the big victory had come at the right moment for the Crusaders, who were heading into a crucial stretch of games.

Drew also was pleased his team had been able to build a big halftime lead, and not let it wither away because of overconfidence.

"I told the team that basically they had two choices: to let [Chicago State] back into the game or to put them away," he said. "They came out with intensity in the second half, and it's a wonderful time to be doing that. Now, the stage is set for two great games this week—Duke vs. North Carolina and Valpo vs. Oral Roberts."

Now that Valpo was 12-9 overall and 7-3 in the conference, players and coaches were becoming mindful of their position in the standings. Youngstown State and Western Illinois both were ahead of Valpo in the conference. That fact was not lost on Drew.

"We control the next two games at home, but Youngstown has five of their next six at home," Drew said. "We've got to defend our homecourt to be in position to have a say in the conference race."

A near-sellout crowd turned out at the ARC for the game, and the student section was on its feet behind the Oral Roberts bench nearly an hour before gametime. This was an important game for Valpo, and the students knew it.

For the third straight game, Valpo shot out from the tipoff like gangbusters. Led by Jamie Sykes, and Bill and Bob Jenkins, the Crusaders jumped out to a 13-point advantage after nine minutes of play. Valpo's defense was also outstanding, holding Oral Roberts All-American candidate Tim Gill to five first-half points. The Golden Eagles crawled closer, thanks to five three-pointers. Still, by the half, Valpo had forced 11 turnovers and led by nine points.

Starting the second half much like the first, Bryce drained two three-pointers to spur a 12-4 Crusader run. Valpo's lead was pushed to 17. Five minutes later, Valpo went on another 14-6 scoring spurt, and the game was put out of reach. Sykes scored on a nifty spin move. Bill Jenkins dunked off a feed from Bryce. Viskovic dunked and drew a foul 30 seconds later. Valpo defenders forced seven more turnovers. Oral Roberts missed five straight shots. The anticipated showdown turned into a one-sided showcase.

With the Valpo lead standing at 26 points and two minutes remaining, Drew cleared his bench. Every player who set foot on the floor for the Crusaders scored. Aric Graham, Aaron Thomason, and, finally, Marko Punda. The game ended. Valpo had a resounding 90-68 victory. The big win surprised even Valpo fans with its unexpected margin, and Drew couldn't do much except express his pride.

"I'm really proud of our basketball team," he said. "The past two weeks we have been working really hard, and we're becoming the team I always felt we could become. The extra work and concentration is paying off for them."

Drew was equally pleased that his club sustained a big lead against a conference contender. The seniors had been showing the tendency to coast with big leads, resulting in some dramatic rallies from opponents and churning stomachs for the coaches.

"The guys did a good job tonight. They kept the momentum going in our favor," he said. "Bryce hit a couple of big threes, Jamie hit some great shots hanging in the lane and did a tremendous job on Gill defensively. Jamie held him to seven shot attempts."

More importantly, Valpo had made a statement that its crown would have to be taken from them, although Bryce shrugged off suggestions to that effect.

"I don't know about statements. We just didn't want anyone to sweep us and beat us here," he said.

Sykes, on the other hand, was a little more willing to concede that the game was the Crusaders' best effort of the season to this point, and that he hoped other teams were paying attention. After all, there was still a lot of basketball to be played, he said.

"I think it was our best game... at first, we struggled because we had so many injuries," he said. "People were counting us out. I mean, we were 5-3 and people were counting us out! That made us mad. But now, we've proven that you can't keep a good team down, and we're showing our colors now."

Drew reminded everyone that the team was finally starting to hit full stride.

"You know, we've won eight of our last 10 games," he said. "We just keep getting better and better as we get healthier..." his comments were interrupted by Bryce coughing loudly. Drew shook his head and chuckled. "...as we cough right through the press conference, of course."

Of course, after going 6-of-6 from the field to increase his field goal streak to 17 straight, Viskovic's sudden tear was a topic of conversation.

"I've been staying an extra 15 or 20 minutes after every practice with the coaches, and it's not been very fun," Viskovic said.

The Croatian native's less-than-ringing endorsement of the extra practice was understandable, considering that assistant coaches Steve

Flint and Scott Drew spent those minutes after each practice pounding on Viskovic with football-style blocking pads while he practiced inside moves and shots. The object of the drill was to toughen him up and get him used to contact so he would finish his shots better, and it appeared to be working. Still, Viskovic wished the coaches could find a slightly less painful way to improve his inside game.

"If you see bruises on my face or my head, it's from those pads," Viskovic said with a laugh. Drew leaned in and interrupted him.

"We check in with our lawyers every week," he joked.

Drew also offered another reason why the Crusaders were finishing games stronger.

"We've been trying to keep our practices short and hard," he said. "We think it keeps them a little fresher at the end of games." He also said the practice time with a healthy squad was allowing the offense to get in sync.

"We're getting our timing together," Drew said. "We had more assists than turnovers tonight, we move better, we screen better and most importantly, we passed up shots to get better shots, which is a great sign."

Sykes and Bryce read over the stat sheet as they got up to leave the media room. On the way out, Sykes grabbed Bryce's shoulder excitedly as he read Bryce's totals for the night: 19 points, nine rebounds, nine assists, six steals, and no turnovers. Bill Jenkins had a double-double with 14 points and 10 rebounds.

"Wow, you almost had a triple-double, man!" Sykes exclaimed.

On the flipside of the jubilation, Oral Roberts head coach Barry Hinson appeared shell-shocked as he headed into the media room. His team had just been thoroughly dismantled, and he looked the part.

"Valparaiso was a far better team tonight," he began. "They completely dominated us in every aspect of the basketball game...their students start chanting 'warm up the bus...'" He shook his head. "It was an old-fashioned whupping."

Suddenly, Drew ducked back into the interview room, to everyone's surprise. He quickly complimented Hinson on the outstanding job he

had done in his first year as head coach at Oral Roberts, and then patted Gill on the shoulder.

"I just want to say that Bryce and Tim have developed a friendship
over the summer training for the World University Games team, and I
feel that too many times we are so concerned with winning and losing we
forget one of the most rewarding bonus of basketball is that of making
friends," Drew said. "No matter what happens, Bryce and Tim have
developed a friendship that will far outlast basketball."

Hinson, who looked startled when he was interrupted, broke into a
smile.

"Like I said, they dominated everything tonight...they're even dominating the media room," he said to reporters' laughs. "I'm only kidding.
Homer's first class, and y'all know that."

Although he didn't mind Drew's interruption, Hinson was clearly
agitated with the Valpo student section, which began chanting "overrated," late in the game to taunt the Golden Eagles' bench. He didn't vow
revenge, but he came close.

"We've got to let this game go, but I'm not going to let 'overrated' go.
It was really hard to sit there the last five minutes of the game," he said.
"We won't forget that.

"Of course, that's a part of college basketball. At least they didn't say
'warm up the tractor' like the students did at Oklahoma State."

Even a few of the Valpo players expressed disappointment that the
students began taunting their opponents. The consensus was that there
was no need to give a conference rival extra motivation.

"Most likely that will come back to haunt us," Bill Jenkins said.
"That's so high school...I was like, 'man, don't do that.' It was pretty
childish."

"You can use all of that stuff as motivation," Bryce said. "In the tourney, we'll be ready, though, and not too much stuff in the past is going
to determine the outcome."

Bryce, himself the object of opposing fans' taunts on occasion, said
that one has to shrug off those types of comments.

"It doesn't really register when you're out on the floor," he said. "People say stuff all the time, but you can't listen to it or it will drive you nuts. You've got to find a way to block it out."

Life long friendships are one of the beautiful values that basketball produces.

Bryce then talked about his friendship with Tim Gill. The two were roommates in Colorado Springs the previous summer for the USA Basketball tryouts for the World University Games. Even though Gill had to head home early with an injury, the pair formed a bond through faith that no basketball game can break.

"Obviously, we both love to play basketball," Bryce said. "But we also talked a lot and we prayed together a lot. He took me out to eat a few times, which was really nice of him."

Over a plate of fries one night, Gill and Bryce discussed the upcoming college season, which would be their final year representing their respective schools. Both players were accused of being too unselfish at times. Both resolved to display leadership for their teams.

"We were both seniors, so we decided we needed to be a little more aggressive for our teams," Bryce said. "Of course, we'll do whatever it takes to win, but we said we would take the open shot a little bit more. Which is fine with me, because I'd rather be the one taking the shot at the end of the game. I can deal with the consequences. I can't deal with not trying."

Two nights after the big victory, Valpo faced a struggling Southern Utah squad. Yet again, the Crusaders looked strong from the outset. Jumping out to a 14-2 lead, Valpo capitalized on Southern Utah's poor shooting. Behind several more inside baskets from Viskovic (whose streak of consecutive field goals ended at 20 when a baby hook spun out of the basket nearly 11 minutes into the game), the Valpo lead stretched to 17 points.

However, led by the outside shooting prowess of Jason Essex, the Thunderbirds rallied to get back into the game. They trailed by only 10 points at halftime after the late flurry. The momentum continued after the break.

Within three minutes, Southern Utah had pulled to within four points. After a Valpo timeout, Bryce scored five quick points and Zoran scored in the paint to give the Crusaders breathing room. The Valpo lead was 11 points with under seven minutes remaining when Southern Utah went on another run, this time led by freshman Jeff Monaco's three-point bombs. With one minute remaining and Valpo up by five, Nuness was fouled. He missed both free throws, giving the underdogs from Utah a chance to pull within one possession in the game's final minute. However, Sykes snagged the loose ball rebound, saving the day for Valpo. Sykes' free throws down the stretch put the game out of reach, and Bill Jenkins' dunk on a nifty lob pass from Nuness sealed the deal. Valpo won, 66-56.

Yet, when the team returned to the locker room, Drew gazed disappointedly around the room. When Valpo jumped out to a big early lead, the players seemed to lose focus and that bothered the coaches. It seemed that the team thought the game was decided after the first 12 minutes, and, as a result, the turnovers, defensive lapses, and mental mistakes prevailed throughout the rest of the game. The final score was deceiving, as Valpo had to gut out the final five minutes and hold on for the victory. As he did after the Purdue game, Drew shared his "two scoreboards" theory. Only this time his team was on the opposite side of the board.

"Even though the scoreboard said we had won, on the scoreboard in our hearts we knew we didn't deserve to win, because we did not play with intensity," he said.

The performance haunted Drew as he made his way to the press room. This was not the time for a lack of concentration, especially with the two biggest road games of the year coming up in the following two weeks. Drew entered the press room shaking his head and wearing an exasperated smile.

"Well, that was fun," joked *Vidette-Times* sports editor Paul Jankowski. Drew broke out laughing.

"Please, Paul, tell me who it was fun for," Drew replied. Then, perhaps to illustrate to his players how obvious the lack of focus and intensity was to the game's observers, Drew asked each of the four reporters seated around the media room table what the Crusaders did wrong. The answers were diverse: the team didn't take care of the basketball, they did barely enough to win, they lost their focus on defense and allowed too many easy shots, etc. The answers all had one aspect in common: they were the result of a lack of team focus.

"I think you analyzed it well for us," Drew told the press. With that, he jokingly got up to leave. He returned to his seat a few seconds later and continued the press conference. Although their coach could have a laugh over it, the players made no excuses for their subpar play. Drew was relieved to see that the seniors weren't happy with the game. He knew they were looking ahead to the road game against Buffalo three nights later, but like most coaches, Drew realized if he allowed his team to do that, it would cost Valpo eventually.

"We came out excited on Thursday, tonight was a test to see if we could do it again," Bryce said. "We didn't come out with the same emotion."

Bill Jenkins hoped that the game would send the message to the entire team that every opponent, no matter how far behind, is to be respected.

"We're going to see what this team is all about in the next few games," he said. "But we were fortunate to win this game."

Although the seniors felt they got away with one on this night, they weren't about to give the win back, either.

"Hey, a win's a win," Sykes said. "We just weren't very happy with the way we won. We made too many silly mistakes." The difference between a win and a loss was also evident in the loose attitude in the Crusader dressing room when Bill Jenkins attempted to explain that his last-second slam relieved his frustration.

"That was like an aggression dunk, because I was so mad with the way I was playing at that point," he said. His brother Bob interrupted.

"Oh, give it a rest! You were smiling after you dunked it!" Bob exclaimed. "You were running around out there saying, 'oh, yeah.'" Bob imitated Bill begging for high-fives after the dunk. Bill smirked, then turned back to the reporter.

"You see, as long as you win, it makes it a heck of a lot easier getting up the next day," he said before returning the teasing on his brother.

However, the test looming ahead for the Crusaders was no laughing matter—venturing on the road to take on Buffalo in the hostile confines of Alumni Arena. One player joked to the press that Buffalo ought to have metal detectors at the door to protect Vilcinskas after his near run-in with a Buffalo player one month earlier. That was a bit extreme, but there were reminders all over the Buffalo campus that Valpo was not on friendly ground. A large banner was hanging from the entrance to the campus.

"WE WANT VALPO!" it screamed. "BEAT VALPO!" read the lighted sign above another campus building.

"It's like we're heading into the lion's den," Drew remarked. "They are ready."

As the season's largest crowd filed into the Bulls' home court, Drew was hoping that his team could start fast one more time, in order to neutralize the home crowd.

Neutralize they did. Sprinting out to a 17-2 lead, the normally wild building was relegated to pin-drop silence. Buffalo was able to narrow the gap, but Valpo still led by 10 points at halftime. Drew encouraged his team not to fall prey to complacency.

Led by a strong second half from Jason Jenkins and key rebounds by Viskovic, Valpo was able to hold the Bulls at a comfortable distance for most of the game. Valpo won, 73-64, to improve its record to 15-9 overall and 10-3 in the Mid-Con.

"They were warriors tonight," Drew said from his hotel room. "This was a big game and everyone played like it." He passed around the praise to all of the team.

That early run really quieted the crowd," he said. "Then, we played an immaculate floor game. The senior leadership was obvious tonight."

Drew singled out Viskovic for his play, as well as Bill and Jason Jenkins, who combined to go five-for-five from three-point range.

"Zoran's playing his best basketball right now...he's just exploding to the ball," Drew said, before exploding off to a late lasagna supper.

Valpo was now just one-half game behind Youngstown State for the conference lead, and the Crusaders would get a second crack at the Penguins the following week. However, there would be a non-conference game before venturing off to Youngstown State—a home rematch against Belmont.

Belmont visited on a Saturday afternoon. Similar to the first meeting, the game was close in the first half. Valpo led by only seven points at the half. The highlight of the day came at intermission, when the inaugural class of athletes and coaches were inducted into the Valpo Athletic Hall of Fame. Among those inducted were former head basketball coach Gene Bartow; Bob Dille, captain of the 1944-45 team that went 21-3; as well as former Valpo football and Green Bay Packer standout Fuzzy Thurston and major league outfielder Lloyd McClendon.

In the second half, Valpo was jumpstarted by two big spurts. First, a 14-0 run four minutes into the half transformed a five-point lead into a 19-point edge. Seven points from Viskovic during the run were key. Later, two Bryce three-pointers spurred another 14-0 run, blowing the game wide open. Valpo strolled to a 95-61 win. The efficiency and intensity with which the Crusaders overwhelmed the struggling Bruins pleased their coach.

"It was a very enjoyable day," Drew said. He also felt the first Hall of Fame class made the afternoon special.

"Bob Dille and Fuzzy Thurston are sensational to begin our Hall of Fame era, and Gene Bartow is just the topping on the cake," Drew said. "I have had the privilege of knowing Gene for several years now, and he has always gone out of his way to help me and he has been so loyal to Valparaiso University."

The team now had four days to prepare for the Youngstown State game. The contest was absolutely a must-win for Valpo, if it was to have any chance at winning the regular season conference title. However, in a bit of unexpected help, Buffalo defeated Youngstown State later that evening, erasing the half-game deficit in the standings. Youngstown and Valpo were now tied for the top spot.

This game had several storylines to underscore its importance, but perhaps one of the themes was most compelling: the Beeghly Center, Youngstown's home court, was the one building in the conference where the seniors had never won, going zero for three. That fact gnawed away at the seniors during the five-hour bus ride to northeastern Ohio.

The desire to finally shake off the Youngstown jinx was evident during the game's first half. The Crusaders dictated the tempo of the game, stifled Youngstown's opportunities to get into a transition-heavy track meet, and thanks to Vilcinskas' 10 points, grabbed a six-point lead at halftime.

The Penguins responded quickly in the second half, eliminating the Valpo lead, and building a lead of their own. Behind the hot hand of guard Anthony Hunt, YSU sprinted to a 10-point advantage with approximately six minutes remaining in the game. Valpo called timeout.

Inside the huddle, Drew reminded the players of the goals they had been working towards.

"This is our last stand," he said. "You all have the ability, the heart, and the experience to make it four-for-four and set yourselves apart, not only in the history of Valpo, but also in all of Division I. Now put your hands in here. Let the power that's inside each one of you bring out our best!"

The team broke the huddle and went to work. With their backs being pushed toward the wall and their championship hopes on the line, Valpo countered with intensity and determination. Bryce later told the *Vidette-Times* that the team "drew the line," and decided it was time to take care of business. Bryce led the way.

Utilizing Viskovic's inside prowess, the Crusaders slowly climbed back into the game. With under two minutes left, Valpo pulled within two points. With 1:18 to go, Bryce knocked down a running jumper in the key to tie the game. After a Youngstown basket, Valpo came down with the ball. Working the shot clock down, Bryce got the ball in the corner. Hounded by defender Devon Lewis, Bryce stepped behind the three-point line with 22 seconds left and let fly with a three-pointer. The ball dropped through the hoop, and the Crusaders had a one-point lead. Bryce fell to one knee near the court's baseline and prayed joyfully. After another Youngstown miss, Bryce hit one of two free throws to reach the final margin: Valpo 70, Youngstown State 68.

Finally, the Crusaders had rid themselves of the burden of not winning in Youngstown. Finally, after a long, tumultuous season, the Crusaders were leading the conference race. Both remaining regular season games were at home—the Crusaders controlled their own destiny. Win both games, and a fourth straight Mid-Con season championship would be theirs.

"This was huge..." Bryce told the *Vidette-Times*. "Because we haven't won here before and that's something we talked about the whole trip and even during the game."

The first of the final two home games was a visit from Missouri-Kansas City. The Kangaroos were on their way to a sixth-place finish in the conference. Still, all of the emotions of the seniors, not to mention the possibility that the team might be looking forward to a Senior Night showdown with rival Western Illinois, caused Drew some concern.

"This is a dangerous game," Drew warned minutes before tipoff. "They are well coached and they have everything to gain tonight."

For the game's first 10 minutes, the coach looked prophetic.

UMKC capitalized on some early Valpo shooting woes, and eight minutes into the game took a 15-8 lead. Valpo quickly righted itself, and within eight minutes had used seven points from Bryce and four points from Bob Jenkins to reclaim a nine-point lead. The Crusader defense clamped down the final few minutes of the half. After forcing a shot clock violation against UMKC, Bryce swished a three-pointer from the left baseline. Valpo took an eight-point lead into the locker room.

As they had done so many times before, Valpo turned to its inside game in the second half. Viskovic and Vilcinskas were thrown the ball in the post on nearly every possession. The easy baskets piled up. However, UMKC, to its credit, refused to give up. They stayed within two or three baskets of Valpo the entire half. With 2:23 to go, UMKC was within four points.

Finally, in the game's last minutes, the Cruaders sealed the victory at the foul line. Hitting seven of eight free throws in the final 48 seconds, Valpo hung on for a 75-65 win.

The Crusaders had one regular season contest left: 48 hours later at the ARC against longtime nemesis Western Illinois. While Valpo held a one-game lead over the Leathernecks, it was crucial that the Crusaders win the game. Western held the tie-breaker over Valpo, so the Crusaders needed to win the regular season title outright to earn the number one spot in the conference tourney. Balancing all of the emotions along with a heated rivalry was a tricky situation, Drew said. Furthermore, Western Illinois coach Jim Kerwin always had his team ready to play.

"I'm very concerned, because they beat us on our home floor last year and that doesn't happen often," he said. "We need to find a way to stay focused without losing the sentiment of the evening."

Drew was heartened by the business-like approach most of his players were taking heading into the final home game.

"I try not to think about it," Sykes said. "I appreciate having played here for four years, but I don't think I'll sit back and appreciate it fully until the job is done."

Even so, there was no denying the sentimental impact of such a game on all of the graduating seniors. Bryce admitted as much.

"I've been thinking about this game all year," he said.

CHAPTER TEN

You Only Get One Senior Night

"Whatever you do, work at it with all your heart, as working for the Lord not for men, since you know that you will receive an inheritance from the Lord as a reward."

–Colossians 3:23

Beginning the conference season with a 5-3 record seemed like a distant memory as the Crusaders found themselves in a more comfortable and familiar position, awaiting a showdown for the Mid-Continent Conference title.

One game—in the friendly confines of the ARC—would decide if Valpo would win its fourth straight season title. More importantly, the game would determine if Valpo would get a first-round bye in the Mid-Con Tourney the following week. After the one-point loss to Western Illinois in Macomb earlier in the season, the Crusaders longed for another shot at Western. Drew knew the game would be an emotional test. There was a lot of respect for Western coach Jim Kerwin and his staff. Over the years, in many sports, the two institutions had squared off in many memorable contests, several of them with conference championships on the line. Still, there was no question: this was a rivalry. Bill Jenkins sized up the team's feelings after the win against UMKC.

"We owe Western," he said.

Watching his team warm up from the bench, Homer Drew seemed calm before the game. Had the emotions of Bryce's final home game kicked in yet?

"Oh, they've been going all day long," he responded with a glossy-eyed smile.

Earlier in the day, Drew told the seniors that it was important to thank the fans, since they were the ones who had stuck with Valpo through the good times and tough times. Drew told the players that they owed a large debt of gratitude to the Valpo fans, because while they understood the game, they also appreciated effort and teamwork, whether the Crusaders won or lost. He also told them that it was okay to cry, and when he did, Drew got choked up himself.

"You're simply the best team I've ever had the pleasure to be around," he said. "Thank you."

Just prior to pre-game introductions, each senior was introduced with his parents. For most players, this is a memorable moment. However, for Tony Vilcinskas, whose parents were still 8,000 miles away in Lithuania and unable to attend, the brief ceremony was not going to be easy.

"I've tried not to think about it," he said two nights earlier. "Everyone will come out on the floor with their parents. I'm not looking forward to it, because my parents are not going to be here. It will be tough."

The same night, Bill Jenkins also expressed disappointment with Senior Night, but for a different reason.

"There's this realization that it's coming to an end, and it's gone by way too fast," he said. "Right now, I keep thinking that I've got one more year left...it seems like only yesterday that Bob and I were laughing at Bryce, this skinny kid with braces, at Krider Camp. And yet, here we are..."

When the Jenkins twins were announced, Bob walked on to the floor first, escorting their mother. Then Bill followed, with his arm around their father. All four Jenkins hugged as Bill wiped away his tears.

Finally, Bryce walked onto the floor with Drew and his wife, Janet, accompanied by a huge ovation. Public address announcer John Bowker read the lengthy list of Bryce's accomplishments—over the chanting student section.

"M-V-P! M-V-P! M-V-P!" they shouted. Bryce smiled and acknowledged the crowd with a wave.

Double Trouble...Bill and Bob Jenkins. (Sam Riche/THE TIMES of NW Indiana)

The coaching staff: Coach Scott Drew, Coach Jim Harrick, Coach Homer Drew...going over strategy during the Mid-Continent Tournament. (Sam Riche/THE TIMES of NW Indiana)

Five seniors...claiming Valparaiso University's fourth consecutive Mid-Continent Tournament Championship. (Sam Riche/THE TIMES of NW Indiana)

Like father like son...going over practice plan, Coach Homer Drew and Coach Scott Drew. (Sam Riche/THE TIMES of NW Indiana)

Die-hard Crusader supporters followed the team to St. Louis. (Sam Riche/THE TIMES of NW Indiana)

Another one of Zoran Viskovic's many rebounds...on his way to 19 points against Ole Miss. (Sam Riche/THE TIMES of NW Indiana)

The celebration after "the shot." (Sam Riche/THE TIMES of NW Indiana)

"Have you hugged your child today?"
The coach and the player...the father and the son... "the hug."
(Sam Riche/THE TIMES of NW Indiana)

Coach Homer Drew and Bryce Drew enjoying comments on "the shot." (Sam Riche/THE TIMES of NW Indiana)

At the NCAA Tournament, Dale Brown and Craig James shine the national spotlight on Valparaiso University. (Sam Riche/THE TIMES of NW Indiana)

Tony Vilcinskas...the celebration begins after scoring a put back basket over Florida State in overtime. (Sam Riche/THE TIMES of NW Indiana)

Bryce Drew driving to 22 points against the Seminoles. (Sam Riche/THE TIMES of NW Indiana)

Jamie Sykes spins in the lane on his way to scoring 19 points against Florida State. (Sam Riche/THE TIMES of NW Indiana)

Bryce thanks the crowd after NCAA victory over Florida State University. (Sam Riche/THE TIMES of NW Indiana)

At NCAA news conference the media enjoys conversing with Valparaiso University Crusaders...left to right Bill Jenkins, Coach Homer Drew, and Bob Jenkins. (Sam Riche/THE TIMES of NW Indiana)

Dribbling toward daylight, Bryce Drew fights past a Rhode Island defender. (Sam Riche/THE TIMES of NW Indiana)

Valpo fans echo the thoughts of the nation during the Rhode Island game. (Sam Riche/THE TIMES of NW Indiana)

Finally, it was game time. Bryce wanted to make sure his last game at the ARC would be one of his very best.

Right out of the gate, Bryce drained a three-pointer from the right side. Western Illinois' guard Brandon Creason followed with a three of his own to tie the score. Bryce hit another three, this time a pull-up in transition. Another three-pointer from Bryce, following two baskets from Western, put Bryce ahead of the Leathernecks, 9-8.

Even though Bryce had his shooting touch, Western was dominating the boards, getting two or three shots on every possession, while Valpo was kept squarely away from the offensive boards. Western was able to move in front.

Enter Bryce yet again. After a Valpo miss, the ball bounced loose. Bodies went flying and hit the floor in pursuit of the basketball. Despite a lot of contact, no fouls were called. The loose ball was tipped in Bryce's direction, and he grabbed it, stepped behind the three-point line on the left side, and buried a three. The crowd roared as Valpo pulled ahead again. Bryce had 12 points and the crowd wasn't even warmed up.

It was truly a scoring outburst to behold. Bryce canned another trey to put Valpo back in front with just under five minutes remaining. Then, Bryce pulled up from the left side and fired a three. It rattled around the basket, rolled around the rim and dropped through the hoop. The ARC crowd, sensing they were witnessing a special performance, leaped to their feet.

He wasn't even close to being finished, either. With 3:18 left, Bryce leaned in past his defender and kissed in a soft bank shot from 12 feet away. One minute later, Bryce sent his defender airborne with a head fake and dropped in another three-pointer. Valpo headed in at halftime with a 31-27 lead over the Leathernecks. Bryce had 23 of the Crusaders' points.

Despite the outstanding half, Western coach Jim Kerwin had to be pleased. His team only trailed by four despite an All-American guard hitting nearly everything he shot. Coach Drew was displeased for the same reason.

The Crusaders were playing solid defense, but Drew didn't want Bryce to score 70 percent of the team's points in the second half. Valpo had a tremendous size advantage on the Leathernecks, but were being outhustled on the glass. At halftime, Drew told his team it was time to turn on the defensive intensity.

"Defense is not a variable. It's a constant," he said. "We need to expand this lead with our defense. Defense takes heart, energy, and intelligence. You have all three, so let's show it in the second half."

"Defense is not a variable. It's a constant." –Homer Drew

To start the second half, the Crusaders started to work their inside game. Viskovic scored on two spin moves, and Bryce knocked down another three-pointer to push the Crusader lead to eight. Bill Jenkins tied up the ball when his man moved toward the basket, giving Valpo possession. Kerwin called timeout to settle his team, but the stoppage gave Drew time to call a familiar play.

When Valpo took possession and set up its halfcourt offense, Bryce dribbled the ball on top of the key. His defensive man sealed off by a backscreen set by Viskovic, Bill Jenkins began sprinting towards the hoop. Bryce casually flipped the ball towards the backboard. Like clockwork, Bill Jenkins timed his jump, grabbed the ball in mid-air and buried a monstrous dunk, to the crowd's delight. The lob pass—also known as the "alley-oop"—had worked to perfection again. The Crusaders had a 10-point lead.

Once again, the Crusaders turned to their size advantage. Vilcinskas was fouled and hit a free throw. Then he scored on a turnaround jumper. Bill Jenkins broke free for a layup. By the time Bryce stroked another three with 10:40 remaining, the Crusaders had completed a 10-1 run to take a 52-37 lead.

While the Crusaders had taken command, they still were having trouble putting away Western. With 9:11 remaining and Valpo up by 13,

Sykes stole the ball and headed up court, all alone. He lifted into the air to dunk the ball, only to watch the ball spring off the back of the rim. Nuness grabbed the rebound, but missed the layup and Western came down with the rebound. Sykes, who had several prior dunks in games despite his 5-10 frame, shook his head as he jogged back downcourt. Later, he spoke of his embarrassment regarding the miss.

"I've never missed a dunk in a game before in my life," he said. "I don't know what happened or how I missed it. Everyone's going to be giving me a hard time over that one."

Fortunately for Valpo, Western was only able to get two points out of its next two possessions. However, Bob Jenkins fouled out with 7:52 remaining on a play away from the ball. While the last foul was pretty obvious, some of Bob's earlier fouls could fall into the "ticky-tack" variety, meaning that they were fouls where there was little contact. The disparity of fouls between Bob Jenkins and his brother led Bob to comment after the game.

"We look alike but we don't foul alike," he quipped.

After a timeout, the Crusaders looked to settle things. Western never got closer than 10 points. Bryce's spectacular running one-hand basket with 4:27 left seemed to ice the contest as well as close out a memorable evening.

As the final minute ticked off the clock, Valpo attempted to let the seniors leave to a standing ovation. The clock kept running, however, and Drew never had a chance to insert his subs. A long shot clanked off the backboard as time expired, and Valpo had its fourth straight regular season Mid-Continent Conference Championship. Final score: Valparaiso 66, Western Illinois 56. As the buzzer sounded, the seniors embraced on the floor in the middle of a mob of students. After a tumultous early season, the Crusaders had rallied to capture the regular season title, the #1 seed in the conference tourney, and a first-round bye.

David Joseph Schwartz once said that "all great achievements require time." It may have taken all season, but Valpo was finally achieving its season-long goals. One goal down, two more to go: winning the Mid-Continent Tournament and winning a game in the NCAA Tournament.

The capacity crowd in the ARC rose to its feet for the final seconds of the game, sending off the most successful group of seniors in school history with a loud ovation. It somehow seemed so fitting. Not many exited, either, for they knew this group would be honored after the game.

One goal down, two more to go: winning the Mid-Continent Tournament and winning a game in the NCAA Tournament.

After the conference trophy was presented, Drew took the public address microphone to speak to the Valpo faithful. He thanked the students, who responded by chanting the head coach's name.

"HO-MER! HO-MER! HO-MER!" they shouted.

It certainly had been a love affair between the head coach and the Valpo students. Drew valued their support, and the students offered unwavering loyalty in return. Before games, Drew made a point of stopping by the student section and offering a few words of encouragement and sharing a laugh. He occasionally would buy pizzas for the student section and help them secure tickets for road games. The dynamic between the coach and the university population was unique and special. Drew waved to the students, and then introduced his seniors.

"These six gentlemen are something very special," he began. "These six have written most of the records here at Valpo. Our school was founded in 1859, and the last four years have been the most successful in the history of Valparaiso University. These six gentlemen are mainly responsible for that."

With that, he introduced his group of seniors, led by Jay Phifer, the player who had the frustrating experience of sitting out his senior season with a shoulder injury. Drew praised his perseverance.

"He's always upbeat, he's always kept a positive attitude. He's a winner in life," Drew said. Phifer stepped to the microphone and quickly thanked the fans for their support. So quickly, in fact, that Drew had to laugh.

"That's the fewest words he's ever said," he joked.

Next, he introduced Vilcinskas, who also stepped to the microphone and briefly thanked the fans and his teammates. The brevity of his statement also left Drew humorously puzzled.

"Gosh, he says more words to me during a timeout," Drew said, chuckling.

Sykes was introduced by Drew as "someone who had risked his professional future" to be a part of the team. The crowd roared. Sykes waved to the crowd as he took the microphone. He started thanking everyone. He thanked his girlfriend, something that led to immediate teasing from the twins and a collective "aawwwww" from the crowd.

"Oh, you just stop that now," he laughed.

Sykes then credited Assistant Coach Harrick as a big reason why he came back for his senior year, instead of heading to the world of professional baseball.

"[Coach Harrick] kept the fire burning," Sykes said.

After Sykes finished his remarks, Drew introduced the Jenkins twins, who were obviously caught up in the emotion of the moment.

"We have the best twins in Division I basketball right here," Drew said to the crowd's approval. Bob took the microphone first.

"Hi. I'm Bob," he said. The crowd laughed. "And yes, we are separate people."

"I just want to tell you that I consider all of you my family," Bob continued. "It's been four great years."

Bill agreed when it was his turn.

"I wouldn't trade these past four years for anything in the world," he said. "Thank you all."

Then it was time to introduce the player who had made everything possible. Drew paused before introducing his son, Bryce.

"I just want to tell you that I consider all of you my family. It's been four great years."–Bob Jenkins

"I got a phone call this afternoon, and the person on the other end said, 'Dad, don't cry tonight,'" Drew began. "I told him I would not...but I am crying right now.

"And what makes me happiest is the fact that he's a much better son than he is a player," Drew said. "Ladies and gentlemen, Bryce Drew."

The Valpo student section broke into alternating chants of "MVP! MVP!" and "NBA! NBA!" as Bryce stepped forward.

"He's a much better son than he is a player..."
                                    –Coach Drew introducing son Bryce

---

"I want to thank God for making this all possible," he said. "And I want to thank all of you for coming out these four years." Then, he reflected. "You know, when my dad first took the job here, you guys were all gone," he said, motioning towards the balcony of the ARC that was empty in Drew's first years as head coach. "You don't know how many times I would sit here, staring up at that curtain, and dream about what this place would be like if we could fill this place, and get it rocking and be able to win here.

"When I was being recruited out of high school, I told a certain coach from a bigger school that I wasn't going to come play for him, and this coach said, 'what's the matter, don't you want to be big-time?'" he continued. "But during last season, I realized that's a lie, because what we have now is big-time basketball right here."

The crowd roared its approval. Bryce then singled out his brother Scott for making him the player that he had become.

"I want to thank Scott for yelling at me all those years," he said, laughing. "No, really, I want to thank him for making me be the best." Bryce hugged his brother, and then his father.

Drew had a few final comments before relinquishing the microphone.

"I want to thank the fans who have come out loyal all these years," he said. "And mostly, I want to thank God for giving us the opportunity to work with these six seniors. It's really something, we have six gentlemen of different races, different religions, and even different countries, yet they have all come together to work for their dreams... and that is what made America great, and it's what made these young people great."

With those words, the students rushed on the floor again to watch the Crusaders cut down the net in celebration. Viskovic was surrounded by fans.

"Seek ye first the Kingdom of God and all these things will be given to you."
−Matthew 6:33

"It was a rough game, so I'm glad we won," he said, rubbing his chin. "Especially for the seniors, this is great. Now we've got two games to play, and we want to go to the NCAA again."

Scott Drew also expressed his joy for the seniors going out in style in their final home game.

"This is the best way for them to come out of the season," he said. "The rivalry we've had with Western Illinois has been pretty intense, so this is a fitting ending for the seniors... but the big goal is the one coming in Moline."

Vilcinskas slowly waded through the mobs of well-wishers and autograph seekers. He was asked about his emotions after his final home game. The center shrugged his long, angular shoulders.

"History repeated itself, and, hopefully, it will keep repeating," he said. Anything else?

"Yeah, I finally didn't foul out," he said with a smile.

A few moments later, Jim Kerwin reflected on the loss in the media room. He also took a look back at a team that has been Western's achilles heel for four straight years.

"In the last four years, we've played Valpo 11 times, and we've always played 'em in the tournament," he said. "Sometimes you're able to do it, sometimes you're not. Tonight we weren't."

While Kerwin acknowledged that Viskovic and Vilcinskas overpowered his team inside, he pointed to one main reason why the 'Necks had been unable to get over the hump against Valpo.

"Bryce Drew... that's the reason they won," he said with a slight twinge of envy in his voice. "Heck, give me Bryce Drew and I'm in the NCAA two years in a row, too."

Drew entered the room following Kerwin's exit, and began with his traditional opening statement.

"I'm really proud of these seniors," he began. "I'm honored to have worked with them. It really was a magical moment out there tonight. It shows that great things can happen when you stick together.

"You know, a lot of teams would have folded and given up after some of the losses, but these gentlemen fought through it until we got everybody healthy. A lot of people were saying our reign was over, but these young men were warriors and they bonded together. It takes a team to win."

Bryce confessed to not thinking about the game much due to the emotional symbolism of the evening. After his stellar 33-point performance, not many Crusader fans minded.

"I really didn't think about this game today, I've been too busy reminiscing about the last four years," he said. "I'm actually kind of sad right now, because this was our last home game. I didn't want to lose our last game."

As for explaining his lights-out shooting display, Bryce was typically humble.

"I don't know... I did a lot of extra shooting this week, and I somehow found the bottom tonight," he said. "The team did a great job of finding me tonight, where I was at on the floor. I definitely wanted it."

Sykes was asked if there was a particular point during the game when he knew Bryce had a hot hand. He laughed.

"I did a lot of extra shooting this week...and the team did a great job of finding me tonight."–Bryce Drew

"I especially knew it when my shot wasn't going in," he joked. "This is extra sweet, because so many people were counting us out."

Drew was asked to reflect on coaching his son for four seasons—each one ending in a conference title.

"Tonight was a special moment in a father-son relationship," Drew said. "Bryce really complements these other guys here...it's been far harder on Bryce than it's been on me. He puts a lot of pressure on himself, but that's what makes him so good."

Later, Drew reflected on Bryce's childhood, when he first became enthralled by the game of basketball. The Drew parents taught Bryce that basketball is only a game and that he needs to have fun playing it first and foremost. However, like everything else in life, Bryce was encouraged to give basketball his best effort. Drew felt that explained Bryce's success more than anything.

"Why did he become so good in basketball?" Drew said. "Because he always works hard and always does more than expected. His self-discipline and work habits have provided him with success."

Drew then commented on the team play that put Valpo back on the winning track and onward to the conference championship.

"That's always been our philosophy: one guy cannot carry you. It takes a group to be successful," he said.

Drew subscribed wholeheartedly to John Wooden's notion that teamwork was the key to winning championships.

"Greatness can happen when everyone is willing to give what they have and sacrifice a little 'I' for 'we,'" he said. "Talent alone cannot win championships. It takes both talent and chemistry, and chemistry is much more difficult to discover than talent."

"Greatness can happen when everyone is willing to give what they have and sacrifice a little 'I' for 'we.'"

Now that Valpo had gotten the top seed in the conference tournament, a reporter wondered aloud whether the team might get complacent. Drew didn't seem overly concerned with that prospect.

"We know what it takes to win there, we know how to find that edge,"
Drew said. "We have to make sure that we don't let up...that's experience."

Drew agreed that his team's experience was instrumental in its recent success. The Crusaders had won nine games in a row, and they
were still hungry for more. They still had the will to build on the momentum, Drew thought.

"It has to come from within," Bill Jenkins added. "That's what great
about this team, is that we're all winners."

"Coach always says that great athletes compete, and that's what we
try to do," Vilcinskas said.

Back in the Valpo locker room, the mood was festive and happy.
Jason Jenkins smiled as he dressed quickly.

"It feels good, I really felt into the game after I hit my first three. This
is why I came here, to win championships," he said. However, he knew
there was still one big unknown for a freshman. "The tournament is a
completely different ballgame. I'm relying on these seniors to show me
what it takes to win there."

Bill Jenkins stood in his locker, applying lotion to his scalp. For him,
the turning point came early in the second half, when he, his brother,
and Vilcinskas took over the rebounding game.

"If I feel like I'm not into the game and I'm not playing well, then I
always try to make up for it by getting on the boards. Usually that
helps," he said.

While Bob Jenkins was frustrated with his early exit, Bill Jenkins
said at the very least there was a small benefit to his brother fouling out.

"It shows me what I can't get away with," he said, laughing. Bob
Jenkins saw his accumulation of "cheap" fouls a little bit differently.

"Man, cheap is right," he declared with a broad smile. "What can I
say, sometimes you don't get the calls. Although that seems to happen
to me a lot."

Still, when he's on the floor with Bob, Bill spoke of a non-verbal communication that the two use to motivate each other.

"That's a twin thing," he said. "We don't have to say anything. I'll look at him. He'll look at me, and we'll know it's time to step it up."

Both thought the win erased many of the doubts from earlier in the year.

"This could have been a disappointing year, but this win takes care of all that," Bob Jenkins said. "That's why this team is so good. Despite all the downfalls, all the injuries, our heart kept us in it."

A few minutes later, Bill and Bob's father, William, Sr., walked into the locker room.

"Hey, is there any pizza left?" he asked.

"No, check in the other room," Bill responded.

"Man, that's the only reason I come in here is to get some pizza, and now you guys eat it all," he replied with a smile and a laugh. He left for a minute and returned with a slice of pepperoni pizza. Munching away, he looked back on the four years of the twins' career.

"This is the end of a tough chapter," the elder Jenkins said. "They're the babies of the family. Their two sisters both played basketball in college, but somehow it didn't feel like this when they graduated.

"Bill and Bob were both being recruited out of high school, but most schools would offer one of them a scholarship and not the other," he went on. "We got worried, because Minnesota, who had been recruiting them, dropped away. Then, they signed with Valpo right as the conference was being restructured. There was a lot of uncertainty with that. They kept coming to me and asking, 'Dad, did we make a mistake?' But everything here has been a blessing."

William, Sr., and his wife, Cassandra, who made the three-hour drive to Valparaiso from Glendale, Wisconsin, for each home game, confessed to suffering a basketball-related empty nest syndrome.

"We've got no more babies at home, so we're already bored," he said. "I think next winter the car's going to automatically head for Valpo whether there's a game or not."

Being in a similar situation with his youngest son ready to graduate from college, Coach Drew could relate, as could other basketball parents.

"The Jenkins family is representative of the type of family that follows Valpo basketball," Drew said. "Many of the parents follow their sons to all of the games, even making road trips to Hawaii 'a family affair.' Their interest is not merely wins and losses but the overall positive development of their children through participation in our program. We always welcome them to share in this period of growth and enjoyment."

Meanwhile, Bryce Drew sat in his corner locker with a look of total relief on his face. While Valpo still had two tournament games left, it was obvious that winning the regular season title lifted a big burden off of his shoulders.

"I couldn't have picked a better way to go out," he said. "We've gone seven for seven in championships, now I want to go eight for eight."

That achievement would put the Crusaders in some elite company. Only three schools in Division I history had won four consecutive regular season and conference tournament titles: Kentucky, North Carolina State, and Massachusetts.

Overcoming the early season adversity to take the season crown made the victory even sweeter for the 6-3 senior captain.

"We've gone seven for seven in championships, now I want to go eight for eight."–Bryce Drew. Only three schools in Division I history had won four consecutive regular season and conference tournament titles: Kentucky, North Carolina State, and Massachusetts.

"This is one of our greatest accomplishments as a team, because it's been a really difficult year," he said. "We've had to battle back all season, and we stuck together and got it done."

While admitting that the emotions of the evening had gotten the best of him early in the day, Bryce also knew that the team couldn't rest for very long with the Mid-Con Tourney beginning in four days.

"We know we've got to re-focus quickly, because the real battle is about to start," he said. "Still, all day I've been kind of sad. I made sure I got all the tears out before we got here tonight. Then again, you only get one senior night, so you've got to enjoy it."

As Bryce was talking, Bob Jenkins sarcastically leaned over and mockingly sobbed at Bryce, holding out a box of Kleenex. Drew laughed and shook his head. With the win, the Crusaders could afford to joke around a bit. If nothing else, the exchange proved that one constant of sports is still alive: no one on any team—even a guy who had just scored 33 points—is above getting razzed by teammates in the locker room.

Although the team was obviously loose, Bryce didn't fear complacency in the tournament.

"We know we have to get back that hunger to get to the NCAA," he said. "I don't think we'll have trouble getting motivated. We've been there before, and the first-round bye is huge for us. It would have been a real disadvantage if we had to play on Sunday [in the first round] because we need the rest."

Bryce started to talk about the integral role the freshmen would play in the tournament when he was interrupted by one of the team's managers.

"Bryce, there's a whole bunch of kids waiting for you out there," he said.

"Okay," Bryce said, and turned to his interviewer. "I'm sorry. Mind if we cut this short?"

"No problem," the writer replied. Bryce had always tried to accommodate every child who approached him for an autograph, and even the most jaded sportswriter isn't going to stand between 30 eight-year-olds and their hero. Furthermore, watching Bryce tend to the hordes of children who camped outside the hallway leading to the Valpo locker room after each home game was one of the more charming sights in all of sports. Bryce never left until each child had an autograph, and he smiled and chatted with the kids as he signed away.

All of the Valpo players took time to sign and pose for pictures with local children. It explained why Drew liked to recruit "people of character instead of characters." The fact that his players cared for other people was Drew's proudest achievement as a coach.

"The way these gentlemen are an example to children tells why we coaches go overboard to try to help them on the court and off," Drew said. "Basketball is a metaphor for life. Learning to care, to be sensitive and to give back to the community will help these athletes become successful in life."

To emphasize this point, Drew always distributed a poem titled "Little Eyes" to his players every year. He ran across the poem during his days at LSU. An excerpt from the poem summarizes the message.

There's a wide-eyed little fellow, who believes you're always right,
And his ears are always open, and he watches day and night;
You are setting an example every day in all you do,
For the little boy who's waiting to grow up and be like you.

Adding to the evening's souvenir frenzy, the players were giving away their shoes, T-shirts, and towels to the children in honor of the last home game. The kids were so excited that they abandoned their normal practice of waiting patiently down the hall and instead stood right outside the door of the Valpo dressing room.

When the players were giving away shoes, however, a few kids got a little too excited. One boy, who was decidedly smaller than some of the other kids, kept getting muscled out of the way by bigger kids. When the shoes had all been given away, the smaller boy came up empty-handed.

Turning towards his father, the little boy's lip began to tremble and tears welled up in his eyes. Bob Jenkins saw the boy, and ducked back into the locker room. A minute later he emerged, and casually breezed by the rest of the children, who were still focused on Bryce.

Bob Jenkins spotted the little boy who had been denied a souvenir, and gently tapped on his shoulder. When the boy turned, Jenkins slid a shoe—autographed by several players—from under his shirt and handed it to the boy. The boy's eyes lit up.

"Oh, thank you, thank you!" the boy exclaimed. "Dad, look!"

Jenkins laughed, patted the boy on the head, and headed out the door.

A few minutes later, the boy was still proudly displaying his shoe to his father, who smiled as he reminded the boy it was way past his bedtime. But a few seconds later, he realized how wired his son was.

"Yeah, right," the father remarked to a passerby. "Like there's any way he's going to go to sleep tonight."

"Dad, can I wear it home?" the boy asked, prompting more laughter from his father.

The boy hopped up and down as he cradled the shoe. It may have smelled sweaty and had a few scuff marks, but to the boy it was a treasure. The shoe, much like the moment, was priceless.

CHAPTER ELEVEN

Eight-for-Eight

"People acting together as a group can accomplish things which no individual acting alone could ever hope to bring about."

–Frankin D. Roosevelt

The Quad Cities area consists of four cities along the Mississippi River that are all within several miles of one another. Two of the cities, Bettendorf and Davenport, are in Iowa. The other two, Rock Island and Moline, are across the river in Illinois. They are four mid-sized, blue collar cities with few ties to the Mid-Continent Conference, other than being home to one of Western Illinois University's branch campuses.

Nevertheless, the entire area, and the city of Moline in particular, rolls out the red carpet for the conference's basketball teams and fans every March. The Mark of the Quad Cities, a gleaming 12,000-seat arena in downtown Moline, is the home of the Mid-Continent Conference basketball tournament.

The Crusaders arrived a day later than normal for the tournament, thanks to the first-round bye. The coaching staff figured an extra day of practice in the ARC and an extra night of sleep in their own beds would benefit the players. Of course, some of the players were too excited to get much rest. While the team bus was scheduled to depart for Moline at 8 A.M., Bryce Drew arrived an hour early to shoot in the empty, darkened gym. Along with him were two freshmen, Jared Nuness and Jason Jenkins.

"That just demonstrates their dedication," Homer Drew said. "Bryce has earned his status through his work ethic and it's wonderful to see the young players following his lead."

On Sunday evening, three first-round games determined Monday night's semifinal pairings. Oral Roberts defeated Southern Utah. Youngstown State defeated Missouri-Kansas City. Finally, Buffalo topped Western Illinois, 81-74, to earn a berth in the semifinals against Valpo. The Bulls' win guaranteed that Valpo would not play Western for the fourth year in a row in the tourney. While Valpo may have been excited not to have to play a long-time nemesis in the semifinals, they were not thrilled about playing Buffalo. Considering the intensity between the teams over the years, which had resurfaced earlier in the season at the ARC, it's little wonder that Valpo fans were apprehensive about the matchup. Many of them no doubt remembered Bryce crashing to the Mark floor the season before, courtesy of an elbow to the head from Northeastern Illinois' Daveeno Hines, and wondered if similar tactics would surface in the Valpo-Buffalo matchup.

"Every time Valparaiso and Buffalo play, something strange always seems to happen," wrote Paul Jankowski in the *Vidette-Times* after a brawl nearly erupted at the end of the Valpo-Buffalo game at the ARC in January. Not to mention the potential for rust, which Drew spoke about.

"By playing in the first game, it's a disadvantage to us because Buffalo has one game under its belt. They come in with confidence. We come in having sat and watched," Drew said. "If we can get to the championship, then, hopefully it will be our advantage."

The night before the game, Drew decided to make a list during a team meeting.

"Let's list the reasons why we can win," he said.

The Crusaders came up with many different reasons. Drew wrote down the top eight:

1) We know the feeling of being a conference champion.
2) We have momentum.
3) We are well prepared.

4) We want to accomplish another one of our goals for the year.

5) We have the experience.

6) We have the edge mentally.

7) We have improved all season long.

8) We can still raise our level of play.

Drew summarized by saying that everyone on the team needed to make a contribution in order to wear another championship ring.

The Crusaders didn't show too many signs of rust at the outset of the game. Bryce was especially ready, and he came out firing. He hit seven of 10 shots from the field in the first half, including three three-pointers. Behind Bryce's 17 points and Viskovic's nine points, Valpo used a late 11-2 run to propel themselves to a 42-28 halftime advantage. Also aiding the Crusaders was Buffalo's 27 percent shooting in the first half. To the disadvantage of both teams, the game was being officiated tightly. Perhaps aware of the physical history between the two clubs, the referees blew their whistle at nearly every contact. This not only sent both offenses out of rhythm, it also made both coaches struggle to find a defensive set that wouldn't promote more fouls. After 20 minutes, the teams had been called for a combined total of 21 fouls. Drew knew that putting Buffalo at the line in the second half was the surest way to let them back into the game. Apparently, Sykes also knew this.

"No more fouls!" he said to his teammates before taking the floor in the second half. "They have to make big shots to get back into this. Make them hit those shots!"

Valpo heeded this advice. In the second half, Valpo was called for just six fouls. The Crusaders increased their lead to 17 points at the start of the half, only to see Buffalo embark on a 10-0 run to pull within seven. The lead remained in that range for the next several minutes, until Buffalo's Matt Clemens was called for a technical foul for arguing with an official. Bryce hit both free throws, Jason Jenkins hit a jumper on the ensuing possession, and Buffalo was only able to trim the lead to single digits once after that. Valpo went on to win, 84-73, earning a berth in the Mid-Con title game for the fourth year in a row.

While Buffalo coach Tim Cohane credited the Crusaders' accomplishments as "amazing" and "a credit to their school," he was clearly upset after the game about the technical foul on Clemens. He felt it thwarted Buffalo's final push and put the game out of his team's reach.

"It seems like every time we come to the state of Illinois, we get called for a technical foul. It doesn't seem to happen anywhere else...it stinks," he said. "I just want to know who the referees are accountable to."

However, Bob Jenkins said later that the technical didn't come out of the blue.

"The refs told us at the start of the second half that they would be looking to call a T," he said. "The reason was because we were out of control in the first half. We were all talking back to the refs in the first half. Both teams were doing it, and the refs were fed up with it. Everyone had been warned."

Despite the fact that this was at times a bitter rivalry, the teams were cordial and sportsmanlike to each other at the end of the game. Two Buffalo seniors, Rasaun Young and Mike Martinho, came over to the Valpo bench and hugged Drew and Bryce at the end of the game. Bryce had developed a strong friendship with Martinho during an off-season visit to the East Coast. While Bryce was working at a basketball camp in New Jersey, Martinho and his brother took Bryce to New York City's Times Square, where he had never been before. Drew remarked that this is yet another beautiful thing about sports.

"Friendships develop out of respect for each other," Drew said. "It certainly was impressive that Mike and his brother would go out of their way to befriend Bryce when he was visiting back east."

Cohane was similarly complimentary of Valpo after the game, saying that the Crusaders were definitely one of the top 50 programs in the country.

"So much publicity is given to the Big Ten and Big East..." Cohane said. "They've won four straight titles. How many times in NCAA history has that happened?"

In the evening's other semifinal, Youngstown State cruised past Oral Roberts to set up a rematch of the dramatic regular-season games the two teams had played. Both Valpo and Youngstown had won a close, emotional ballgame on the other team's home floor. Now, on a neutral floor, the season series—and Mid-Con title and NCAA berth—would be decided.

"We've got our work cut out for us," Nuness said.

"We're definitely going to have to play better to win tomorrow night," Drew said.

Bryce, however, wasn't about to let the anticipation of the next evening's championship game keep him awake that night.

"I'm just going to pray about it," he said. "We'll come out and give it 100 percent. If we're meant to win, we'll win. That's all you can do."

About four hours before the tipoff of the Mid-Con Championship game, a group of Valparaiso University alumni sat around a table at TGI Friday's, a chain restaurant next door to the Mark of the Quad Cities. Over a platter of calamari, the group laughed, reminisced, and talked about old times. As the subject turned to the game at hand, one of the men noticed former Valpo star Casey Schmidt walking by.

"Hey, Casey! How ya doing?" the man shouted over.

Schmidt turned and came over to the table. After sharing a few jokes, he explained that his season playing professional basketball in Europe was cut short by an injury. Valparaiso now has 12 players in the last six years playing professionally. Since Casey had returned to the U.S. for treatment and rehab, there was no reason he couldn't drive over to Moline to check out his alma mater.

Valparaiso now has 12 players in the last six years playing professionally.

The group professed trepidation about playing Youngstown State for the title. The athleticism, quickness, and other qualities worried these Crusader fans, especially the poise they displayed in an earlier victory before a hostile crowd at the ARC. However, Schmidt had no such worries when asked his opinion of the evening's opponent.

"I say VU will win by 12, unless Youngstown gets hot," he said. "But I don't think they will...they're nervous. They've gotta face the champs now."

With that, he bid farewell to the group, who began nodding at each other, seeming to show with a little more confidence in their team. This group of fans was now ready for the game.

About 30 minutes before game time, Valpo assistant coach Steve Flint saw Youngstown State head coach Dan Peters in the hallway leading to the locker rooms at the Mark. They greeted each other with a handshake and a smile.

"How are you?" Peters asked.

"I'm nervous," Flint replied.

"I'm not," Peters said flatly. "I'm ready to play."

"Oh, I wish you and I could play tonight," Flint said with a laugh. "That would make it much easier." Peters nodded in agreement.

The exchange underscored how difficult big-game situations have to be on coaching staffs. You can watch all the film in the world, practice for hours on end, mentally prepare your team in every way possible, but if the players aren't able to execute at gametime, coaches are viewed as being unsuccessful.

Drew was determined to exploit a physical advantage that his team had over Youngstown State: Youngstown was playing its third game in three nights, while the Crusaders were playing only their second game. Drew saw that advantage on the defensive end of the floor.

"Three games in three days does take a toll on you physically and mentally," he said. "We wanted to extend our full-court pressure, not really to try and force us to steal the ball, but to make them bend their knees. In three-point shooting, when your legs go, your shot goes. So, we really wanted to make them wear out their legs."

A few minutes before tipoff, the Crusaders gathered in the tunnel prior to taking the floor. Sykes reminded the team of the keys to the game.

"We're gonna have rebounding by committee tonight!" he shouted. "Now let's play our game and break 'em down! Let's go!"

"Break 'em down!" the team responded in unison, and then ran out on to the floor.

As the lineups were introduced, the Valpo crowd knew they were on national television. Outnumbering the Youngstown faithful by a 4-to-1 margin, Valpo fans held up signs for the cameras. "Look out NBA: The Bryceman Cometh," one read. "VU 3-peat is SO SWEET," read another. Still another offered the correct pronunciation of both the town and school's name: "Hey ESPN! It's pronounced 'Val-pa-RAY-zo.'"

Nearly two minutes into the game, the Crusaders made it clear they had not left their intensity in the locker room. After Youngstown forward David Brown tied the game at 2-2 on a dunk, Bryce Drew hit a three, and Valpo never looked back. The Crusader defense was stifling in the early going, a relentless man-to-man switching to a matchup 2-3 zone that kept the Penguins from getting a clean look at the basket on several straight offensive trips.

Bill Jenkins knocked down a jumper from the wing. Bryce pump-faked then gently kissed a jump shot off the glass and in. Bob Jenkins hit a 15-footer. With 13:02 remaining in the first half, Zoran Viskovic tossed in a jump hook to stretch Valpo's lead to 13-2.

Meanwhile, in an attempt to test the energy and stamina of the Youngstown team, Drew applied full-court pressure on defense. The move was a gamble—Youngstown's quickness had done in the Crusaders at the ARC in January. Drew figured that the Penguins, weary from playing three nights in a row compared to Valpo's two, would eventually wear down in the second half. What Drew didn't figure on was Youngstown's legs tiring in the first half.

The Penguins couldn't get good looks at the basket the entire half. Only a few of their field goals came from open shots. Every time a red jersey stopped to shoot, a Valpo player had a hand in his face. The pressure on defense was ferocious—and it was frustrating Youngstown. Just over 10 minutes into the game, two Youngstown players jawed at each other after another fruitless possession.

What also helped Valpo was the fact that the referees were letting the teams play. As opposed to the night before, when every bump and grab was met with a whistle, the physical play in the championship was hovering near the edge of control. The first foul of the game—for either team—was called with 8:58 left in the first half.

While the defense flustered Youngstown, Valpo's lead grew and grew. With 5:28 left, Bryce swatted the ball away from Devon Lewis and took it the length of the floor for an easy two, increasing the margin to 24-10. When Bill Jenkins scored an easy layup off of an interior feed from Bryce, Valpo had its largest lead at 29-12. As the half wound down, Sykes tipped in a shot at the horn to send Valpo to the dressing room with a 33-17 advantage.

The Crusaders' swarming defense had held Youngstown to 32 percent shooting and forced seven turnovers. Several Youngstown players were shaking their heads in disgust as they walked off the floor. Valpo was dominating this game.

With 20 minutes standing between Valpo and a third straight trip to the NCAA Tournament, both Drew and the team captains wanted to make certain the 16-point cushion did not evaporate.

Youngstown switched to a half-court trapping defense out of the intermission. While it closed some of the passing lanes, Valpo was still ready for the set. On Valpo's first two possessions, Bryce found Viskovic wide open under the basket. He hit two layins to boost Valpo's lead to 37-17. With 18 minutes remaining in the game, Youngstown coach Peters furiously signaled for a timeout. The game was now fully under the Crusaders' control.

Youngstown pulled within 14 on two occasions, but it became obvious that they had no energy for a full comeback. The Penguins' knees looked rubbery, they were hunched over gasping for breath at the free throw line, and they walked up floor slowly on every dead ball. Their legs had been worn out by the Crusaders' strategy of pressing all evening.

"We were hoping that we could wear them down for the last five minutes, so we were surprised when their shots fell short early," he said.

Bryce didn't score much, nor did he get many shots in the second half, but his leadership and distribution of the basketball controlled the game. Sykes, Bill Jenkins, and Viskovic took over the game. Sykes penetrated the lane for a pair of baskets. Viskovic posted up his man, scoring from the box twice and got to the foul line on another play. Valpo ruled the boards, limiting Youngstown to one shot on numerous occasions.

Meanwhile, Valpo's defensive pressure continued much like the double-digit lead. With just over five minutes to go and the Valpo lead at 23 points, Bill Jenkins trapped Youngstown forward Willie Spellman near the sideline.

"Gotcha!" he yelled gleefully before helping to force a turnover. Tonight, there would be no remorse and no mercy. With an NCAA bid on the line, there was no time to worry about the score. Valpo would press until the matter was settled. Firing as one cylinder, the Crusaders were going to finish the job. The lack of chemistry that frustrated Drew early in the season was long gone. The team was playing in full harmony and loving every minute of it.

Finally, Youngstown found a play that broke the press easily. If there was time for a miracle rally, it would have to start now. Still, Youngstown couldn't get a good look at the basket, and Valpo came down with the ball again off another missed shot. With 4:23 remaining, Sykes drove in the Penguins' final dagger. Left alone at the top of the key, he took a pass and buried a three-pointer, stretching the Crusaders' lead to 61-35, and for all practical purposes, ending the game. Sykes paused and stood with his arms outstretched after hitting the shot. Youngstown called a timeout, but there was no postponing the inevitable—Valparaiso University was going back to the NCAA Tournament.

The teams traded baskets during the game's final minutes. Bryce scored his only points of the second half on a pair of free throws with 3:17 left. Bill Jenkins added two more free throws to pad his already impressive stat line.

With just under a minute remaining, Drew pulled all of his starters. One by one, each exited to a standing ovation. Each senior got a quick hug from each of the coaches—very little emotion considering the roller coaster nature of the season. The Valpo fans on hand at the Mark whooped it up, chanting, "N-C-double-A! N-C-double-A!"

Quickly, Drew huddled with his five seniors at the end of the bench. What he said explained the lack of boisterous celebration. Patting each player on the leg, Drew held up his index finger.

"He told us that we still have one goal left," Bill Jenkins said later. "He's right. We can't be satisfied with just going back to the NCAA. We have to win a game there."

A few moments later, however, the result of the Crusaders' dominating performance was starting to sink in, leading the seniors to celebrate. Bryce playfully swatted Sykes and the twins with his towel. Sykes looked at the scoreboard and turned to his teammates.

"We did it! We did it!" he said as he pumped his fist in the air.

The clock ticked down to zero, and the Valpo fans erupted into a loud cheer. Final score: Valparaiso 67, Youngstown State, 48. The seniors had achieved their goal of "eight-for-eight."

The team gathered at mid-court for a quick huddle. At the end of the huddle, the team bounced up and down, in what had become their traditional post-championship celebration. After the ESPN cameras had moved to some other part of the country, Valpo accepted its championship trophy. The team was introduced, and then the All-Tournament Team was announced. Three Crusaders: Sykes, Bill Jenkins, and Bryce, were named to the team. Bryce was named MVP of the tournament, although a case could have been made for any one of the three. As Bryce accepted his award, he motioned for his teammates to come and accept the honor with him. They respectfully declined.

"I personally think Jamie could have gotten it," Bryce said later. "But Jamie told me 'you're the engine,' so I went up to get it."

Then the team walked to one end of the floor to do something many had doubted they would do, especially after the shaky start to the season: cut down the nets in honor of the Mid-Continent Conference championship.

A few minutes later, Sykes stood in the tunnel leading to the dressing rooms. He was grinning from ear to ear. One reporter brought up his speech in that very tunnel at the start of the game, and he smiled even bigger.

"In the second half, the whole team stepped up," he said. "It was great."

His coach was equally pleased with the convincing second stanza.

"Early in the year, we had a lot of big leads and lost them because we became complacent," Drew said. "This team did not allow for complacency, they did not allow Youngstown to come back on us, and I was very proud of that consistency on the part of our team."

Later, Nuness said being prepared for Youngstown's second-half adjustments helped put the game away.

"We had that big halftime lead, but we knew we had to pour it on them, because they were capable of coming back," he said. "Those first two buckets after halftime took their heart."

Sykes also admitted to feeling some vindication, not only for making the decision to hold off on pro baseball, but for winning when a lot of people had said that Valpo's run was done earlier in the year.

"When you've got people counting you out, you come together for your team, and we took it upon ourselves to make this happen," he said.

Assistant Coach Steve Flint walked by. He was asked if he was still nervous, as he told the Youngstown coach he was before the game. Flint smiled and shook his head.

"No, but I think I've got an ulcer," he quipped.

Peters gave Valpo total credit for the defensive showcase.

"Tonight was the best that I've seen Valpo play as a team," Peters said. "When you have a great player like they do, sometimes you have a tendency [as an opponent] to focus on that kid, and you forget everyone else on the team...and teams win championships."

Peters was asked if he thought Valpo had a shot at winning a game or two in the NCAAs. He shrugged.

"So much of it is the draw," he said. "But they have a couple of guys who are battle-tested...so you never know."

After Peters exited the stage, Drew and all five seniors walked into the cramped press conference room. Drew was beaming as the players took the podium.

"I brought all five seniors up here because this is a very special and very unique group," he said. "I've been truly blessed to work with these young men. They've carried me for the past four years."

Drew then stepped aside to allow the players to answer questions, and the assembled media fired away. Sykes said he never doubted the game's outcome after the pre-game drills.

"That was the best warmup we've had all year. I knew we were ready for this game," he said. "I have never seen us that focused and that crisp during warmups."

Bill Jenkins said his improved shooting was the result of hard work and getting up enough confidence.

"It's something I've been working on a lot in practice, but I didn't have enough confidence to use in a game," he said. "But my legs were feeling great tonight."

Drew was asked how Valpo officials would have reacted during his 1988 job interview if he had told them he would win four consecutive conference regular season titles and tournament titles. He laughed.

"They probably would have wondered how much I was drinking," he said. "We never could have envisioned this much success, and a lot of the credit goes to Scott Drew, Jim Harrick, and Steve Flint. They have found so much hidden talent, and done so much behind the scenes... those three have done an outstanding job. Our assistant coaches are the backbone to our success. Their loyalty and hard work has helped this team achieve its goals." However, those weren't the only ones working together, he said.

"This whole team really became a family during the season," he said.

"Our assistant coaches are the backbone to our success. Their loyalty and hard work has helped this team achieve its goals."—Homer Drew

Drew also alluded to the team's remaining goal, which he mentioned on the sideline to his seniors.

"The only thing this group has left to do is win a game in the NCAA Tournament," he said. "And you can't replace experience. This time, we'll be going in much better prepared and more focused."

If Bill Jenkins was any indication, the team had already begun its preparation less than 20 minutes after the game.

"It was great to win. I'm all out of adjectives," he said. "And it's great to be part of the field of 64 again. But we've been here three years now and each year we seem to get a little closer. This time, we've got a mission to beat a major team. This team has great motivation—the fire comes from within."

Bob Jenkins agreed that the low-key reaction from the team was an indication of its unrelenting pursuit of the next goal.

"I know our focus is outstanding because the level of excitement in here was down," he said. "Oh, man, you should have been in here the first time we won [the Mid-Con]. Everybody was dancing, screaming, and tackling one another. We were happy tonight, but nothing like that. That's good. It shows we're staying focused for the tournament.

"It's about getting past your obstacles, which this team has done all year. Youngstown State was an obstacle. Now, we have one obstacle and one goal left: winning in the NCAA. And I'm going to do everything to make sure we achieve that goal."

To achieve that goal, Valpo first had to qualify for the tournament. After doing so, Bryce admitted publicly what many Valpo fans had already said quietly throughout the year.

"Going to the NCAA really makes or breaks our season," he said. "Anything less than winning the Mid-Continent Conference would have been considered a failure in our eyes. Now, we're happy, because we can put everything towards that higher goal that we want."

His father admitted that high expectations can be a double-edged sword. Very seldom can a team live up to the expectations set by others.

"All we can do is live up to what we do best," Drew said. "I think a big part of our early difficulties was that expectations were so high that we were never able to find a comfort zone or get in our cocoon to concentrate on achieving our peak performance until we got everyone healthy.

"Expectations can get coaches old...and fired," he continued. "What's wonderful about this group is they always try to surpass the expectations."

While the victory was euphoric for many of the players, especially the freshmen, for some players it was a reminder that the good times would soon be coming to an end. Tony Vilcinskas sat in the Valpo dressing room at the Mark less than 30 minutes after the game. He was trying not to get emotional over the victory, but the reflective nature of a college senior was evident. Dressed in a European soccer jersey and jeans, the native Lithuanian sighed, as if he were looking back on a long journey.

"I'm kind of sad, actually," he said. "I'm going to miss college basketball, because it's been so much fun and it's soon going to be over. It will be time for me to step into the real world, I guess."

However, Vilcinskas made it perfectly clear that he wasn't going to let emotions overwhelm his focus for the NCAA Tournament game.

"Two years ago, we were going nuts [after winning the Mid-Con]. We've been there and we've gone back, so we know how it is there," he said of the "Big Dance." "Now we know what we have to do there. We're excited, but we know we have to get focused again."

According to Vilcinskas, Valpo could have punched its ticket to the NCAA after the semifinal victory over Buffalo.

"After the Buffalo game, I had no doubts that we were going to win because we were playing like we should," he said.

The players dressed quickly to attend a post-game reception for Valpo fans being held in one of the adjacent conference halls. It appeared nearly all of the Valpo fans on hand stayed for this post-game celebration—the pep band included. Aaron Thomason deliberately waited for the seniors before entering the hall.

"I want to milk some more applause out of this," he joked.

During the reception, Drew thanked everyone in attendance for their support. He introduced each player, giving special mention to each senior. However, when he got to the twins, someone decided to play a joke on Drew.

"Hey, Coach, can you even tell them apart?" someone shouted from the audience.

"Sure, I can," Coach responded. "Let's see..." The crowd chuckled as Drew took 10-15 seconds to survey each Jenkins. Finally, he pointed to one twin. "That's Bob," he said. A few in the audience clapped after the correct answer.

"Their mom and dad gave me a few tips on telling Bill from Bob," he said.

Turning more serious, Drew smiled and imparted an important message on the crowd.

"What makes this so special is that our players, the university, and the entire community of Valparaiso are one big family. You have treated us like family, and I believe we are family. We are family. Please repeat that with me. We are family." The audience responded. "We are family! We are family!"

Walking out after the reception, Scott Drew offered quick thoughts on the win, and the long road of the season.

"I was stressing out all day," he said. "All day, I was praying that we would get one more chance to go to the NCAA Tournament, and we did it. This was a fantastic way for the seniors to go out, because everybody contributed."

After the press conferences, interviews, and receptions were over, Janet Drew stood in the hallway outside the Crusader locker room, leaning up against the wall with a relieved smile. She was, of course, proud of her husband and two sons, but she also felt good for their classmates.

"It was so cool to see the seniors do this and go out this way," she said. "They got 20 victories again, and won four regular season and four tournament titles. We never had started a real tradition of winning until these seniors came here."

Like some of the seniors, she also reflected on the long journey, and recalled how the puzzle slowly was completed: Bryce, Scott, Jim Harrick, the twins, and on. Could she ever have envisioned this level of success at Valpo? Janet paused, smiled, and shook her head slowly.

"It's something you would dream about happening, but you never wanted to bring it up, because you were afraid if they didn't win, it would be too much," she said. "But everyone has put in so much work behind the scenes, and, with all the injuries, to stick to it and win is just wonderful."

So, Mom, what's the lesson to be learned by this Crusader team, which went from a 3-5 start to the NCAA Tournament?

"To know that hard work pays off someday," she said. Homer Drew approached and hugged Janet. He, too, wore a look of proud relief.

"You can't write a better story for our seniors," he said. "It just shows that you can't out-give God. If you work hard and have faith, anything is possible."

Drew's positive attitude was instilled early during his career by Dale Brown at LSU. Many years before, Brown sent Drew a quote which read, "the impossible is what no one can do until someone does it."

"It just shows that you can't out-give God. If you work hard and have faith, anything is possible...the impossible is what no one can do until someone does it."–Homer Drew

---

"Dale has such an infectious personality for positive thinking," Drew said. "His theory on enjoying life rubbed off on me, and so I was able to thoroughly enjoy watching these players complete their mission and make it 'Mission Possible.'"

With that, Drew and the Crusaders set off on making the most of their last chance at the dream and final goal: a win in an NCAA Tournament game. The way they persevered to a championship proved Valpo wasn't going to let go of the dream without a fight. Win or lose, the dream would be pursued to its fullest extent.

CHAPTER TWELVE

Overcoming Adversity:
The Miracle at the Myriad

*"These young people believed in themselves–they had the power to endure.
They never gave up."*

–Homer Drew

Late on a snowy March evening, the Valparaiso team was headed from Chicago after claiming its third consecutive berth in the NCAA basketball tournament. The mood was relaxed and jovial as the charter bus passed through Joliet, Illinois, until the bus suddenly lurched to a halt, rousing the players and coaches from their seats.

"What's going on?" asked one player, voicing the question for everybody as they rubbed their eyes and peered out the icy windows.

"We can't be out of gas yet," the driver said. "The tank on this thing holds enough fuel for 500 miles." Then he looked down at the trip odometer. It read: 509 miles. Audible groans were heard from the back of the bus.

Coach Homer Drew, who had promised to give the players a few days off to relax and get recharged before the NCAA Tournament, also was disappointed. In a season filled with overcoming adversity, this was just one more hurdle to handle. Bundling up against the chilly winds and blowing snow, Sports Information Director Bill Rogers and Assistant Coach Steve Flint left the warm bus to hike to the nearest station about a mile away.

148

As Rogers and Flint disappeared from the view of the bus headlights, Drew leaned back in his seat and exhaled. Not even in victory were the Crusaders immune from the travel snafus that had plagued them all season.

The Valpo road journal from the 1997-98 season read like a traveler's worst nightmare: a missed flight to Kansas City, a mysterious illness that a majority of the Valpo contingent suffered upon arrival at the Big Island Invitational in Hawaii, countless delays due to road construction and bad weather, and now this.

As Rogers and Flint trudged through the messy slush towards the nearest exit, they were rescued by a passing police officer who gave them a lift to the station, where they got enough fuel to get the bus back to the pump. After the refueling, the Crusaders again set out for home, finally arriving after 5 A.M. Only the previous night's victory kept it from being an incredibly long night, Drew said.

The rain poured on the Crusaders during the season. Coming off of a 24-8 season in 1996-97, the most wins in school history, created high expectations for the 1997-98 Valpo squad. Four starters were returning: athletic point guard Jamie Sykes, towering center Antanas "Tony" Vilcinskas, deft power forward Zoran Viskovic, and senior Bryce Drew.

Bryce, the coach's son, also was the team's All-America shooting guard. One of the nation's hot prospects his senior year of high school, Bryce turned down marquee programs across the country to stay home and play for his dad. The move had paid off so far. During his sophomore year, he led Valpo to its first-ever NCAA Tournament appearance. However, memories of that experience were bittersweet as Arizona crushed Valpo, 90-51, in the first round of the tournament. Bryce's junior year, the 1996-97 season, also ended with a loss in the first round of the NCAA Tournament in Salt Lake City, a near-miss upset loss against Boston College. During Bryce's first three seasons at Valpo, the Crusaders won three straight regular-season and conference tournament championships. Certainly, with such a team coming back, most Valpo fans reasoned, the Crusaders were destined for grand things in 1997-98.

Then the adversity kicked in. Vilciskas injured his ankle playing in his native Lithuania over the summer. Sykes was drafted by baseball's Arizona Diamondbacks to play in their minor league system. Two days before the exhibition season, Bryce injured his right leg. He missed the first two regular season games, and even when he did return, the team didn't click right away.

With a mix of six seniors and five freshmen, Valpo had trouble achieving harmonious team chemistry. As a result, the team struggled during the early part of the season. Midway through the conference season Valpo's overall record stood at 10-9, far below expectations.

While the team flailed away in the early-going, Drew kept in mind a Robert Schuller quote, which read:

"Tough times never last, but tough people do."–Robert Schuller

---

Drew wasn't fazed by the early struggles of the team. He believed that every team, no matter how talented, has problems once in a while. The key was to work through those problems in a positive manner. The coaching staff worked to keep the players focused on fixing the problems, instead of joining in the finger-pointing and blaming of others.

Drew called on his veteran players' leadership, and their mental toughness, as well. He urged them to focus on the positive.

"In every adversity, there is an opportunity," he told them. "Let's take this opportunity and become better."

Using that philosophy, the team kept going. Eventually, they climbed back into the conference race, and in the post-season tournament, the Crusaders delivered, defeating Youngstown State to win their fourth straight title and their third automatic bid for the NCAA Tournament.

When the team bus finally arrived in Valparaiso after that victory, Drew kept his word and didn't schedule a practice for three days. He said he was "locking up the gym" for a few days so the players could get their minds off basketball. However, when the team gathered for practice on Saturday night, Drew felt they were a bit too rested.

"We're not focused on anything right now. After those days off, you'd be surprised how much they have to do to get their legs and cardiovascular back for playing," he said.

The team trudged through a "lethargic" practice, as Drew called it. Bryce Drew, who strained his hamstring against Buffalo in the Mid-Continent semifinals, sat out most of the practice and shot jumpers on the side of the court. Viskovic was nowhere to be found, as he was home in bed running a temperature. To keep the players focused, Drew treated the players to some shooting contests for the last hour of practice. Winners got candy bars, hats, and T-shirts. Breaking from routine and making practice fun occasionally, Drew explained, helped the team remain mentally sharp during the long grind of a season. Surprisingly enough, Vilciskas, the lumbering pivot man who was far from the best outside shooter on the team, won one of the contests. That was a good omen, Drew thought.

"Tomorrow, we want to come out harder, sharper, and crisper," Drew said a few minutes later. "It will be time to prepare for our tournament game."

By the next night, the Crusaders would know their NCAA opponent. This year, instead of having the selection show party at the cramped student union, Valpo officials opted to have the party at the ARC, the school's 4,500-seat arena. Less than 24 hours before the pairings would be announced, Drew wouldn't hazard a guess as to who his team would play or where they would be playing.

"I've seen so many different scenarios, Chicago, Atlanta, Lexington, Hartford, I don't know," he said. "We won't know until it's up on the television screen. I'd love to be kept in the Midwest, though, especially Chicago. That would be a great reward for our fans to be able to come and support us."

Drew had sent the NCAA selection committee a fax containing seven facts about the Valpo team, including the four straight conference titles, and noting that the Crusaders had been sent two time zones away from home in their previous two tourney trips. Such contact is allowed, but not always effective.

"Do they pay attention to those facts? Probably not," Drew conceded. "But at least they have the information in their hands now and information is a most valuable commodity."

The next afternoon, a large group of fans filed into the ARC for the pairings party. Most Valpo students were at home for spring break, and didn't have a chance to join the celebration. A large projection television was set up at center court with a few rows of folding chairs set up for Valpo officials and players. About 15 minutes before the show, the Crusaders were introduced to the crowd with the house lights down and spotlights up.

After the players took their seats, the traditional array of local and university officials addressed the audience. Athletic Director Dr. Bill Steinbrecher reflected on the previous four years, the greatest in school history. Steinbrecher had seen this program at its lowest depths: in the early years of Division I, through the rough times during Drew's first few seasons, during numerous calls from alumni and even some local media to drop the program to Division II, just about every roadblock imaginable. Now, he got to preside over the winningest era in school history.

"It's been a real joy to ride along with this group of young men," he said. "They've had such great success."

Finally, Drew stepped to the microphone and peered out at the audience.

"It was a year of overcoming adversity," he began. "This season shows that when you stick to it, good things can happen. When we were 10-9, not too many people were saying good things about us.

"But these young people believed in themselves—they had the power to endure. They never gave up."

"Never, Never, Never, Never give up."–Winston Churchill

As Drew finished his comments, the selection show began on CBS.

Quickly, they ran through the East brackets for the Hartford and Washington, D.C. sub-regionals. Former Mid-Continent Conference foe Illinois-Chicago received an at-large bid, which drew some "oohs" from the crowd. However, Valpo wasn't in the East.

The next bracket was for the West region. The crowd held its breath —would the selection committee send Valpo cross country yet again? The brackets for the Sacromento sub-regional were announced first. Valpo was absent. A cheer went up from the crowd. Next came the Boise sub-regional. As each pairing was announced, the odds were increasing that Valpo was going to be staying near home. The last pairing in the West region was announced: Cincinnati and Northern Arizona. The crowd erupted.

Next came the Midwest Regional brackets, for Oklahoma City and Chicago. Oklahoma City was first. Each pairing went down the screen and the crowd's anticipation grew. There was no secret here: the crowd was hoping Valpo would be sent to Chicago so thousands of fans could make the 55-mile drive to see them play.

"If they get sent to Chicago, this place will be rocking," said one fan.

CBS got to the bottom of the screen. Then the pairing went up: Valparaiso, a #13 seed, would play fouth-seeded Mississippi in Oklahoma City. The audience clapped politely. The players slapped hands in subdued fashion. The disappointment in the room was obvious.

After the rest of the pairings were announced, Drew returned to the microphone.

"Well, I was hoping to go to Chicago and take all of you, but we're still excited to be staying in the Midwest in Oklahoma City," he said.

Nearly all of the players echoed that sentiment after the party. Each one began with a variation of the statement: "Well, I was hoping they would put us in Chicago so our fans could come and see us." In addition, only Bryce seemed to know much about Ole Miss, and that was because he had been a teammate of Ole Miss All-America forward Ansu Sesay on the World University Games team. Bryce took the glass-is-half-full view of the Crusaders' seeding.

"A 13 seed's not bad, and Oklahoma City's better than a lot of places we could be sent," he said.

Bryce also warmed to the prospect of facing his former Team USA teammate.

"It'll be fun, I haven't seen him much since the Games, so I'm looking forward to that," he said.

Senior forward Bob Jenkins knew a little bit about the Rebels, but not much.

"We'll be all right against Ole Miss. We know they're not TCU and they're not Green Bay," he said, covering both ends of the tempo spectrum.

Jenkins' twin brother Bill also was nonchalant about the team's seeding and placement.

"We're just happy to be going," Bill Jenkins said. "Sure, we would have rather been in Chicago, but there are 200 teams who have already put up their shoes for the season, so I'm just thankful we're going to the NCAA."

Yet Jenkins didn't seem to know much more about Valpo's opponent than any of his teammates, or did he care.

"They're just a basketball team," he said. "They lace 'em up just like everyone else. We'll be ready for them."

Only Vilcinskas would admit that he knew absolutely nothing about the SEC West Division Champions. However, he was planning an online scouting report for that evening.

"It doesn't matter," he said. "I've never heard of the team. When I get home tonight, it should take me about 20 minutes to get all the information on them from the internet."

The unfamiliarity was relatively mutual. A few minutes after the pairings were announced, Ole Miss assistant coach Russ Pennell confessed to not knowing how to spell Valparaiso and told the *Northeast Mississippi Daily Journal*, "they're a good solid team, probably like a Vanderbilt except not as talented."

The Mississippi media didn't know much more about Valpo. *Biloxi*

Sun Herald columnist Jim Mashek wondered in print the next day about the members of the Mid-Continent Conference. Devry—the omnipresent commuter school featured in commercials nationwide—was listed as a candidate.

Later that evening, Valpo hosted a national media teleconference. While there were some local media represented (most notably the *Chicago Tribune* and the *Indianapolis Star*), most of the people on the conference call were from media outlets across the state of Mississippi. They listened in from Jackson, Biloxi, Pascagoula, Oxford, and Gulfport. They all wanted to know more about this mysterious Midwestern team that would be facing their beloved Rebels in the NCAA Tournament.

Reporters asked about the enrollment, the spelling of the players' names, the vital statistics on each player, where the foreign players were from and how they arrived at Valpo and, of course, they asked about the Jenkins twins.

"Are they kin?" one southern reporter asked quickly. So quickly, in fact, that no one could understand the question at first. The fact that the term "kin" is not used much in northwest Indiana probably also had something to do with it.

"Are they what?" Sports Information Director Bill Rogers replied.

"*Are...they...kin?*" the reporter repeated impatiently.

"Yes, they're twin brothers," Drew said. "And we have another Jenkins, a freshman named Jason, who is not related."

"Jason Jenkins is related?" another reporter asked over the static-filled phone connection.

The twins broke into raucous laughter at the thought of the gangly, red-headed freshman being a blood relative. "He wishes," one of them said.

"No, he's not related, but Jason wishes he had some of the twins' talent," Drew said politely.

Upon request, Drew ran through the previous two years for Valpo in the tournament. Then, in a recent tradition, Drew began asking questions to the Mississippi journalists. He wanted to know what the key was to beating Ole Miss.

Most of the reporters laughed. One offered, "ask Eddie Fogler." Fogler is the head coach at the University of South Carolina, which had defeated Ole Miss in the SEC tournament the day before.

Near the end of the teleconference, Drew was asked his assessment of Ole Miss. Not having seen them on film, he answered, "We're working on getting film right now. That's why tomorrow is such an important time for us and our preparation."

As he spoke, Drew was unaware of the gigantic weather-related hurdle that would affect his team in the ensuing 24 hours.

The citizens of Valparaiso awoke the next morning to more than a foot of snow. Making the storm even worse was 70 MPH winds that were whipping the snow everywhere. Power lines were down all over northwest Indiana and Chicago. Most of the city lost power, including the Valpo campus. Most businesses were forced to close. Since the university didn't have enough power in its backup generators to light any gymnasium on campus, the Crusaders were forced to call off practice. It was probably a safe move, as venturing outside or on to the roads in such a blizzard would have been hazardous at best—and life-threatening at worst.

After a mild winter, the storm took the entire region by surprise. Most weather forecasters were predicting freezing rain, or a few inches of snow. Instead, the mid-March storm blindsided a three-state area. Schools and interstate roads were closed. Hundreds of travelers were stranded on the Borman Expressway near Hammond, Indiana, for more than 30 hours when it was closed during the worst part of the severe weather. Many people said the storm was the worst to hit northwest Indiana in more than a decade. Adversity had returned.

To make matters worse, many of the players could not even eat until power was restored. Restaurant and grocery stores were closed. Because the university was on spring break, no cafeterias or snack shops were open. Like most college students, the players didn't exactly have stocked pantries in their apartments or dorm rooms. Some had no food at all.

"During the storm, I don't know of too many players who ate any-thing," Bill Jenkins said. "It was awful, and it happened at the worst possible time."

The storm also created havoc on travel arrangements for the Crusaders and their fans. All travel-related computer systems were down for two days, delaying the team's departure, and making it nearly impossible for the team's band and cheerleaders to find a flight to Oklahoma City. The band and cheerleaders ended up taking a bus for the icy 14-hour trip.

Due to the NCAA's policy of making the teams go through an official travel agency instead of making their own arrangements, the Valpo team did not arrive in Oklahoma City until Wednesday evening. Furthermore, while most commercial flights from Chicago to Oklahoma City stop in St. Louis or Kansas City, the Valpo team plane stopped in Houston, well out of the way for such a trip. This assured the players, coaches, and staff of a very long travel day. It was more adversity, but this time, Drew told his players, "we're used to this, this will have no factor in the outcome of the game."

"I told the players this was just another travel problem like the ones we had faced all year and not to let it affect their focus," he said.

Valpo fans weren't immune from travel hassles either. A fare of $436 per person for a roundtrip ticket between Chicago and Oklahoma City was viewed by many as excessive. Attempting to purchase airline tickets the day after the NCAA pairings were announced, one man had a travel agent laugh in his face.

"For 50 bucks more, I'm sending a guy roundtrip to Amsterdam at the end of the month," the agent said, waving a ticket.

"You should have booked earlier," the agent admonished. Of course, the pairings are announced a maximum of five days before the first game, so there is virtually no way fans can avoid penalties for booking their flights less than seven days in advance. Many fans and media felt there had to be a better way.

When the storm passed the next day, the Crusaders went to practice minus a critical day of preparation for Ole Miss. The ordeal affected the team mentally as well, according to Bill Jenkins.

"The first day of practice after the storm, well, uh, we sucked. I'll let you come up with a better term," Jenkins said. "I mean, we were *terrible.*

I thought we were going to have real trouble getting focused." As usual, though, Drew took the adversity in stride.

"The week leading up to the game was typical of our season, just one obstacle after another," Drew said. "I told the team that it was just another hurdle and that it was nothing new to us. We had already endured injuries, missed planes, running out of gas, everything. I told the players that overcoming adversity will help us now, and later in life."

Yet, whether the Crusaders had time to overcome that adversity in tie for their toughest test of the season—and the biggest game of the seniors' careers—still remained to be seen.

The team arrived in Oklahoma City on Wednesday night. When they went to practice at the Myriad on Thursday, Drew had some pre-game strategies mapped out. In scouting Ole Miss, he had found two things that stood out.

"To be successful in the tournament, I think you have to have a lot of quickness with your guards, which is what they possess. If you had a chance to watch Arizona that was evident on their team and we all know what happened," Drew said, referring to the defending national champions. "The quickness factor is the thing I'm really concerned about with Ole Miss...also, the thing that Sesay does so well is go to the glass, so we're really going to have to rebound well against this team to put ourselves in a position to win."

Drew had one major thing going for him, however. Bryce felt comfortable in the arena. A psychological factor, to be sure, but not a factor to be ignored.

"This is a good shooting gym," Bryce said at the Thursday press conference. "I was really impressed with the set-up of the place. Hopefully, we can have some success here."

At the same press conference, Jamie Sykes expressed confidence in the team's ability to put aside the hype and distractions of the tournament.

"The first time we were here, we were like a kid in a candy store, so to speak. We were really excited and didn't come out and take care of things. This time around, we're more business-like in our attitude and more focused for this game," Sykes said.

Before the team's final pre-tournament practice session, Drew adapted an Abraham Lincoln quote to fit the moment, a quote with his players. "You have studied, you have worked hard, you are prepared, your chance is now...and you can do it!" Drew said.

"I will study, I will work hard, I will prepare and sometime my chance will come."–Abraham Lincoln

---

At the Myriad on Friday morning, the press room was a hub of activity. For those who have wondered what it's like to go behind the scenes at a NCAA Tournament game, the experience is nearly overwhelming.

In the large conference hall underneath the Myriad stands, dozens of tables, equipped with phones, modems, and electrical outlets stretched to the back of the room. Several television sets were set up at strategic points around the media's work area. Through an adjacent doorway, the NCAA video distribution area was set up, along with room for television production trucks.

Back towards the main entrance of the area was a long table featuring information, media guides, and photos of all eight teams present at the sub-regional. The table was next to the entrance of the interview room, which features television-ready cameras, lighting, and sound—not to mention the large podium up front with the bright blue NCAA backdrop that viewers see in every tournament interview segment during the month of March. All the while, reporters and photographers from around the country hustled about.

The Myriad is an older arena—approximately 20 years old—and is relatively small by NCAA standards with a seating capacity just over 13,000. The hall and seats are trimmed in red upholstery, giving the feel of a Las Vegas cabaret.

About a half-hour before tipoff, Assistant Athletic Director Carl Hensley walked by press row to chat with a couple of local reporters. He looked exhausted, and with good reason.

The snowstorm that had battered northwest Indiana a few days before had done more than strand motorists, blow over trees, and knock out power to thousands of people. It also had made life miserable for those responsible for the Crusaders' tourney preparation. Valpo officials put in some very long hours—and did quite a bit of scrambling—on Tuesday and Wednesday to find flights and transportation so the school's contingent could get to Oklahoma.

To top it off, the allotment of tickets for Valparaiso fans did not arrive in Hensley's office before school officials had to leave.

"We kept waiting and waiting and waiting for the tickets to show up, but they never did," Hensley said. "Finally, we couldn't wait any longer if we were going to get out here on time, so [NCAA officials] had to reprint the tickets on-site. Thankfully, we got everyone their tickets on time."

Valpo was expecting several hundred fans at the game—hardly a bad turnout for a team playing more than 800 miles from home. Despite that fact, Hensley shook his head.

"You know, if they would have put us at the United Center (in Chicago), we could have gotten five or six thousand tickets, and we would have sold them all, too," he said with a sigh. "Oh, well."

Inside the dressing room, Drew recalled a scene from the movie *Hoosiers*, where Coach Norman Dale, played by Gene Hackman, stresses the importance of fundamentals. "We've been completing passes, cutting hard to the ball, and going to the boards with intensity. That's why you have won."

"We have won 11 in a row because of fundamentals," Drew told his team.

Drew then saluted individual players in front of the group.

"Bill and Bob, your screens have allowed Bryce, Jamie, Jared, and

Jason some wonderful looks," he said. "Tony and Zoran, you two have been finishing strong inside. Improve through fundamentals today. In order win it is important that each of you get one more assist, one more rebound, and one more loose ball. Fundamentals. Now, let's get a good warmup."

The players huddled, yelled "TEAM," and headed out into the arena.

The two teams took the floor for pre-game warmups. Ole Miss was warming up casually at the near end of the floor. A few players laughed and joked during the pre-game. If these Rebels were nervous, they weren't showing it.

Paul Jankowski, sports editor of the *Vidette-Times*, Valparaiso's daily newspaper, took his seat on press row. Several reporters watched in awe as Mississippi's All-American Ansu Sesay warmed up, burying jumper after jumper, but Jankowski thought the reigning SEC West Division champions might be guilty of overlooking Valpo. Indeed, Jankowski had predicted a Crusader victory in his column that morning.

Back in the locker room, Drew reiterated the theme for the game: Find a way.

"Each one of you has made a contribution for us to get here," Drew said. "Each of you must do something extra to beat a good team. You must find a way. That way can be a pass, a shot, a rebound, a defensive steal—but just find a way. *Find a way!*"

Vice President of Business Affairs Charley Gillispie led the team in a pre-game prayer, after which Aaron Thomason began clapping rhythmically. The entire team joined in before huddling with hands touching and arms lifted high. In unison, the players shouted, *"Find a way!"* Then, the Crusaders sprinted on to the court.

"Each one of you has made a contribution for us to get here. Each of you must do something extra to beat a good team. You must 'find a way.' That way can be a pass, a shot, a rebound, a defensive steal–but just find a way. Find a way!"–Homer Drew

The arena was less than half-full when the game started. Despite the national stature of the tournament, the only people cheering at the start of the game were about 1,500 Ole Miss fans and about 600 from Valpo. A mixture of TCU fans, Florida State backers, and curious locals trickled in slowly. Gradually, the arena filled up, and, by the second half, a large noisy crowd was present.

The game tipped off to a sloppy start. On Valpo's first possession, Ole Miss forced a turnover, but then the Rebels came down and missed a shot. Valpo took the ball back upcourt. Dribbling across the top of the key, Bryce stumbled and fell, losing possession again. The Rebels again failed to convert on the offensive end, and Vilcinskas, fresh off of his first foul of the game a few seconds earlier, put the Crusaders on the board with a lay-in in the paint 95 seconds into the game. Fifteen seconds later, Ole Miss' Keith Carter drained a 20-foot three-pointer to put the Rebels up 3-2. As the ball fell through the net, Vilcinskas picked up a silly frustration foul by shoving Ole Miss' Anthony Boone, earning him a quick seat on the bench.

Ole Miss increased its lead to seven points, 18-11, before Valpo fought back and went over with just over five minutes remaining in the half. The back-and-forth pattern continued, however, as the Rebels responded and went ahead by six with less than a minute to play. Drew signaled for one shot, and Bryce held the ball near mid-court for most of the half's final 30 seconds. With seven seconds on the clock Bryce made his move, dribbling to the top of the key. Keeping his dribble, he spun his body so that his back was facing the basket, then quickly spun back, forcing his defender to back off a step. As soon as the defender stepped back, Bryce launched an 18-footer, which splashed through at the buzzer. At halftime, Ole Miss led 38-34.

Drew felt good about his team's position, mainly because it was only down four points and he knew the team could play better. The defensive strategy required some tweaking, as well.

"Initially, our game plan was to take away their inside quickness and make Ole Miss hit the perimeter shot," Drew recalled. That worked well—

except for the fact that the Rebels went 5-of-10 from three-point range in the first half. It was time for some adjustments.

After briefly consulting with his assistants, Drew outlined a three-pronged approach for the second half. He scrawled the priorities on the locker room chalkboard:

Valpo vs. Ole Miss...Keys for Second Half

1) Challenge the three-point shot and give early help on defense if they penetrate around us.

2) Ole Miss had eight offensive rebounds in the first half. Our goal is no more than six in the second half.

3) Mix up the defensive sets more often from man-to-man to zone. This will slow their tempo.

Drew sent his team back out on the floor with a positive message.

"Remember to 'find a way,'" he said. "You can win...we're in a perfect position to do so. *Find a way!*"

Valpo came out strong. After a defensive stop, the Crusaders came downcourt and threw inside to Viskovic. He spun towards the hoop and drilled the baby hook shot. After another defensive stop, Valpo came down in transition and Bryce knocked in a three to put the Crusaders back in front, 39-38. Twenty seconds later, Vilcinskas' layup made it a three-point lead. Ole Miss head coach Rob Evans called a timeout to try to stop the brown-and-gold momentum.

Its momentum interrupted by the timeout, Valpo was forced back into a nip-and-tuck game. Just when one side enjoyed a small run and built a narrow lead, the other team came clawing back and went in front by a few points. A five-point Valpo lead with 5:33 to play disappeared on the strength of Ole Miss free throws, and the Rebels were on top, 69-67, with 2:14 remaining when Drew signaled for a timeout.

The coach diagramed a play to get Viskovic open, and as he made a quick back cut, Bryce fed him the ball. As Viskovic spun toward the basket for what looked as if it would be the tying basket, Sesay leaped seemingly out of nowhere and rejected the shot. Ole Miss ran down the loose ball and called timeout with 1:35 left, still protecting its two-point lead.

The Crusaders had picked an inopportune time for a scoring drought. The Mississippi zone defense was giving them fits, and, worse, the Rebels had the ball, and the lead, with 95 seconds to play. To the average observer, momentum had clearly shifted to Ole Miss.

Nevertheless, when the team came over to the bench during the timeout, Drew was heartened by what he saw.

"I looked at each of the players, and I saw that the look their eyes showed confidence and determination," Homer said. "It was the determination to find a way, which was our theme for the game. I didn't know how, I didn't know who was going to do it, but I knew we were going to respond."

No doubt running through the players' minds were all of the obstacles in their path during the course of the season: the injuries, the expectations, the chemistry problems, the frustrations, the early losses and even the travel problems—the *adversity* that dogged the Crusaders this season. Each time, they had responded to the situation with a win or an improvement. Drew hoped they had one response left.

Out of the timeout, Valpo got the defensive stop they so desperately needed. Sesay attempted to drive the lane and kick the ball outside. Sykes stepped in the passing lane and picked the ball off. A couple of quick passes set up Sykes for a wide-open three-point shot, but the ball bounced off the iron. Bill Jenkins grabbed the offensive rebound and passed back to freshman Jared Nuness, who stepped behind the line and let a jumper fly with 45 seconds left. The shot and rotation looked true, but the ball bounced off the front of the rim. This time Ole Miss cleared the rebound, and the Rebels walked the ball upcourt, further running down the clock.

Once again, the Rebels couldn't convert. Flanigan drove to the baseline and left his five-footer short. Viskovic tipped the rebound, and Nuness corralled the loose ball and sprinted downcourt with 13 seconds left. Nuness passed to Bryce who faked a shot and passed to Viskovic a few feet away. He quickly gave the ball back to Bryce, who found himself with an open look at a three-pointer with seven seconds to play. This was the Crusaders' best hope, and most likely, their last chance. Bryce's shot appeared to be on target, but yet again, the shot rattled out. The Valpo fans deflated. Sesay grabbed the rebound, and Viskovic fouled him with 4.1 seconds remaining. The Ole Miss bench began celebrating, and Sesay raised his arms anticipating his team's escape.

Bryce's shoulders sunk visibly. His father and coach, sensing his team might have just taken its last shot, smiled while applauding and encouraging his players.

Sesay, one of the Rebels' best free-throw shooters, stepped to the line. His first shot bounced off the front of the rim and fell off to the side. The Valpo fans leaped to their feet. Drew quickly called a timeout—the team's last—to try to ice the shooter.

At the time, people questioned the timeout call, because Ole Miss could now intentionally miss and Valpo would have to go the length of the floor—off a rebound—and get off a shot, a difficult proposition against the quick hands and athleticism of the Rebels.

Sesay did miss the second shot strong off of the back iron. The ball bounced on the floor. In the scramble, the Rebels' Keith Carter knocked the ball toward the sideline, in hopes the clock would run out. It didn't. 2.5 seconds remained as the ball rolled out of bounds. The Crusaders would get one final chance, but they'd have to go the length of the floor.

"Pacer!" Sykes yelled. "Pacer!"

"Pacer!" Bill Jenkins replied.

"Pacer!" Bryce shouted.

"Pacer" was a play the Crusaders had rehearsed for just such an occasion. It was a desperation play, a basketball "Hail Mary," if you will. The seniors groaned all through their four years whenever they had to practice gimmick plays like Pacer. "They all complained, 'Coach, we never get to use this,'" Drew said.

The play was designed for Sykes, the minor-league baseball player, to throw a long pass just beyond mid-court to Bill Jenkins. Bryce would take two steps towards the ball to fake the defender into thinking that the pass was intended for him. Once the defender turned to run for the ball, Bryce would cut back as Jenkins caught the ball in mid-air. If the play worked correctly, Jenkins would catch the pass and feed Bryce, who should then have enough of an opening to get off a 20-to-25 foot jumper. The play required expert, precise timing, an incredible jump, and soft hands, in succession. Furthermore, the play was not game-tested Still, there was no time for regrets—or second-guessing. There was one final chance.

The fact that Valpo would be attempting the play was enough to satisfy Drew.

"I was very proud as a coach, because at that moment, they didn't need me. They knew exactly what to do," he said.

"Pacer!" Sykes yelled. "Pacer!"
"Pacer!" Bill Jenkins replied.
"Pacer!" Bryce shouted.

Sykes took the ball from the official. Hounded by the Rebels' Keith Carter, who had a five-inch height advantage over the 5-11 Sykes, he pump-faked once and lofted a perfect pass to Jenkins. On the bench, Drew breathed a sigh of relief when he saw the ball in the air.

"Once Jamie got the pass off, I knew we had a chance," Drew said later.

Two Old Miss defenders surrounded Jenkins, but he still was able to leap high into the air, over Sesay and Lockhart, to grab the ball. In one fluid motion, he turned and flipped the ball to Bryce, who had shaken off his defender and had much more than daylight—he had a wide-open look at the basket from 23 feet away. Bryce stopped behind the three-point line, and, with one second on the clock, launched the Crusaders' last dream into the air. All the work, all the sacrifice, all the sweat, tears, and love of the past four years came down to one shot, spinning airborne towards the hoop. For a brief second, the arena fell into stunned silence.

CHAPTER THIRTEEN

The Celebration

"Apparently, they're going to remake Hoosiers, only this time they're going to use real Hoosiers."

–CHICAGO TRIBUNE, March 16, 1998

The ball hung in the air for what seemed like an eternity. The entire crowd of 13,269 at the Myriad held its collective breath. Homer Drew stood on the sidelines quietly, his arms folded across his chest. He was no more than a few feet behind his son, Bryce, who was firing up possibly the last shot he would ever take for his father's team.

The shot looked flat at first. Even Bryce admitted later that he thought it was short. Instead, the ball kissed the front rim slightly and rattled through as the buzzer sounded. The entire crowd in the arena, save about 1,000 Ole Miss fans, went berserk. Bryce dove onto the floor at the top of the key as his teammates joyfully piled on him in celebration. Final score: Valparaiso 70, Ole Miss 69.

The Crusaders had accomplished their mission in the most dramatic way possible. After the players unpiled, Drew and his son found each other in the midst of the chaos. They hugged in the middle of the floor—a picture that would run in nearly every major newspaper in the country the next morning. The journey wasn't over yet.

"We did it, Dad," Bryce said.

"I love you, Bryce," Drew replied into his son's ear.

The beautiful simplicity of the moment was charming. Yet, sometimes eloquence is found in the simplest things. Poet Maya Angelou once said that a simple gesture of love between a parent and child can transcend any situation.

"There's nothing more eloquent than a parent saying to a child, 'I love you,'" she said. "That's eloquence."

The play blew everyone away. Ole Miss players stood with their hands clasped on their foreheads in disbelief. TV and radio announcers shrieked with delight along press row. Photographers ran onto the floor to capture the moment, a no-no by tournament guidelines. According to one local photographer, NCAA officials later scolded and threatened to yank the credentials of those who went out on the floor at game's end. Even the Texas Christian University band, which had arrived early for its school's game, was jumping up and down and high-fiving each other as if its team had just won.

As the team headed for the dressing room to a standing ovation, the Crusaders turned to their fans and raised their arms upward. Sykes had tears welling up in his eyes. As they walked off the floor, Drew embraced Harrick, Scott Drew, and Flint. The remaining goal in this group of se- niors' four-year journey—the win over a "major conference" opponent— had been attained at long last.

As Valpo fans danced and hugged each other in the stands, press row buzzed with activity. Reporters from newspapers around the coun- try who, just minutes before, had been half-heartedly paying attention to the game sprung into action. Some craned their necks toward a nearby TV monitor to get a look at the replay. Others scurried off into the press room to call editors and file stories. Still others sat for a mo- ment, trying to take in the entire scene.

Rushing off into the interview area, an Oklahoma sportswriter smiled and summed up the situation.

"The shot of the tournament, right there," he said with a smile. "No matter what happens from here on out, that's the shot of the tournament."

Another reporter, hustling into the media room, gushed about the play to a colleague.

"The shot of the tournament, right there. No matter what happens from here on out, that's the shot of the tournament."

"That's an ESPY winner if I've ever seen one," he said, referring to the awards given out by a major sports network in recognition of outstanding plays.

As the Valpo players reached the locker room, they huddled with the coaching staff. Drew knew there wasn't much he could say to top what had just happened.

"I'm proud of your poise and composure," he told the team. "Enjoy this moment. This is very magical for all of us. Enjoy it. When you wake in the morning, let's start focusing on our next opponent. We are playing our best ball right now, so let's make it a 'lucky 13.'"

The symmetry was striking: Valparaiso University, the 13th seed in the NCAA Midwest Region, playing on Friday the 13th, had scored a dramatic victory to earn the chance to win its 13th game in a row two days later.

The seniors were overcome by the magnitude of the win and many broke into tears of joy. Sykes, who had successfully fended off all the emotions of senior night and the Mid-Con Tournament, finally let it all out and sobbed uncontrollably.

"Yeah, I was weak," he would say later with a laugh. "I cried like a baby when we first got back in here."

Once his tears dried, though, Sykes' sense of humor returned.

"I started screaming, 'What's Christian Laettner got on that?'" he said, referring to the famous jump shot in the Duke-Kentucky regional final in 1992.

A few moments later, Drew walked to the podium in the interview area, along with Sykes, Bill and Bob Jenkins, and of course, Bryce Drew. All five were still clearly caught up in the emotion of the moment.

"I'm still wiping away the tears," Drew began. "I'm so proud of this basketball team. They really found a way. All week, our motto was, 'Find a Way,' and they did."

Drew broke down the final play, commending all three players involved. The play was unique in that it took three players executing perfectly to make it work.

"We had the heroics by Bryce...and I think you see why Jamie is playing baseball," he said. "And I still don't know how Bill got that high in the air."

"All week, our motto was, 'Find a Way,' and they did."–Homer Drew

---

Bryce was a focal point in the press conference, and, obviously, the first question he fielded was about the game-winning shot. In typical Bryce fashion, he directed the praise to his teammates, and a higher power, as well.

"I didn't practice all week, so I'd like to thank the Lord Jesus Christ for allowing me to be healthy today," he said. "We five seniors...we've worked so hard and come so close to upsetting teams in the past. To come in here and do it our senior year, well, it's certainly the best game-winner I've ever hit in my life."

Bryce confessed that he thought his missed three-point attempt with seven seconds left was his final shot in a Crusader uniform.

"I was scared that might be it," he said. "I was hoping and praying that I'd get another chance, and I'm thankful that I did."

Drew said that even if the Crusaders hadn't gotten that final chance, he was proud of his team. The teacher in him was thrilled that the players knew exactly what to do in such a unique situation.

In the months since the shot, Drew has been asked numerous times how he could appear so calm as Bryce took the shot. The answer was simple, he said.

"The fact was, I was actually proud of them before the shot, and now I just thank God for letting those three young men share a memory that will last a lifetime," he said.

The pride also extended to the fact that his team displayed no fear in the game's final minutes.

"Make or miss, Jared and Jamie and Bryce had the courage to take the shot, and that's what's most important to me," he said.

Later, walking in the cavernous hallways under the Myriad stands, Drew admitted he didn't think his team would get the final opportunity to win the game.

"After Bryce missed with seven seconds, I thought, 'well, at least we got our chances,' which is all you can ask for," he said. "Those were some of the best looks we had all day, and I was hoping for one more chance... and then things happened so quickly, it was a bang-bang play."

As for the fateful final shot, the one that both Bryce and Drew thought was short when it left Bryce's hand?

"I guess divine intervention made it get over the rim," Bryce said with a smile.

Later, in the dressing room, Bob Jenkins said he felt no such doubt when the shot went up.

"I knew it was going in," he said. "A player like Bryce, you *know* he's gonna drop bottom. Especially since he had that miss, you knew he was not going to let this one go."

Bryce was asked to characterize the odds of the Pacer play working in a game situation.

"I'd say it's 50-50," he said. "I'm glad it was the 50 percent that worked today."

Drew said the shot was a testament to the years of hard work that Bryce had put into the game.

"It goes to show that hard work can pay off," he said. "All those thousands of jump shots that Bryce has taken in practice...I just thank God that he got that angel to direct the ball in the basket to reward Bryce."

A reporter complimented Sykes for making a great pass, and the praise was again passed along to a teammate.

"I just threw it. I give most of the credit to Bill because he had to go up and get it," he said. Bill Jenkins said he knew the ball would be there when he jumped because of a look he gave to Sykes.

"Our eyes met and we knew what to do," Jenkins said.

Even Ole Miss players professed admiration for the way the Crusaders pulled off the win.

"They executed to a T," said Rebel guard Keith Carter. "We knew it would end up in Bryce's hands, and he hit a great shot."

"It was a great pass," said Mississippi guard Jason Flanigan. "Everybody was rushing to the ball, and no one noticed Bryce."

All of the Valpo players noticed the wonderful, almost overpowering, feeling of winning a tournament game after two previous attempts. The final play sparked a spontaneous reaction and celebration that none of the players will ever forget. Freshman Chris Sparks, who was redshirted for the season and was on the bench in street clothes, literally jumped out of his shoes when the shot went in. Television replays show two empty Reeboks left behind at the end of the bench where Sparks was sitting.

"I have never experienced that feeling before," Tony Vilcinskas said. "I just wanted to scream and fall down. I mean, you watch stuff like that on TV, and you think, 'Come on, it can't be that exciting,' but it is."

Bill Jenkins called the post-game celebration on the floor "the most legal way to get high."

"It was just instant screaming...I lost my voice in one minute. One minute! Have you ever lost your voice that quickly and not even noticed?" he said. "We came back in here and I was so happy that I was crying my eyes out."

When the ball went through the hoop, Bryce Drew became an instant national celebrity. Within five minutes, ESPN was already calling to get Valpo radio announcer Todd Ickow's call of the play. Writers from *Sports Illustrated* and *The New York Times* showed up in the Crusader dressing room. Yet, Bryce was left somewhat speechless by the fantastic ending. It took him a moment to respond when asked how he felt after the game.

"It's hard to describe...it's one of the greatest feelings you could ever have...it was pandemonium in here after the game, everyone was just hugging each other," he said. "We've tried so hard, and we knew this was our last chance. That's why we all had tears in our eyes."

Bryce also grasped the national implications of a Valpo win in the NCAA tournament.

"We've come and gone the last two years in the first round, so we never really earned our respect," he said. "And some people were picking Ole Miss to go to the Final Four, so that was motivation for us...this is definitely going to open some eyes around the country."

The grand predictions for the Rebels by many national basketball pundits—anticipating that Ole Miss would reach the Final Four—also rubbed Sykes the wrong way.

"It bothered me, because we had seen them on tape, and to hear all these people talking them up, it made me think, 'do these people know something that we don't? Have they seen something that we haven't?' We knew we could compete with this team," he said. "This gives us notoriety. People have to respect us now."

Bob Jenkins sat grinning from ear to ear watching all of the players being interviewed. No one was clamoring for a quote from him, as he fouled out with two points and two rebounds in just 15 minutes of playing time. Yet, his meager stat line did not bother him.

"I'm still letting it sink in," he said with a smile. "This feels so good."

Despite fouling out with over 12 minutes remaining in the game, Bob Jenkins felt he needed to serve as a role model for the younger players on the team by staying upbeat.

"I didn't consider myself helpless sitting on the sideline," he said while munching on a cookie. "I try to stay positive and keep everyone's head in the game. Like when Jared had a turnover, I saw him hang his head a little, so I jumped up and encouraged him a little. And the other players see that and think, 'this guy had a bad game and he's staying positive, so I'll stay positive, too.'"

Nevertheless, he still was surprised to have fouled out so quickly.

"I had a tough assignment [Sesay]," he continued. "And when the ref called the fifth foul on me, I honestly thought he was kidding. I mean, there were still 12 minutes left. But then I realized he wasn't joking, so

I made that long walk back to the bench and sat down. And that's when it hit me that I may have just played in my last game."

That realization may explain why Bob Jenkins was one of the first players to jump on the pile of happy Crusaders after Bryce's last-second trey found the net.

"The whole thing is like slow-motion in my mind right now," he said. "I saw it happen, but it's like it didn't happen, you know what I mean? Jamie's never made that perfect of a pass, it was two perfect passes, actually. Bill jumped so high. I can't wait to watch the replays. It's one of those plays that will be famous, and to see a face you recognize is going to be just great."

Sykes concurred with Bob Jenkins' viewpoint of the final play. Sykes said he was merely hoping to get a pass off in the face of Keith Carter, who was jumping up and down less than three feet away.

"I knew the shot was going in, because that play is not supposed to work," he said. "Bill's not supposed to catch that ball like that, but when he caught it and got it to Bryce, I knew. I just knew."

Although Bryce would be making headlines the next day, it was Zoran Viskovic who was one of the game's biggest heroes as well. Viskovic finished with 19 points on 5-of-8 shooting and a clutch 9-of-10 from the foul line. The 6-11 forward confessed to having a premonition about the game the night before.

"We know what it takes to win here now," he said. "I talked to Bryce last night, and we both said 'we're going to do it.' I can't explain the feeling... we've put so much work into it this year and now this. It's a great accomplishment for us and our program."

In addition, Viskovic had a different perspective on the final shot than either of the Drews.

"I knew it was going in because I was standing under the basket," he said. Then he closed his eyes and broke into a wide smile. "I heard it go 'swoosh' and I thought, 'oh, maaaaaan.' I couldn't believe it. I ran over to Bryce and then everyone jumped on the floor."

Bryce was asked why he fell on the floor after he hit the winning shot. His dad asked the same question.

"When you look one way and you've got Bill and Bob running at you, who are both 6-6 and chiseled, and then you look the other way and Tony and Zoran are running at you, who weigh a combined 500-plus pounds, you've only got one place to go, and that's down," Bryce said, laughing, before turning deadpan serious.

"Honestly, it was such a blur," Bryce said. "All I really remember is lying on the floor saying, 'thank you, Lord.'"

Within hours of the game's end, "The Play," as CBS was already calling it, was shown on every sports highlight show in the country. The Crusaders were the lead story on both the early and late SportsCenter on ESPN—complete with Ickow's call dubbed in over the highlight. By the time people on the East Coast turned in for the night, most of America had heard Ickow's voice-cracking description along with the stunning video.

"They're going to have to go the length of the floor...Sykes...to Jenkins...TO DREW! FOR THE WIN...GOOOOOOOOOOOOOD!!! VALPO WINS! VALPO WINS! VALPO WINS!"

The next morning, nearly every American opened a newspaper to find Valparaiso staring at them from the sports pages. *The New York Times* ran a front-page story. The front page of the *Chicago Tribune*'s sports section blared the headline: "Just like they Drew it up." A picture of the happy head coach ran in the upper left hand "Hit & Run" column. It read: "Good Morning, Homer Drew: Father Knows Best." In one instant, the Crusaders went from being projected SEC road kill to the talk of the tournament—and of an office-pool-crazed nation. Aaron Thomason acknowledged as much in the dressing room after the game.

"Guys, we just messed up a lot of people's brackets," he said with a laugh.

In sports bars and restaurants across the country, Valpo made instant fans with the last-second miracle. At a crowded restaurant in Chicago's financial district, stock traders on their lunch hour hooted and hollered when Bryce's last-second prayer was answered. In Washington, Boston and New York, folks playing hooky from work—suffering from a unique mid-March ailment known as NCAA Fever—reveled in the Crusaders' dramatic victory at local watering holes. Closer to home, at Valparaiso High School, the cheering echoed down the school's corridors as the shot was shown on television monitors in classrooms.

Even inside the walls of ESPN world headquarters in Bristol, Connecticut, the shot reverberated throughout the building. Darin Riter, a studio technician at ESPN, was down the hall from the screening room where several dozen production assistants watch sporting events and prepare highlights for the evening's news programs.

"I was just working in another studio, and suddenly I heard everyone let out a roar," Riter, a native of Fort Wayne, Indiana, said. "About 40 production assistants all screaming and yelling at once. I ran down the hall to see what was the matter, and they told me that Valpo had just beaten Ole Miss. Then I saw the play, which was amazing. One of the guys said, 'that's what the tournament's all about, right there.' I have to agree."

For those with a connection to the program, the university or the city, "the shot" was destined to become one of those special moments, where everyone will remember exactly where they were when they saw or heard it.

More important than the coverage and the hoopla, however, was the fact that this team, through hard work and perseverance, had achieved the one goal that had eluded it for so long: an NCAA Tournament win.

It was especially sweet for Bryce Drew. The win finally silenced those who had mocked his decision to come to Valparaiso University, the coaches who ridiculed him for "not wanting to be big-time." There was no denying that Valparaiso basketball had arrived at that magical place that the Drew family could only have dreamed of several years earlier. During the TCU-Florida State game broadcast, CBS announcer Ted Robinson summed it up with one sentence.

"Today, Valpo was big-time."

CHAPTER FOURTEEN

Capturing America's Heart

"Far better it is to dare mighty things, to win glorious triumphs, even though checkered by failure, than to take rank with those poor spirits who neither enjoy nor suffer much, because they live in the gray twilight that knows not victory nor defeat."

—Theodore Roosevelt

With all the hype surrounding the Valpo team during the two day following Bryce's "Miracle at the Myriad," it was natural to wonder about the team's focus and intensity level going into its second-round game against Florida State. After all, there are upsets every year in the NCAA Tournament, but in most cases the second round serves as a reality check for starry-eyed teams.

Florida State was capable of leaving teams starry-eyed, but in an entirely different manner. The big, muscular Seminoles had easily dispatched favored Texas Christian, 96-87, following Valpo's dramatic win over Ole Miss. The bruising frontline of 6-9 Corey Louis and 6-11 Randell Jackson combined for 40 points in the TCU win, overpowering what many considered to be a quicker, more athletic Horned Frog team. With the win, the Seminoles were able to silence critics who had complained about them being awarded an at-large bid to the tournament despite a very ordinary 17-13 record and a subpar 6-10 record in the Atlantic Coast Conference.

"I think that probably inspired our guys to play a little bit harder,"

Florida State head coach Steve Robinson said of the critics. "I think our guys felt that they were really slighted."

"We felt it was us against the world," said senior guard Lamar Greer. "When everyone said we were overrated, we just had to stay together and not fall apart."

"The Crusaders are popping up all over the nation, on syndicated talk shows and every Web site from here to Guam. What's next, the Wheaties box?"
                                                                    —VIDETTE-TIMES

Nevertheless, both Jenkins twins were confident of Valpo's ability to put the heart-stopping win behind them and prepare for the next opponent.

"We're a veteran team," Bill Jenkins said. "Our focus shouldn't be a problem."

"We've enjoyed this, but now it's time to get focused," Bob Jenkins concurred. "We know what we have to do."

Homer Drew, however, knew that the temptations to settle back and be content with the Ole Miss win were very real.

"I'm really concerned about our focus for Sunday," he said while watching the TCU-Florida State battle from an arena tunnel. He expressed awe at the Seminoles' overpowering inside game. "Florida State is just huge, but what's more impressive is their quickness. What's even worse for us is that they have quickness at every position."

After a long evening studying film, the coaching staff came up with a theme for the Florida State game. The Crusaders' theme would be, "own the paint." Owning the paint would cut down on easy baskets, and with Florida State's size and athleticism, those were of chief concern. To accomplish this goal, Drew and his staff came up with three keys for success:

First, Valpo would have to rebound with impunity. By keeping the

Seminoles in a "one and done" situation on each possession, their inside game could be neutralized. Second, Valpo wanted to limit the Seminoles to just two dunks for the game. If the Crusaders could limit the number of Seminole dunks, that meant the Florida State fast break was being slowed and easy baskets were being kept under control. Finally, Valpo needed to commit fewer than 10 turnovers. In addition to giving Valpo extra opportunities to score, taking good care of the basketball would help the Crusaders control the tempo of the game.

If Valpo could do all of these things, Drew knew the game would be close. He wanted the game to be close to put the pressure on Florida State.

In his Saturday press conference, which was televised on ESPN, Robinson said he warned his team about Valparaiso.

"We're smart enough to know that we've got to respect whoever we play," he said. Oddly enough, however, he didn't mention Valparaiso by name once during the five minutes the conference was carried live.

Sunday afternoon arrived in Oklahoma City. The weather was dreary, and a cold, steady rain fell all morning. Just a few blocks from the Myriad in the city's downtown is the site of the Alfred P. Murrah Federal Building, which was bombed April 19, 1995. It was the worst act of terrorism ever to occur on American soil—a tragedy that still affects and haunts the city residents.

Passing by the bombing site, it's easy to see why. Nothing remains of the federal building itself—the ruins were cleared a few months after the bombing. However, the entrance to an underground parking garage still sits undisturbed as a chilling remembrance of the 168 people who lost their lives due to a despicable act of cowardice. It was not hard to picture the victims arriving at work, pulling into the parking garage as millions of other working Americans do, not knowing that they were walking into the path of one of the most hateful acts ever committed. It's enough to bring a horrible chill up the most hardened person's spine.

Surrounding the site where the building stood is a chain-link fence turned makeshift memorial. "The Fence," as locals refer to it, is covered with flowers, prayers, poems, pictures, teddy bears, and just about every other type of memento one could imagine. Drew took his players to the bombing site, a painful, albeit necessary experience.

"I wanted the team to have a sense of history and to impress upon them that they need to keep basketball and life in perspective," Drew said. "It was a reminder that they need to know what is really important in their lives...it was very touching, and it was hard for some of the players to be there for very long."

The bombing site hit particularly close to home for the team's foreign players. Tony Vilcinskas has seen sites where Lithuanians fighting for freedom were killed in his native country. In Lithuania, memorials are not erected on such sites.

"I didn't want to take a picture because I didn't feel like it was a tourist attraction," Vilcinskas told *The Daily Oklahoman*. "It's nobody I knew, but it was painful inside."

"I wanted the team to have a sense of history and to impress upon them that they need to keep basketball and life in perspective."–Homer Drew

---

Zoran Viskovic told the newspaper that the bombing site reminded him all too well of the strife in his war-torn homeland of Croatia.

"It hurt so many people," he said. "I've been through a war in Croatia, so I've seen lots of people getting killed...it's just so inhuman."

A woman who was a local resident saw the team near the bombing site. She approached and gave each player a commemorative pin as a token of appreciation. Many Oklahoma natives were touched that numerous visitors in town for the NCAA games took time out to stop by and pay their respects at the memorial. However, it was the Valpo players who were touched by the local woman's offering. As she presented the pins, several players were on the brink of tears.

Looking around the area surrounding the bombing site, one gets a sense of the magnitude of the bomb's force. A YMCA sits down the street, condemned from being knocked off its foundation by the blast. Another large limestone building sits shuttered, also rendered unsafe by the massive bomb. Then the terrible images of that sad day return to one's mind.

It served as a reminder of the grieving process that Oklahomans were still going through, nearly three years after the fact. More importantly, it reminded everyone that no matter what happened at the Myriad that day for any of the teams involved, it was still just a basketball game and nothing more.

As the two teams took the floor at the Myriad, it was obvious who the fan favorite would be. Fresh from the win over Ole Miss, everyone suddenly knew Valpo's name. Kansas and Rhode Island would be meeting in the day's second game following Valpo and Florida State, but that didn't stop hundreds of red, dark blue, and baby blue pom pons from being waved when the Crusaders took the floor.

Despite being the lower seed, Valpo was wearing its home white uniforms, which was a break from tournament protocol. Yet, it was a legal one—the higher seed gets its choice of home jerseys. The Seminoles chose their gold uniforms, and since Valpo's road uniforms were gold, the NCAA allowed Valpo to wear its home whites.

The starting lineups were introduced. Each Crusader player received a louder cheer than his Florida State counterpart. A loud roar went up when Bryce Drew was introduced. The Florida State players huddled at mid-court when the lineups were finished and began dancing and hopping—before the game.

Other than a few hundred Seminole fans who had made the journey from the Florida panhandle, most heard the early reactions and figured this would be a pro-Valpo crowd. However, the notion that the afternoon would be a Valpo lovefest ended the second the Florida State pep band struck up one of the most well-recognized songs in all of college athletics: the Seminole war chant, otherwise known as "The Chop."

Florida State fans began moving their arms back and forth, simulating a tomahawk chopping, all the while chanting along with the band's tune. Those who have never seen FSU fans do this should watch an Atlanta Braves' game, because Braves fans co-opted the "chop" several years ago. While Seminole fans view the song with reverence and pride, fans of Florida State's opponents, especially those down the road in Gainesville at archrival University of Florida, generally dislike the tune, mainly because the band plays it incessantly. Apparently, the song is less than popular with the press corps as well.

"Oh, man, I forgot all about this stupid song," said one southern sportswriter sitting on press row. "They play it too much."

Much like a prizefight, the two teams cautiously surmised each other for the first moments after tipoff. Players surveyed the floor to get a feel for offensive and defensive setups. Bill Jenkins missed a layup on the game's first scoring opportunity. Just over a minute into the game, FSU's Lamar Greer wound around a screen and drained a wide-open three-pointer. Valpo couldn't get a good look at the basket, and FSU guard Kerry Thompson came down in transition for an easy lay-in. It was 5-0 Seminoles, and Drew signaled for a 20-second timeout. Florida State's quickness advantage over Valpo was showing, and Drew wanted to make sure the Crusaders didn't get rattled and fall too far behind at the start.

Two Valpo three-pointers countered the Seminoles' push. With Valpo ahead 6-5, FSU missed yet another shot, and Greer was called for a pushing foul. On the next possession, Sykes drove the lane and hit a floating one-hand jumper off the glass. Valpo went up 8-5, and the Crusader fans were on their feet cheering. After Bill Jenkins scored on a driving layup, the score was 12-7 in favor of Valpo heading into the first media timeout. The Crusader bench jumped up and down and high-fived the players as they reached the sideline.

Three minutes later, Bill Jenkins capped a 7-0 Valpo run with a three-pointer from the right corner that touched every part of the rim before finally falling through. The Crusaders had a 19-12 lead, and the Myriad crowd loved it.

Sensing a need for momentum, Lamar Greer took over for the Seminoles. First, he hit a three-pointer from the right side. Then, he caught a pass from Karim Shabazz and connected on a three from the left side. Within one minute, another Crusader lead had evaporated. Valpo embarked on a four-minute scoring drought. At the same time, Kerry Thompson hit another three, and Louis and Jackson each added two points. When the media timeout at 7:53 mercifully arrived, Valpo found itself trailing 27-19. FSU had rattled off 15 unanswered points, and Valpo appeared to be getting tired chasing Florida State's athletic players around the offensive end of the floor.

The Crusaders looked shell-shocked heading towards the huddle. However, Drew felt the Seminole blitzkrieg was a positive for the Crusaders.

"I told the team it was actually a good thing for us because now Florida State would be overconfident," Drew said later. "I told them that we needed to re-establish our game and get back into the game slowly with inside-outside play, and there was plenty of time for us to do that. We needed more ball movement on offense. Let's get more touches on offense and let them chase us around the screens."

Out of the timeout, Valpo finally snapped the dry spell with a Bill Jenkins layup off a pass from Jared Nuness. However, 27 seconds later, Ron Hale drilled another three and the Seminoles had their largest lead of the game at 30-21. With 6:01 left in the half, the FSU lead was 32-23 when Nuness spotted up, Sykes threw the cross pass to him, and the freshman calmly swished a three from the right corner.

Even though the Seminoles had the lead, they weren't able to dictate the tempo as they had earlier, a by-product from Drew's instructions in the earlier timeout.

"On defense, we had to keep switching up our defenses to slow down Florida State," he said. "We couldn't stay with anything for too long."

The two teams played evenly for the rest of the half. This time, as the clock ticked down, Bryce's spin move produced an open shot, but without the results of two days earlier. His shot clanged off the back iron, and the two teams headed for the locker rooms with Florida State on top, 41-38.

In the locker room at halftime, Drew knew his team trailed, but once again he liked its position. If Valpo could keep it close and then grab the lead in the last five minutes, they could win, he thought. He stressed the need to be physical in the paint, to utilize the Crusaders' bulk over FSU's quickness. He also felt the Crusaders' execution could be better in the second half. "We haven't played our best yet."

"Own the paint, come meet the pass, remember our fundamentals," Drew reminded his club. "We can do it! Remember that talent can win games, but teamwork and intelligence on the floor will get us to the Sweet 16! Second half let's give them our best."

Valpo got the ball to start the second half. Much like the game against Ole Miss, the Crusaders wanted to start strong and avoid having to dig out of a hole for the remainder of the game. Within two minutes, a Viskovic three-point play put Valpo ahead 43-41.

For the next six minutes, the teams seesawed back and forth. Bryce hit a three from the left wing. Greer counter-punched with a three of his own. Sykes hit a fall-away jumper in the lane and a pull-up shot from the foul line. Florida State's Ron Hale delivered a spectacular rebuttal with an alley-oop jam. The exchange induced a loud roar from the thoroughly-entertained crowd in Oklahoma City.

With 11:32 left, Valpo made its move. Clinging to a two-point lead, Nuness corralled a loose ball and drained a three from the left corner— 59-54 Valpo. After another media timeout, Nuness flipped the ball to Bryce standing open in the right wing. He came through with another three, and the Crusaders had a 62-54 lead with 9:43 remaining. The crowd, sensing that Valpo wasn't going away, rose to its feet.

After whittling the lead down to five points, the Florida State defense began trapping and turning up its defensive intensity. On two straight trips, the Crusaders couldn't get a clean look at the basket. After an FSU basket, Valpo got sloppy against the press, and Ron Hale made a backcourt steal and went in for the jam. Florida State led by three, and the maroon-clad Seminole fans jumped up and down with glee.

The Seminoles' up-tempo pace looked like it was wearing on the

Crusaders' legs. On Valpo's next offensive set, Bryce missed three open looks from beyond the arc that would have tied the game.

With 3:30 left, Vilcinskas was fouled again, sending the big seven-footer to the line. As the two teams set up for the free throw, Valpo players leaned over, pulling on their shorts and gasping for breath. Vilcinskas, likely breathing harder than any of his teammates, missed the front end of the one-and-one.

Fortunately for the Crusaders, the Seminoles' half-court offense wasn't producing many good shots, either. Valpo was having trouble defending when the Seminoles would get out running on the fast break, but the Valpo defense was strong when FSU was forced to set up in its half-court game. Knowing that his team, down three points, desperately needed a basket, Drew signaled for a timeout with 2:24 left in the game.

On the critical possession, Valpo made certain the passes were safe and crisp. After working the ball around through their set, Bill Jenkins passed to Sykes, who knocked in an acrobatic, hanging 12-footer off the backboard. The crowd rose to its feet again. Sykes sprinted back on defense. The Crusaders got the defensive stop that they needed when Bob Jenkins poked away an errant pass. Sykes brought the ball upcourt with the season on the line.

The Crusaders worked slowly through their offensive set. After a series of backscreens, Bryce faked a shot and threw the ball inside to Viskovic, who had a clear path to the basket. Like a horrible case of déjà vu, a defender appeared out of nowhere. With 1:06 left, Randell Jackson swatted away Viskovic's layup. Drew ran up the sidelines, arms above his head, protesting the non-call. Indeed, the replay showed that it could have been called goaltending. Obviously, the Crusader fans thought so as they screamed at the officials for a call. More compelling evidence was offered by the fact that the entire Kansas section rose to its feet in a chorus of boos. The way the blue-sweatered fans were waving their hands at the refs and booing, one could have easily thought the call went against the Jayhawks.

Meanwhile, Kerry Thompson split two defenders and knocked down a one-hander in the lane to stretch the FSU lead to 75-72. With 42 seconds left, Drew called timeout. The booing continued as the teams headed for the sidelines.

Out of the huddle, Valpo wasted no time in throwing the ball inside to Viskovic, who was hacked as he went up for a shot by Jackson. With 34 seconds remaining, he calmly sank both free throws. Valpo trailed by one. Nuness quickly fouled Thompson, who stepped to the line for a one-and-one. He missed the front end and Bill Jenkins grabbed the rebound. Jackson fouled him over the back. The Crusader bench jumped up and down. With 30 seconds remaining, Jenkins could give Valpo the lead.

Jenkins exhaled and stepped to the line. He dribbled and released the first shot. It fell off the front of the rim. Jenkins' shoulders sunk briefly. A Florida State player began jawing in his ear, sarcastically telling him "not to be short" on his second shot. Jenkins exhaled, then said a prayer under his breath.

"Lord, please help me." he said.

The second shot looked on target, and it was. It rippled through the cords and Valpo had tied the score at 75-75. Florida State pushed the ball across the timeline, and Steve Robinson called timeout. Once again, Valpo's tournament hopes were going down to the last possession.

As the Crusaders broke from the huddle, all five seniors—Bryce Drew, Jamie Sykes, Bill Jenkins, Bob Jenkins, and Tony Vilcinskas—headed onto the floor for their final defensive stand. Near midcourt, the five huddled in a tight circle. It was time to leave everything on the floor.

"This is everything we've worked four years for, right here!" Bryce told his teammates. "We've come too far to quit now!"

The team broke the huddle and set up its defense. Florida State inbounded the ball, and ran the clock down. Thompson looked at the clock, and with 10 seconds left, he made his move. From the right side of the floor, he dribbled across the top of the key, and gathered to make his move into the paint. Forced to pull up sooner than expected after Bryce got his fingertips on the ball, he lost the handle with four seconds left. Bryce grabbed it and prepared to make a final charge down the court. However, the ball eluded his grip, so in a safe play, Bryce heaved the ball downcourt to run out the clock. Bill Jenkins pumped his fist. The game was headed into overtime.

In the huddle before the start of the overtime, Drew exhorted his players to not hold anything back, to reach deep inside for the drive to win. He reminded them that they had won 12 games in a row, so they knew what it took to win a close game.

"Let the power be released," Drew said. "Leave every ounce of energy out on the floor!"

The defensive stop seemed to give Valpo a lift going into the extra five minutes. The Crusaders played smothering defense at the start of overtime. Unfortunately for Valpo, so did Florida State. Finally, Bryce cracked the overtime scoring column by sinking an eight-foot runner in the lane with 3:18 remaining. After an FSU timeout, Louis missed a tip-in slam. The ball bounded off the rim and Bryce corralled the loose ball. With 2:30 left, Bryce was hand-checked by Baker, sending him to the foul line for two shots. Finally, the Crusaders had a chance to put some distance between themselves and the Seminoles.

Drew's first shot rattled out. Then, his second shot fell short.

"Oh, no!" one Valpo fan exclaimed. "He never misses 'em both!"

With 2:03 left, Karim Shabazz was fouled as he went up for a layin by Viskovic, his fifth foul. Viskovic received a standing ovation as he slowly walked over to the bench. Shabazz, a 45-percent free-throw shooter, drained both shots perfectly. The game was tied yet again.

Valpo came downcourt and set up its offense. After working the ball through the paint, Sykes found himself wide open for a three-pointer. The shot was long, but Bob Jenkins leaped over Jackson to snag the rebound. He went up strong and stuck the ball back in for another Valpo lead with 1:33 left. Florida State pushed the ball back upcourt and ran its set play. After swinging the ball around the outside, the ball was thrown in to Jackson who turned and made a move toward the basket. Vilcinskas followed his every move and got his hand on the ball. A whistle blew. The referee signaled jump ball. On the alternating possession rule, the Crusaders were awarded the ball. With 56 seconds left, Valpo had a two-point lead, and, more importantly, possession of the ball.

After the timeout, Valpo got into its offense slowly, wanting to use every available second of the shot clock. Finally, Bryce ran off a screen and fired a three from the left side. The shot hit the rim and rolled off. Vilcinskas batted the rebound off the backboard, grabbed the ball and softly tossed in a right-handed jump hook. The entire arena roared. Kansas and Rhode Island fans jumped up and down while Valpo fans dissolved into a state of collective bedlam. Florida State signaled for a timeout with 19 seconds remaining. Valpo was up four, 81-77.

After a missed FSU three-pointer, Bryce stole the rebound. Baker finally slapped his arm to stop the clock with eight seconds remaining. Bryce bounced up the floor, giddy and pumping his fist. By that point, the entire nation knew this was Valparaiso's day. Bryce hit both free throws. Kneeling in front of the bench, Drew grinned.

"He can see St. Louis coming up right into view," said CBS commentator Rolando Blackman as Bryce aimed his second foul shot.

FSU failed to convert a desperation three, and the clock hit :00. Bryce held both arms up and pointed skyward. Drew was nearly knocked to the ground in a sea of hugs from Scott Drew, Jim Harrick, and Steve Flint.

Not even the players could have imagined this at the start of the season. All of the struggles: the early season losses, Drew's injury, Sykes' baseball issues, the mid-season inconsistency, the challenge of blending in so many freshmen; all of it seemed so distant at that moment. The players danced and hugged each other on the court. This team had captured the nation's imagination with the Ole Miss win. With the 83-77 victory over Florida State, it had captured their hearts as well.

"Valparaiso, Going to Town; The Little Team that Could Enchants a Nation and Community"-WASHINGTON POST, March 18, 1998

Near the free-throw line on the opposite end of the court, the Crusaders quickly huddled before leaving the floor and did a little dance of their own. Drew had one request of his players before they continued the celebration.

"There's a whole bunch of your friends, family, and fans who made the long trip out here," he said. "Let's go over there and let them know how much we appreciate them."

With that, the Crusaders sprinted to the end of the floor in front of the section of Valpo fans. Aaron Thomason high-stepped over and nearly broke into a full-blown dance move. The seniors all raised their arms in triumph, and Bryce and Homer Drew waved to the crowd. The Valpo contingent, still cheering with ballistic fervor, loved every second of it. The Crusaders—the Valparaiso Crusaders—were going to the Sweet 16.

Nuness said later that thanking the Valpo fans that had traveled across the country to cheer them on was a no-brainer for the team. He echoed a line from the movie, *Jerry Maguire*.

"They complete us, at home and on the road," he said. "We're a family with everybody from Valparaiso, and we couldn't do it without them."

Getting a brief moment to celebrate with the Valpo fans was also important to Bill Jenkins, if for no other reason than the fact that many of the people in the Valpo section had gutted it out through the lean years.

"It felt great out there," he said. "Some of the fans were even happier than we were, if that's possible. But when you think about it, that makes sense, because most of them have been through the worst seasons and have stuck with the team through thick and thin."

As the team headed into the locker room, the players chanted "Sweet Sixteen!" and other school cheers. Quickly, they gathered in the center of the room and Drew addressed them. He complimented each person individually, emphasizing that above all else, this was a team victory.

"Bob and Tony, what great efforts on the offensive boards, the determination to not only get the offensive rebound but to convert it for two points...both of you were keys in the overtime for our win," he said. "Jamie, you did a beautiful job again on defense against Greer and then to add your offense was superb. Zoran, your presence in the paint versus their quickness and leaping ability wore them down.

"Bill, you got us to overtime. What a pressure free throw, especially after missing the first, you hit the second. See, God does answer prayers."

Drew turned to his son, and then to the freshmen.

"Bryce, your two points in overtime got us going, but the way you controlled the tempo of the entire game was masterful," he said. "Jared, you were three-for-three and each one was a big shot. More importantly, your ballhandling and passing were huge for us. Jason, your quality minutes handling the ball and playing defense were important.

"As for the bench, I know it's hard for you to watch and not get in the game. But your enthusiasm and support got us over their spurts of momentum. This truly was a team victory."

Drew surveyed the dressing room and flashed a huge smile.

"Gentlemen, this is kind of fun. Let's go to St. Louis!" he said to a roar of approval.

Back in the press room, Drew took the podium for the post-game interview along with all five seniors. Each player wore a weary smile. The physical exhaustion of the players was evident as they slowly climbed the steps of the stage.

"We at Valparaiso University really enjoy meeting you like this," Drew said, surveying the room. "I'm very proud of these five seniors and this team. They played this game with all of their heart, all of their soul, and all of their might. They really left it all on the floor."

Drew said his team's courageous nature was evident near the end of the game. Valpo seemed to have the stronger team at the end, diving after loose balls and making key plays on defense. Above all, the team remained composed.

"Their will power was the difference in this game," he said. "They just refused to give up...they deserve all the credit they can get. They defeated a well-coached, athletic team today."

He also felt that game sent a more emphatic message to the nation than the Ole Miss win.

"You know, the win over Ole Miss wasn't just one shot—we played them well the whole game," he said. "So we were confident of our own ability [today]."

Sykes seconded that notion. He was named CBS Player of the Game after his 19-point performance.

"This is truly a blessing for as much as we've worked this year...we were the only ones who believed that we could play against these big schools and beat them," he said.

Many of the reporters seemed to take the position that Sykes' defense on Lamar Greer in the second half was a key for the Crusaders. Both Drews said they weren't surprised at his outstanding defensive play.

"He does that game in and game out," Bryce said. "He always puts that kind of effort out."

"Jamie has done all year what you have seen here this weekend," Homer Drew concurred.

Bill Jenkins was even more succinct. He said simply, "Jamie is awesome."

As for his hot shooting touch, Sykes said he had a premonition that he was going to have a big day from the moment he woke up.

"I knew early this morning...I was telling people, 'Man, I feel really good today,'" he said in the locker room. "I passed up a lot of open shots against Ole Miss, and I decided I wasn't going to do that today."

The Crusader dressing room was a portrait of things to come. For most regular season games, there would be two or three local beat writers in the Valpo locker room after games. There was a decent crowd of reporters after Bryce's game winner against Mississippi. However, after the Florida State win, the Valpo locker room at the Myriad was packed wall-to-wall with camera crews, national sportswriters, and photographers.

They had become America's darlings. Every sportswriter wanted a part of this feel-good story. The down-to-earth nature of this team won over most of them, too. Jay Mariotti, a sports columnist for the *Chicago Sun-Times* known for sardonic, biting wit in his columns, fell for the Crusaders head over heels in his column the next day.

And the Winner is...Valpo
One thing's for sure, no matter
how this blockbuster turns out, it
certainly won't have a tragic ending.
Two thumbs up, Valpo.
    –Chicago Tribune, Editorial Page, March 20, 1998

"You walked back to the press room with a smile," he wrote. "The Valparaiso story is that precious."

Outside the entrance to the dressing room, the Jenkins brothers sat side-by-side talking to reporters and eating sandwiches. The twins had become fan favorites in Oklahoma City, as evidenced by the fact that a uniformed police officer who was patrolling the area near the locker room took time off the patrol to shake hands and congratulate the pair.

Impossible Dream? The Crusade Continues
They are Beanie Babies, Tickle Me Elmo,
Cabbage Patch Dolls and Pet Rocks. They are
Hula Hoops, Rocky and the Beatles in America
In 1964. They are Elvis...and they haven't yet
Left the building. They are the Valparaiso
Crusaders, the biggest, hottest item in this
Year's NCAA men's basketball tournament.
    –San Antonio Express News

"You guys were great today," he told them with a huge smile. "Way to go."

Bob Jenkins finished with only two points, but they were the two biggest points of his life—the putback of Sykes' miss in the overtime to put Valpo on top to stay. He said in the press conference that he was "just doing his job," but that explanation didn't satisfy Bill Jenkins, who was bursting with brotherly pride in the locker room.

"He went in like a *Jenkins*," Bill said. "He made a great play!"

Drew was proud of the way the team utilized its rebounding fundamentals.

"Rebounding is one of the most overlooked reasons for victory in the game of basketball. The more you rebound, the more shots you get, and the more games you win," Drew said. "A good rebounder has to be aggressive, enjoy contact, and have great desire."

The coaching staff taught the Valpo players a three-step method for rebounding. First, the player needs to step toward his man. Secondly, he needs to make contact with that player. Finally, the rebounder needs to react to the ball aggressively. Offensive rebounding played a key role in the Florida State win, and Drew mentioned that there are three specific offensive rebounding tactics that the Crusaders learn each year.

"The key to offensive rebounding is to assume that every shot is going to be a missed shot," he said. "We teach them to spin and roll off their man, to fake one way and go the opposite way to the glass, and we teach them what we call the 'Moses Malone move,' where a player gets under the basket and literally slides in front of his man."

Bob Jenkins said he had struggled most of the contest, so being able to come through down the stretch was a big relief.

"The whole game, I was just trying to find some way to contribute," he said. "I couldn't get going offensively, but I knew if I could get a few rebounds that would be a big contribution. Rebounding has been our forte all season long."

The Seminoles were a physical team, but not in the bruising way expected of a team that's been through the rigors of a season in the ACC, Bob Jenkins said.

"They were physical, and we expected a physical type of game," he said. "But they were more about throwing little elbows, and little pushes in the small of your back. It was like they were thinking, 'I can get away with this,' so they weren't as tough as we thought they would be."

Bob Jenkins said that the seniors were determined to get the crucial defensive stop before the end of regulation, and that he provided inspiration for his classmates.

"I knew it all was coming down to this," he said. "All of the hard work was on the line. I kept reminding them: 'Bryce, this is why you rehabbed your knee,' and 'Jamie, this is why you came back from baseball,' and this is why I got the stitches in my thumb. All of it. We didn't want the season to end."

While Bill Jenkins admitted to being "fatigued with a capital F," he wasn't too tired to mention that this team was not afraid of anyone—and that the players didn't consider their wins "upsets."

"We will do our best no matter who we play...we were not afraid to play Ole Miss, we weren't afraid today," he said. "You know, any Division I team can play, it doesn't matter what conference they're from. Anyone can beat anyone."

With 10 points and nine rebounds, Bill Jenkins was one of the game's heroes. However, he was well aware that he could have been the goat if he had missed the second free throw with 30 seconds remaining in overtime.

"When we got into overtime, I was kicking myself, thinking, 'if I had hit that first one, we'd have won the game," he said. "I knew I couldn't choke...I always make fun of people who choke like that. Fortunately, the second one went in. If I had missed the second one, you would have seen a black man turn blue."

In the tunnel after the game, Bryce said the team had set out to prove that its win over Ole Miss wasn't merely a one-shot deal.

"We had a team meeting yesterday, and we all said that we wanted to show people that we weren't just a fluke," he said. "The other day was a big milestone for us, we've waited four years for a win like that, it was the last thing we had to accomplish. Now it's all bonuses, and everybody knows that game wasn't just a fluke."

Bryce finished with 22 points and four assists, but he said he was happier that four Crusaders ended up in double figures.

"Last year, I had a couple of games where I scored 38 and 34 and we ended up losing," he said. "Going back to the beginning of the year, we knew we'd have to have more people score, and I'd much rather have the win than the points.

"I never really imagined this. Our first goal was to get back to the tournament and win a game, and we had to go through a lot just to get back here... I'm just thanking God for blessing us."

Although Bryce had gotten a taste of the national media crush in the locker room, he was trying to keep everything in perspective.

"Fame is really fleeting," he said. "As soon as you start to lose, all those people won't be here. So you've got to prove yourself day in and day out."

Vilcinskas turned in a clutch performance of 13 points and five rebounds, and probably no play was bigger than his rebound and layup with 25 seconds remaining. As Vilcinskas recalled the play, he said he heard a stranger's voice inside his head.

"In my head, I was thinking of Dennis Rodman, because some guy in the airport came up to me and told me that Rodman gets so many rebounds because he tips the ball off the board to himself," he said. "So, I tipped the ball off the board, and I got it and made the shot. So whoever that guy was, he was right."

The whole time Vilcinskas was talking, he was wearing a black 10-gallon cowboy hat he had purchased at the Houston airport during a layover on the flight to Oklahoma. The first time he wore the hat, his teammates teased him about it, but Assistant Coach Steve Flint told him to bring the hat to the arena that day.

"He said it would be a lucky hat," Vilcinskas recalled. "Hey, I guess he was right. We're going to St. Louis now. I'm bringing it there, too."

CHAPTER FIFTEEN

America's Team

*"But it was in defeat that the real character of the Crusaders–and their fans–
came to the fore. Few teams have ever bowed out with such dignity, grace
and class."*

–INDIANAPOLIS STAR, March 22, 1998

The plane, on final approach to Chicago's O'Hare Airport, carved its
way through the frigid morning sky. Inside, Homer Drew was getting
mixed signals from himself. He was far too excited to sleep, but he was
slowly dozing off here and there due to being awake for nearly 24 consecutive hours. Many of the players fell into the same category.

The plane landed, and as the Valpo entourage walked up the jetway,
they caught a glimpse of what life would be like for the next week at
least. Several camera crews and newspaper reporters were waiting at the
gate. They wanted sound. They wanted pictures. They wanted quotes.
With the win over Florida State, Valparaiso was suddenly the country's
hottest sports story. Everyone wanted in.

Although everyone was exhausted, the players happily yawned their
way through interviews as they walked toward the team bus. Drew recalled his early days at Valpo, when just having the team's name mentioned in the Chicago papers was cause for celebration. No one ever
envisioned this type of interest.

After battling through rush-hour traffic near the airport and stopping for lunch near the state line, the bus finally arrived in Valpo nearly

196

two hours later. As the bus approached the campus, a Valparaiso police car pulled it over. An officer poked his head inside the bus.

"There's a crowd of people waiting for you by the gym," the officer told Coach Drew.

"Great. That's exciting," Drew replied. "Well, we'll be there in a minute."

"No, no, you don't understand," the officer said. "It's a huge, huge crowd. You're going to need our help getting through."

With that, bleary-eyed players shot awake in the back of the bus. As the police escort turned onto Union Street, the players caught a glimpse of what the officer was talking about. Nearly 1,500 fans were waiting outside the entrance to the ARC. Students sat in tree limbs. Shirtless fraternity brothers raced down the block, their bare chests painted to spell V-A-L-P-O. Bystanders stood on rooftops. The crowd roared and surrounded the bus. The Crusaders were flabbergasted.

"We had goosebumps running up and down," Drew said. "It truly was a magical moment."

Students had called one another a few hours earlier, alerting the campus of the team's arrival. Apparently, everyone got the message. The students started pounding on the sides of the bus, which never made it closer than a half-block from the entrance. As the team disembarked, they slowly made their way through a sea of arms and signs and television cameras. Scott Drew high-fived everyone in sight. Bryce Drew signed autographs, as did Jamie Sykes and the twins. After capturing the nation's heart, the Crusaders finally had a chance to celebrate with their fans at home.

Only this time, the nation and world were watching. CNN cameras rolled and *New York Times* photographers snapped away as Valpo held an impromptu pep rally in old Hilltop Gym.

"I don't know what's more amazing, the way this team won two games or all of you waiting here for us," Drew told the crowd.

"There's no doubt who has the best crowd," Sykes said to a roar of approval.

Zoran Viskovic got up to speak, and he surveyed the audience with a sly grin.

"Shouldn't you be in class?" he said, eliciting laughter from the students. Indeed, many professors had either called off class, dismissed class early, or simply looked the other way as Valpo students ditched to head to the rally. After all, it was Monday. Yet, it was a Monday like no other this campus had ever seen.

That night, scenes of the pep rally ran on most sports shows and local news sports segments around the country. The eyes of a nation were on the Crusaders. Their hearts were cheering right along. Many national sportswriters echoed the sentiments of the people: for the moment, the Crusaders were America's Team.

"This is nuts. Beautiful and nuts," wrote Jay Mariotti in the *Chicago Sun-Times*. "You thought it was a one-shot fairy tale, a fluky moment in time. Instead, it was a prelude for more."

Against Florida State, "they were given little chance against the quicker, more athletic Seminoles...," wrote David Leon Moore in *USA Today*. "But desire never seems to be in short supply at Valparaiso."

"A grown son hopping onto a basketball court into the joyous arms of his father..." wrote Joe Drape in *The New York Times*. "The transformation into National Collegiate Athletic Association tournament Cinderella was strictly family business."

Even though the players, coaches, and athletic department were getting more used to dealing with national media during the NCAA Tournament, they had no inkling what they were in store for this week. The phones literally rang all day and all night long. Besieged with interview requests, as well as questions about the school, the program, and the coach, Valparaiso's sports information staff worked late into the night. Ticket requests were another matter altogether, as hundreds lined up overnight outside the ARC ticket office.

"We were not prepared for the media crush," Drew said two months after the season. "I still have a big stack of letters and several hundred e-mail messages to return. I will answer them all, but it will take some time."

Next door, at the university bookstore, Valpo clothing and memorabilia flew off the shelves. T-shirts and sweatshirts could not be printed quickly enough to meet demand. Newly acquired fans from all points around the globe called to purchase their souvenirs. Brown and gold was suddenly the sizzling new fashion trend.

However, phone calls from newspapers weren't the only media that Valpo tried to accommodate during the week leading up to the Sweet Sixteen game. "Good Morning America" visited the Drew home to tape a segment. Valpo players and coaches were guests on numerous call-in radio shows. ESPN arrived on campus to tape a piece for "SportsCenter." Nearly everywhere the Crusaders would go that week, it seemed that a television camera was in tow.

The best by-product of all the attention, according to former Valpo player Anthony Allison who now plays overseas, was that the town's name was finally being pronounced properly: Val-puh-RAY-zo.

Drew was understandably concerned that his team would get caught up in all of the hype and publicity surrounding the team's magical run and forget about the task at hand: the NCAA regional semifinal game against the University of Rhode Island.

Like Valpo, few experts predicted Rhode Island to be in the Sweet 16. They had followed up Valpo's win over Florida State with an impressive upset victory over top-seeded Kansas. Adding to the intrigue of the matchup was the fact that there would be another family connection during the game, aside from the Drew family.

Jim Harrick was the head coach of the Rhode Island Rams. He was also the father of Valpo assistant Jim Harrick, Jr. The Harricks and Drews had developed a close friendship during the younger Harrick's tenure at Valpo. In fact, after Rhode Island completed its win over Kansas, Jim Jr. and Drew joined him on the floor in Oklahoma City. They embraced and smiled through interviews. It was a great day for both families.

"God bless the Harricks," Drew said in a televised interview.

Both families were looking forward to the game. However, Drew rarely enjoyed playing against family members or close friends. On several occasions he has mentioned that one of the most difficult games to coach was an 84-65 win over Toledo in a Hawaiian tournament at the start of the 1994-95 season. Drew's son-in-law is former Toledo center Casey Shaw, drafted later by the Philadelphia '76ers. At the time, Shaw was playing for the Rockets.

"It was extremely difficult for me because Casey's part of the family, and you want to see him and his team succeed, but yet, you have a job to do," Drew said. "I was happy when that game was over."

While it might be a similarly awkward situation against the Rams, Drew needed to keep his players focused on the game and not on the relentless swirl of media attention given to the Crusaders' success. His efforts appeared to be working.

"We really haven't had time to sit back and appreciate all of this yet," Drew said in mid-week. "We've been too busy preparing for Rhode Island and getting our practice and travel schedules worked out."

Finally, the team traveled to St. Louis for the NCAA Midwest Regional Finals. It was a homecoming for Drew, returning to his roots and the place where he grew up. Drew was greeted by the media and by many friends, such as childhood friends John Martz, Randy Richardson, Perry Thompson, and Dave Schroeder. Most important was his own family—his mother and sister Diane and her husband Wayne Marks. "My mother was always 'there' when I was growing up," Drew said, "and, along with my wife Janet, has really shaped my life. My dad, who passed away in 1996, always believed in me and my sister and brother-in-law provide a great support system."

Ever since beating Florida State, Drew had been repeating the famous phrase, signifying his team's journey to his family's hometown.

"Meet me in Saint Looie," he said with a huge grin.

When they arrived at the Kiel Center, where the games would be played, the media interest continued. Every player was interviewed. Every story angle was re-examined. Even Janet Drew had several TV microphones surrounding her as she watched a Crusader practice session.

Even in the hallowed halls of Congress, people were talking about the Crusaders. U.S. Rep. Peter J. Visclosky praised Valpo and Drew during a speech on Capitol Hill the week before the game.

"He has been a positive influence on his students, a model of sportsmanship on the sidelines, and an example of the type of hard work that make the people of Northwest Indiana great," he said from the House floor.

> *"On behalf of Northwest Indiana, I rise to congratulate the Valparaiso University men's basketball team on their impressive wins in the first and second rounds of the NCAA tournament...Not only has Valparaiso University continued to shine on the basketball floor, but the school itself has a stellar academic record."*
> *–Rep. Pete Visclosky in the Congressional Record, March 17, 1998*

The attention was welcomed by the university and the city. However, there was one aspect of the coverage that irked longtime residents of Valpo as well as students, coaches, and players for the university.

In their zeal to link the Crusaders' dramatic run with the movie, *Hoosiers*, many national media had taken to portraying Valparaiso as a small town in the middle of nowhere. Among the images presented to the nation were a grain silo several miles outside of the city, a bingo hall, a rusted-out sign on the outskirts of town, and, of course, cornfields.

This bothered many residents. In reality, Valpo is a white-collar, suburban college town. Locals identify themselves more with Chicago, an hour away, than with Indianapolis or any areas downstate. While no one who lived there would argue it was midtown Manhattan, they resented their town being portrayed as a backwater.

"I thought all of that stuff was baloney," Bill Jenkins said. "They wanted their small-town story, so they were going to portray us however they wanted to."

One former Valpo resident joked that he had to call his parents' house to see if they still had running water and electricity following a segment he had seen on national television. Even the mayor, David Butterfield, joked about the town's portrayal during a post-season banquet.

After all of the hype, however, the players were itching to play the game. Finally, game night arrived, and the Crusaders took the national stage once again. Although Rhode Island came into the game with two highly touted guards, Tyson Wheeler and Cuttino Mobley, Drew told the Crusaders that the team that executed best as a unit would win the game.

"No single person is going to win this game," he said in the locker room. "It takes a team."

Both teams suffered from jitters at the game's outset. Neither team was able to score for nearly two minutes, until Viskovic tipped in a missed shot to give Valpo a 2-0 lead.

Rhode Island quickly gained its composure, driving the lane for layups and easy shots. When Luther Clay converted a three-point play nearly five minutes into the game, the Rams held a 12-6 advantage.

After a television timeout, Valpo sought to re-establish itself. Bryce hit a jumper. Sykes knocked down a three from the wing. Bill Jenkins scored on a tip-in. The Crusaders were back within one point. Then, his brother took over.

First, Bob Jenkins rattled home a three from the top of the key. Thanks in part to consecutive defensive stops, Bob Jenkins was able to run off nine straight points for Valpo. Capped by a layup, Jenkins' burst had propelled Valpo to an eight-point lead, 24-16. The crowd of more than 23,000 rose to its feet. The Rams were backpedaling.

On the next possession, however, the momentum shifted. Bob Jenkins was called for an intentional foul for shoving Rhode Island's Arigabu. He drained both free throws. Then on the ensuing possession, Mobley drained a three-pointer. The Crusader lead had been trimmed to three.

The teams played close for the remainder of the half. Rhode Island finally took a small lead right before halftime. With five seconds left in the half and the Rams leading by two, King buried a three-pointer to give Rhode Island a five-point lead at the break.

At the start of the second half, Valpo's offense seemed to be out of rhythm. They missed their first four shots and had two turnovers, while Rhode Island scored in the paint to open up an 11-point lead. Suddenly, it appeared as if the Rams were on the verge of putting the game away. However, after a Viskovic tip-in and back-to-back threes by Sykes, the Crusaders pulled to within three points with under 14 minutes remaining.

Two minutes later, after a Jason Jenkins' three-pointer, Bryce hit a jump shot off the glass to tie the game. The crowd roared. On the next Rhode Island offensive set, Mobley missed a three-pointer and Valpo grabbed the rebound. The crowd rose to its feet once again. With 11 minutes left, the Crusaders had a chance to take the lead.

But the Crusaders could not convert on their next two possessions, and the Rams were able to regain a one-point lead. Valpo had two more chances to take the lead, but Bryce and Bill Jenkins both had shots rim out with just over eight minutes remaining. Finally, Wheeler gave the Rams some breathing room by hitting a three-pointer. Bryce countered with a three of his own. Antonio Reynolds-Dean scored after an offensive rebound to put the Rams back in front by five points.

Less than four minutes remained, with the Rams up by three, when Mobley was whistled for an intentional foul on Sykes. Sykes thanked the official for the call, and then calmly sank both free throws. Valpo was within one point, and had possession of the ball.

Once again, Valpo couldn't capitalize. The Crusaders turned the ball over, and Reynolds-Dean converted a three-point play to put the Rams ahead by four points. After Bob Jenkins had his shot blocked, Rhode Island scored again, extending the lead to six with 2:31 remaining. Valpo would have to play catchup the rest of the way.

With just under a minute remaining, the Rams still led by six points, until Bryce hit a three-pointer to pull within three. With 41 seconds left, the crowd roared and Valpo fans began to dream. Drew confessed that he thought another miracle was possible.

"When Bryce hit that shot, I honestly thought we were going to pull the game out," he said. "I got that feeling." Rhode Island players felt the same way.

"I started thinking, 'please, don't let this game come down to a three-pointer,'" Reynolds-Dean said later.

After Valpo fouled to stop the clock, Wheeler hit one of two free throws to increase the lead to four. Valpo set up for a crucial possession. Rhode Island played suffocating defense, however, and with 12 seconds left, Bryce launched a desparation three-pointer. It never reached the rim, and Clay hauled in the rebound. Rhode Island held on for a 74-68 win. The dream had come to an end for the Crusaders.

The Drews and the Harricks embraced as the teams left the floor. The loss stung for the Crusader players, especially the seniors. They had given the nation some magical moments during the past two weeks, but now, it was over. The tears flowed as the players reached the locker room. Their coaches cried right along with this special group.

"I told them it was okay to cry," a misty-eyed Drew said.

As the team was fighting off the bitter disappointment in the locker room, something unexpected happened. There was a sharp knock on the door. It was an arena security guard.

"Your fans are calling for you," he said. Realizing how much the fans have meant to his team over the years, Drew had his team gather themselves and return to the floor. As they walked down the tunnel, they never envisioned what they were about to see. Four to five thousand thousand Valpo fans, chanting in unison:

"WE WANT THE TEAM! WE WANT THE TEAM!"

"WE WANT VALPO! WE WANT VALPO!"

Sykes and the Jenkins twins were the first to emerge from the tunnel. Bob leaned against Sykes. Both had tears streaming down their face. It was a bittersweet moment, but as the wave of cheers washed over the players one final time, the team realized that to their fans, their four-year run had meant much more than wins and losses. This team, and this group of seniors in particular, were the pride of the city. The fans wanted one last curtain call.

The loss was disappointing, to be sure, but the fans' reaction after the game helped to take the edge off the disappointment. Fans cheered and cried. Players cried. The warm embrace did not go unnoticed by the national media who were present.

"Usually there's not much a team can learn from its fans," wrote Phil Arvia in the Chicago *Daily Southtown*. "But the Valparaiso story has been about nothing but confounding expectations."

As they headed off the floor, Drew turned to the fans, held out his arms and simply said, "thank you."

The seniors thought the send-off was just what they needed.

"It was very therapeutic," said Bob Jenkins.

"It made me feel a lot better," said Bryce.

"It was the perfect ending to my basketball career," Sykes said.

"It was the comforting hug that all of us needed at the time," Bill Jenkins concurred.

"There was no dry eye in the locker room," Drew said at the press conference. "There's so much love and respect between each other on this team." Bill Jenkins then summarized the feelings of one outgoing senior.

"There's sorrow and sadness that this great ride has come to an end," he said. "But there's also a satisfaction in our hearts for what we accomplished...the friendships I have made here are everlasting to me. I would die for anyone on this team. That's how close I feel to them."

Afterwards, in the locker room, Jenkins was asked what his favorite memories would be of playing at Valpo. He smiled.

"The friendships I've made, the places I've gone, the things I've seen," he said. "There's too many of them. I couldn't even write them all down."

"The friendships will stretch further than anything," Sykes said.

Bob Jenkins talked about what he would miss most about playing for Coach Drew.

"I'll miss his fairness, his smile, his intense competitive nature, all of it," he said. "He's a great leader."

In the locker room, all five seniors in uniform took turns embracing one another. Although their feats on the court as a group were coming to a close, all five would go on to have professional athletic careers. Sykes was headed to the Arizona Diamondbacks training camp the following week. Bob Jenkins would be drafted by the Cincinnati Reds as an outfield prospect. Bill Jenkins signed to play basketball in Portugal and Vilcinskas was going to play professional basketball in Poland. Then, there was Bryce, who was expected to be drafted by an NBA team.

However, it was the coach who would be missing these players more than anything. Drew said he would miss watching the group practice, because they always gave full effort and had an outstanding work ethic as a team. He was thrilled that all of their hard work had paid off.

"They have touched America," Drew said. "And it all couldn't have happened to a better bunch of young men."

CHAPTER SIXTEEN

The Dream Lives On

"That's when I come alive: on the basketball court. As the game unfolds, time slows down and I experience the blissful feeling of being totally engaged in the action...That's when you realize that basketball is a game, a journey, a dance—not a fight to the death. It's life just as it is."

—Phil Jackson

Although the season-ending defeat was heartbreaking, along with the reality that these six seniors would never take the floor for Valpo again, something funny happened to this Crusader team as they were supposed to be fading from the public eye: people kept talking about them.

Two days after their return from St. Louis, the Crusaders were the guests of honor at a Chicago Bulls game so they could be introduced in a pre-game ceremony. Bulls vice president of marketing and broadcasting Steve Schanwald invited the team, due to the large following in the Chicago area the team attracted during its tournament run.

The players walked to mid-court before the start of the game, looking around the arena in awe. The Crusaders were honored by public address announcer Ray Clay, who recited the team's accomplishments before a replay of Bryce Drew's shot against Ole Miss on the United Center's enormous video scoreboards. The crowd roared with approval before giving the team a standing ovation.

After the quick ceremony, Homer Drew slipped over to the Bulls' bench to shake hands with head coach Phil Jackson. Drew said he simply wanted to tell Jackson how much he had enjoyed his coaching and his book.

"We only spoke for a few seconds because the game was about to start," Drew said. "But I've always admired Phil Jackson. I've admired his temperament, his style, his coaching philosophy of preparing players mentally. I really appreciated the point of view he brought to the game."

Although Drew and his players may have been floored by the way they were being hailed as heroes in the home of the then five-time world champions, the NBA players on hand expressed their congratulations as well, including one who is considered to be the greatest ever.

"That's what's so great about the NCAA tournament," Michael Jordan told the *Post-Tribune*. "A school like Valpo can really accomplish something. I know they didn't make the Final Four, but what they did I'm sure will help them with their recruiting."

Bulls guard Steve Kerr told reporters that Valpo's run in the NCAA was "awesome," and confessed that the Bulls run a play similar to "Pacer," the now-famous inbounds play.

"That's what's so great about the NCAA tournament. A school like Valpo can really accomplish something. I know they didn't make the Final Four, but what they did I'm sure will help them with their recruiting."
–Michael Jordan

No one wanted to let go of the Crusaders' magic, even though their season had ended. *Chicago Tribune* columnist Skip Bayless said Valpo was "the little school whose name will forever be associated with the 1998 tournament." On the same day the Valpo team visited the Chicago Bulls, *Indianapolis Star News* columnist Bill Benner explained why he couldn't get Valpo off his mind.

"In the news business, we always need to look ahead, not behind," he wrote. "But in the people business, we occasionally need to look back and find a Valparaiso there somewhere, offering inspiration, providing example. Looking ahead, there will be a Final Four and an ultimate one. But in the years ahead, when I look back at the 1998 NCAA tournament, I'll think of Valpo."

Dale Brown, Drew's former boss at LSU, said that Valpo's 1998 tournament run was something he will cherish for many years to come.

"It gave you hope that people can still do things honorably, the right way..." he said. "They were a breath of fresh air in college basketball, and I think that's why they really captured the whole country the way they did.

"I hope everyone remembers this team, because there are some great lessons to be learned from them: the respect for others and the teamwork. They reminded me of my 1986 LSU team that went to the Final Four and the 1987 team that went to the final eight. They were just so fun to watch, I hope their example can be magnified."

Three weeks after the season ended, the Crusaders gathered at the ARC one final time. Instead of donning shorts and sneakers, the players dressed in their Sunday best: jackets and ties. The team banquet was open to the public and nearly a thousand fans paid for a catered dinner and a chance to see this once-in-a-lifetime group together as a team for one last evening.

Graduation was coming in a few short weeks, and the players were allowing themselves to look ahead to their futures. However, for two hours, they reflected back on their four years at Valparaiso University. The emotions overwhelmed several players, including Bob Jenkins. Very few of the player speeches had a main subject dealing with basketball.

"I always told myself that this day would never come," he said, his voice breaking as the tears began to flow. "I learned a lot about love here, I learned a lot about relationships here...I learned how to care."

The twins stood and recited a poem they had written, entitled "No More." The poem was lighthearted and humorous, but it was clear that teammates and coaches alike were moved by the sweet gesture. Then, a player who had ventured thousands of miles to be a part of this basketball team took his turn at the microphone.

"Thanks for the home, the family, and the friends," said Tony Vilcinskas.

Bryce thanked his teammates for their support, and then told a story about when he and the twins were college freshmen, hanging out at the campus library. They allowed themselves to dream about their future at the university.

"I said wouldn't it be something if we won conference and made it to the NCAA Tournament?" Bryce said. "Then Bill said, 'what if we win a game?' Then Bob said, 'what if we make it all the way to the Final Four? Can you imagine it?'"

The players high-fived, hooted, and rolled with laughter—so much so that they caused a bit of a ruckus amongst the bookshelves.

"A librarian had to come over to us and tell us to calm down," Bryce recalled.

Then, Bryce thanked his family, and his brother Scott in particular for being the foundation of his success.

"I'll never forget the bonding time we had as brothers here," Bryce said.

To top off the evening, former Valpo athletic director Dick Koenig rose to present Coach Drew with a gift and read from a thank-you note Drew had sent to Koenig after agreeing to become Valpo's head coach 10 years earlier. The coach's words in the note foreshadowed a great future.

"With God at our helm, no problem is too great or too small...Valpo's greatest moments lie ahead," Drew wrote.

One week later, the community came out to honor Bryce. The city sponsored a "Bryce Drew Night" at the ARC to thank him for the eight years of memories he had given to local residents. Bryce was flattered, yet embarrassed by all of the fuss. However, there was a good cause involved: one boy and one girl would win a scholarship to Valparaiso University, thanks to a Bryce Drew Scholarship Fund being set up at the school.

The event was hosted by former Indiana Pacers legend Clark Kellogg, now an analyst for CBS. However, it was the cavalcade of former coaches that had the best anecdotes and the fondest memories of Bryce. His eighth-grade coach at Immanuel Lutheran School, Phil Bickel, led off the tributes.

"Watching you play has taken us all to a higher level...this is the community's big hug back to you," he said. "Your faith has kept you humble in success and strong in adversity."

Bickel said people were always asking him what he had taught Bryce during his junior high days about the game of basketball.

"I admit it—nothing," he said to the audience's laughs. "I didn't want to delay his progress."

Bryce's coach at Valparaiso High School, Bob Punter, then reminisced about Bryce's days across town wearing the green and white of the Valpo Vikings. More important than his honors on the court, Punter said, was the impact he had on people off of it. Whenever a situation called for someone with compassion, a few kind words, or just a friendly ear, teachers at the high school still look for a "Bryce Drew kind of guy," Punter said.

Punter said that Bryce truly embodied the old adage, "it's nice to be important, but it's more important to be nice."

"I'm glad my path intersected with yours, because it's been a four-lane highway ever since," Punter added.

After Bryce's grandparents were acknowledged, Dana Drew Shaw and Scott Drew took their turns reflecting on their little brother, who was now all grown up. Dana thought long and hard during the four-hour drive from Toledo. She wanted to come up with a funny anecdote, something to tease her brother with during the ceremony.

"I couldn't think of anything bad to say," she said. Instead, she dedicated one of her favorite Bible verses to Bryce. Then, Scott told of the qualities that he most admires in his sibling.

"You always put others first, and you always make time for others," he said.

Finally, Bryce rose and addressed the crowd. He was overwhelmed by the tributes and kind words.

"Wherever I'm going to be next year, and it could be anywhere in the world," Bryce said, bringing to mind a famous quote from Larry Bird about

French Lick, Indiana. "The only place I'd rather be is Valparaiso, Indiana."

He said he would remember his friends the most from his years living and going to college in Valpo.

"Friendship is greater than anything I can hang on a wall or watch on a tape," he said.

However, there would be one item to hang on a wall: his jersey, number 24, which was retired by the university at the end of the ceremony.

Now that the ceremonies were over and the season was completely behind him, there were only two goals left for Bryce Drew. First, finish up his classes and graduate. Second, put himself in the best possible position for the NBA draft.

As soon as school ended, Bryce could devote himself full-time to preparing for the draft, with the help of brother Scott. Working out harder than he ever had before, Bryce prepared for individual workouts with NBA teams and then finally, the biggie: the NBA Pre-Draft Camp in Chicago. Prior to the camp, Bryce was already impressing team officials. Donnie Walsh, president and general manager of the Indiana Pacers, said that Bryce would be a good NBA player.

"He's more athletic than people realize," Walsh told the *Post-Tribune*. "He can do a lot of things, and he's stronger than I thought he was."

This was a goal that Bryce had been working toward for a long time. Less than a month after the 1997 NBA Draft had completed, the Monter Draft Report, a publication which scouts potential pro basketball prospects, listed what the publication viewed as the "Top Players for the 1998 Draft."

The publication ranked the players by what their NBA position would be. This publication listed Bryce as the top point guard prospect in the country. Both Bryce and his father shrugged it off at the time.

"Well, there's about two dozen of those magazines around. Each one has him ranked somewhere else, so I don't know if you can read much into that or not," Drew said. "Still, it's nice that one of these draft experts has him ranked as the best. With the NBA draft expect the unexpected."

Approximately one month earlier, one got the sense that something special was in store for Bryce. It was mid-May and final exams had been over for a few days. Most of the students were relaxing before starting summer jobs or vacations. Not Bryce. He was alone in a darkened ARC, shooting jumpers and practicing his footwork.

"With the NBA draft expect the unexpected."–Homer Drew

"Wouldn't it be great to see Bryce in the NBA someday?" his father asked almost rhetorically. He was beaming from ear to ear the way only a proud parent can. He gestured toward the basket in the gym.

"You know, Bryce came in here and shot for two hours this morning, went and lifted weights at Gold's Gym for two hours this afternoon, and now he'll be here shooting for another two hours," he said. "Most people don't realize what it takes to play at this level. This is why Bryce is so good."

It appeared those hours upon hours of practice and hard work were about to pay off. At the Pre-Draft camp, Bryce wowed the scouts with his performances against the top players in the country. The consensus among NBA general managers was that Bryce had boosted his standing with his outstanding displays. Some even said he was the best shooter in the entire draft.

Bryce knew his chances of being picked in the draft's first round were solid when his father spoke to Chicago Bulls general manager Jerry Krause a few days before draft night. According to Drew, Krause told the family that Bryce would likely already be drafted by the time the Bulls picked at number 28.

Finally, draft night arrived. The Drew family decided to watch the draft on the television set in their family room. The first 15 picks went by without Bryce being picked. Then, NBA Commissioner David Stern stepped to the podium.

"With the 16th pick in the 1998 NBA Draft, the Houston Rockets select Bryce Drew out of Valparaiso University," he said.

The Drews leaped off the couch and hugged each other in celebration. The reaction was spontaneous. The little boy's dream had become a reality. All of the one-on-one games in the backyard, all of the late-night workouts, all of the weightlifting sessions on hot summer days, it had all culminated with a few words on television.

"If I could duplicate the jump I did, I'd go and play in the 50-and-older league," Drew said. "To go someplace where you're really wanted, and have a chance to get some playing time as a rookie, well, that's just an outstanding opportunity for Bryce."

Houston seemed to fit Bryce well, too.

"My initial thought was that I was very excited," Bryce said. "When I visited down there, I came home and told my parents how much I liked it down there. I liked the coaches, and I liked the whole organization, as well as the city of Houston. I'm very delighted to have been picked by them."

During a press conference from his kitchen table, Bryce told the Houston media what he believed his biggest assets on the court were.

"My strengths are, first of all, I have a winning mentality. I always seem to find a way to win. I pride myself on winning, and I hate to lose. I'm more of a positive leader, and I'm a team player. I'm much better playing five-on-five than one-on-one," Drew said. "As for what I need to improve on, first, I know is my foot speed to guard the really quick point guards. I know I'll have to work on that really hard this summer so I can come in and be able to defend better. Right now, I'm really excited to be able to play against the best players in the world, and compete at that level."

Of course, Bryce was asked a tough question, too. A Houston reporter wanted to know what the bigger thrill was, winning in the NCAA Tournament or being drafted into the NBA. Bryce laughed.

"Hoo, boy...that's a good question," Bryce said, glancing sheepishly at the hometown reporters surrounding him. "I'm in Valpo with all the media here, so it's hard to answer. I would say the [NCAA] run was tremendous because it was with my family and with my friends of many years. Coming to Houston is just the ultimate goal. Growing up, it was my dream to play in the NBA, so this is more individualistic. But they are both great periods in my life, and I feel so blessed to get to go through both of them."

Then, Bryce cupped his hand over the receiver and turned back to the reporters around the kitchen table.

"Was that diplomatic enough?" he asked, drawing chuckles from the assembled media. However, he expressed his regret at having to leave Valparaiso, a place he will always consider home.

"Hopefully, they won't forget me here," Bryce said. "Hopefully, they'll still be able to see me on TV and doing well. I pride myself as being a good person, so I hope they'll look at the things I do off the court, as well as on the court."

Judging by the reaction after the draft, that shouldn't be a problem. Approximately 100 people gathered on the Drew front lawn after the pick was announced, one of them waving the Lone Star flag. Finally, after some cheering and chanting, Bryce emerged on his porch to a hero's reception.

After signing autographs and thanking his neighbors, Bryce returned inside the house. Even though his dream had come true, the family still was waiting with anticipation as more picks were announced. Bryce's brother-in-law, Casey Shaw, was listed as a probable candidate for the draft. Finally, he was selected 37th by the Philadelphia 76ers. The Drew household breathed a sigh of relief, and Bryce allowed himself to look forward to playing with two of the game's all-time legends.

"Sir Charles, and Hakeem Olajuwon...two Hall-of-Famers, I'll probably be in awe the first two weeks of practice, watching their moves and seeing what they do," he said.

"What struck me is how friendly everyone is down there. As soon as I walked out to work out, the coaches made me feel so at home, and it made me feel comfortable. There's a lot of honesty in the Houston organization. There wasn't anybody that seemed off the wall."

Surprisingly, Janet Drew did not view the draft as the end of the road in terms of hard work or basketball, nor was it the ultimate goal in her mind.

"It wasn't like that and I'll tell you why, I really enjoyed what he was doing when he was doing it," she said. "I guess I've always just enjoyed the moment for what it was. Tomorrow is never a promise, so I just really appreciated every day that he had and every day that he could play."

Meanwhile, Bryce marveled at how fortunate and blessed he felt.

"I don't know if I'll get to sleep tonight," he said. "When I wake up in the morning, I'll probably get up ready to seize the day, because this is what I've waited for my whole life.

"I just prayed and I put God at the controls of my life, it seems like through high school and college, He's always been there. I have no control over it. I'm so thankful to have this opportunity. It doesn't really feel like it's here or that it's happened. When the draft first came on the TV tonight, I thought to myself, 'man, I just love sitting down and watching this.'

"Then it hit me, 'oh my gosh, I'm going to be in this,' so it was really weird. For the first few picks, it was just like watching it any other year. I didn't really picture myself in there."

However, the Rockets had a picture of Bryce in their minds wearing their navy and red uniforms.

"We had a wish list, and it's so surprising that the top three guys on our list, we got," said Houston head coach Rudy Tomjanovich in a televised interview near the end of the evening. "We feel that they're all-around players, they're winners, they can shoot the basketball and they complement Dream and Charles very well."

A few moments later, the phone rang, and Drew answered. He didn't recognize the voice on the other end. At first, he thought it could have been one of Bryce's teammates or a recruit playing a prank, but his eyes finally lit up as he walked over to the sofa and handed the cordless phone to Bryce.

"It's Charles Barkley," he said with a huge smile. Bryce took the phone and spoke with Barkley for several minutes. Barkley had Bryce laughing with his jokes.

"He said he looked forward to having me down there," Bryce said after hanging up. "That was very cool."

Finally, the boxes of pizza and soda that had been set out for the press were gathered up by Janet Drew. It was getting late, and Bryce had to catch a flight to Houston the next morning. However, there was one final detail that needed to be worked out.

Bryce would not be able to wear number 24 in Houston. The number had already been retired by the franchise in honor of Moses Malone. Bryce needed to pick a new number for his jersey. After several possibilities were bandied about, Bryce settled on the number 11. There was a reason for it. Both Homer Drew and Dana Drew had worn the number during their playing days.

"I can do everything through Him who gives me strength."

—Phillipians 4:13

Drew was touched that Bryce picked the number, and loved the fact that no matter where he traveled in the NBA the next season, his son would be wearing a little piece of family history on his back.

As for Drew, he also needed a good night's sleep. Although he had completed his recruiting for the following season, it was never too early to get a head start on the following season's class. The job of a college basketball coach is never done, and so Drew would be leaving on a recruiting trip in a few days.

Buoyed by the success of the 1997-98 team, Drew headed off on the recruiting trail with a smile on his face. He was ready for the next miracle.

About the Authors

SHAWN MALAYTER is a writer who has observed Valparaiso basketball from both inside and outside of the program for nearly 20 years. A graduate of Ball State University, he has written for several newspapers in Indiana and Illinois. Shawn and his wife, Eileen, reside in Chicago. This is his first book.

HOMER DREW played basketball at William Jewell College in Liberty, Missouri, where he earned a bachelor's degree in 1966. He received a master's degree in Education from Washington University in St. Louis and a doctoral degree in Administration from Andrews University. He coached at Washington State University and Louisiana State University before coming head coach at Bethel College in Mishawaka, Indiana. He has spearheaded the increasingly successful Valpo basketball program since the 1988-89 season. Homer and his wife, Janet, reside in Valparaiso, Indiana. The Drews have three children: Scott, Dana, and Bryce. This is his first book.

ROB RAINS is a 1978 graduate of the University of Kansas who currently works as the communications manager for the Missouri Athletic Club. He resides in St. Louis with his wife, Sally, and sons Mike and B.J. A frequent contributor to *The Sporting News*, this is Rob's ninth book.